THE COMPLETE
SEAFOOD
COOKBOOK

THE COMPLETE
SEAFOOD
COOKBOOK

BETTINA JENKINS

Food Photography by Chris Jones
Food and Styling by Mary Harris

Charles E. Tuttle Company, Inc.
Boston • Rutland, Vermont • Tokyo

ACKNOWLEDGMENTS

With thanks to my husband Matt,
and my parents Tommaso and Iolanda
without whose support and assistance
this enormous book would never have been achieved

Props supplied by
Ventura Design — Sydney, Australia
Joan Bowers Antiques — Sydney, Australia
Made in Japan — Sydney, Australia

CONTENTS

INTRODUCTION

To many, seafood is seen as a luxury, something that is saved for dining out, but it is also many people's most-loved food. Why then do so many opt to eat their seafood out instead of preparing it at home? Frequently the answer is that they don't know how to handle its selection, preparation, storage, and, most of all, cooking. But seafood, particularly fish, is one of the easiest of all foods to prepare – it is quick to cook, needs minimal additions, and is absolutely delicious.

The range of seafood available to us is staggering, from whole fish and fish steaks to tiny living clams, tender baby octopus, and giant crabs. With this abundance of seafood, the taste, texture, and cooking possibilities are endless.

NUTRITION

Nutritionists and doctors have realized just how healthful fish is, and many of them are recommending that we eat it up to three times a week. So what's so good about it?

Seafood is high in vitamins and minerals but low in calories, so it is ideal for people concerned about their weight. An average 5 oz (150 g) piece of fish contributes only 85 calories (360 kilojoules) and twelve fresh oysters have only 60 calories (260 kilojoules).

Fish is rich in protein, with a 5 oz (150 g) serving contributing 30 g. An average woman should aim for a daily protein intake of 60 g, while 75 g a day is needed by men. So by eating one serving of fish, you get up to half your daily protein allowance. Other types of seafood are similarly beneficial:

Shrimp   3 1/2 oz (100 g) = 90 calories
            (380 kilojoules), 19 g protein

Crayfish   3 1/2 oz (100 g) = 76 calories
            (320 kilojoules), 16 g protein

Crab   3 1/2 oz (100 g) = 93 calories
            (390 kilojoules), 17 g protein

Lobster   3 1/2 oz (100 g) = 90 calories
            (380 kilojoules), 19 g protein

Fish is also low in fat, especially in saturated fat, with an average 5 oz (150 g) serving contributing less than 3 g fat. However, it is rich in omega–3 fatty acids — polyunsaturated fatty acids found mainly in fish and believed to have health benefits.

The incidence of heart disease among fish-eating populations such as the Eskimo (who have a high fat intake from seal and whale blubber) is very low. Research into omega–3 fatty acids, which are plentiful in the Eskimo diet, has revealed that they:

- appear to protect against heart disease
- help lower blood pressure
- prevent clots from forming and blocking arteries
- have a tendency to reduce inflammation in our bodies, thereby helping people with arthritis and rheumatism
- help psoriasis sufferers.

All fish and shellfish have some omega–3s, but the best of all are the oily fish species such as tuna, salmon, mackerel, sardines, and mullet. To gain the best possible benefits of omega–3s, avoid plunging seafood into hot fat. Instead try healthier cooking methods like poaching, steaming, and grilling.

PURCHASING FISH

Be flexible when purchasing fish — or any seafood. Always buy whatever is the best quality, instead of deciding on a type before you shop. Many different species can be adapted to the same basic recipes.

Seafood is seasonal, so when a particular species is in abundance, prices are often low. On the other hand, supplies of seafood can be erratic due to the impact of weather on prices. Unfortunately, many cooks stick to their tried-and-true species, paying high prices due to shortages while ignoring more inexpensive fish of comparable quality. For best quality and price, shop around, buy seasonal seafood, and try a variety of species.

As seafood is highly perishable, it is important to buy absolutely the freshest available.

When buying fish, keep the following points in mind:

Whole fish

- Bright bulging eyes are a sure sign of freshness. Do not reject deep-sea fish if the eyes are bulging but bloodstained, as the blood is due to the fish being rapidly brought to the surface. Bypass dull, sunken, or cloudy eyes.
- Fish should have a pleasant sea smell, not a fishy odor. Some fish develop an ammonia smell when stored in plastic bags — even in the refrigerator; simply run fish under cold water to remove.
- Scales should be firmly intact and have a glossy sheen.
- The flesh should be firm to the touch and resilient, not soft and flabby.
- The gills should be bright red, not brown.

Steaks and fillets

- should be moist and shiny, with no dry, brown edges

- should not be sitting in a pool of liquid which is an indication of poor freezing techniques
- should look translucent, not milky
- should have a pleasant sea smell
- should have firm, resilient flesh with clean, smooth edges.

Quantities

To calculate how much fish to buy per person, use the following figures as a guide. The amounts will vary depending on whether you plan to serve the fish as a first or main course, and on what else you plan to serve with the meal.

Whole fish: 10 – 12 oz (300 – 350 g)
Fillets: 4 – 5 oz (125 – 150 g)
Steaks: 7 – 8 oz (200 – 250 g)

PREPARATION

When purchasing fish from a retailer, you will generally not have to undertake much preparation. Fillets and steaks might need a quick rinsing to remove any scales that may be adhering to them, but basically that is it. With whole fish, the retailer will scale and gut for you, so this can also be bypassed by you.

Should there come a time when you need to scale and gut, although the procedure can at times be messy, it is also quite simple. As a child, (and still doing it today) I remember my father scaling fish on the kitchen sink. The scales have a tendency to grip very well onto whatever surface they land, and upon drying are extremely difficult to remove. So for days after the big scaling job, scales were found all over the kitchen.

When I teach people how to scale fish, I show them the method I have found fastest and cleanest: I fully immerse the fish into a sink of cold water while scaling. The scales will come away easily, and fall directly into the water. When you drain the water, be sure to use a drainer, which will collect the scales, so they can be easily discarded.

STORING FISH

Temperature plays an important role in maintaining freshness in fish, so when shopping, take an insulated bag or container for carrying your purchase. Once home, transfer it immediately to the coldest part of the refrigerator.

Shelf life depends on the fish's quality and freshness, but generally it should be consumed within 2 days of purchase. If you are planning to cook the fish on the day of purchase, store it in the original packaging; otherwise transfer it to a plate, rinsing only if the fish is not totally clean or if there is an ammonia smell from the plastic, then pat dry, and cover with plastic wrap. Whole fish that has not been cleaned should be gutted immediately, as spoilage occurs faster with the insides intact. Rinse the cavity well to remove any blood along the backbone. Scales do not have to come off at this stage, as they act as an insulator to keep the fish moist.

Freezing

Fish freezes successfully and, if it is perfectly fresh and is frozen correctly and quickly, it remains flavorful, moist, and of good quality. Although some moisture is lost during thawing, this loss can be minimized by cooking the fish, particularly fillets and steaks, from the frozen state allowing a little extra cooking time.

Freeze fish only in quantities to be used at one time. Overwrap it tightly with plastic

FISH – SCALE, CLEAN, FILLET AND SKIN

One

Two

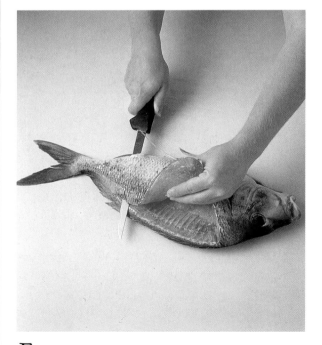

Four

Five

Three

1. Using the edge of a metal spoon, knife, or fish scaler, scrape against the scales with one hand, while firmly holding onto the tail with the other. This may be done with fish immersed in water to prevent scales flinging in all directions.

2. To gut fish: use a sharp knife to slit the belly from head to tail, and gently ease out the guts. Rinse under cold running water, making sure the cavity is thoroughly clean.

3. To fillet fish: begin by cutting the fish crossways, half way through until you reach the backbone, just behind the gills.

4. Holding the knife at an angle and keeping it against the backbone, carefully slice down the length of the fish. Do this in one continuous cut, gently lifting fillet away from body of fish as you go. Sever fillet at tail. Repeat for other side.

5. To skin fish: place fillet on work surface, skin side down. Hold tail firmly with salted fingers. Begin at tail and, staying close to skin, run knife between flesh and skin, keeping knife flat to work surface. Push down firmly while cutting and flesh should lift as you slice.

wrap, excluding as much air as possible. Fillets and steaks can be interleaved with plastic so individual pieces are easily removable while frozen if the entire package is not needed. Then place in a freezer bag, sucking out all the air with a straw – this is important, as it helps prevent freezer burn, or drying out of the flesh. Seal the package with tape and label with type of fish, date, and quantity.

As a guide, white-fleshed fish will freeze for up to 6 months, but oily fish for only 3 months. Oily fish oxidizes faster than white fish because of its fat content.

Ice glazing whole fish

As whole large fish can be difficult to wrap, ice glazing is an ideal method to protect it from freezer burn. To ice glaze fish or lobsters and crabs that have already been killed (see page 22), freeze on a tray until solid. Dip into cold water, freeze until solid, then dip into water again. Continue this process until a thin layer of ice is formed, then place in a freezer bag and return to the freezer. To defrost, simply run fish or seafood under cold water to melt the ice, then thaw as suggested below.

Thawing frozen fish

The best way to thaw fish is in the refrigerator overnight. This provides a controlled temperature that prevents spoilage, minimizes moisture loss, and maintains texture. Place the package on a plate to catch any juices. There is no need to unwrap the package, as the plastic wrap will protect the fish from drying out. This method takes quite a bit of time, so you will need to plan ahead.

Defrosting in the microwave oven can also be successful if done correctly. But fish will defrost around the edges first, so it can

CUTTING STEAKS OR CUTLETS

Steaks or cutlets are cross-section slices cut from a fish that has been scaled, gutted, and cleaned (see page 10).

One

Using a strong, wide-bladed knife, or small saw, start at tail and cut fish into 1 in (2.5 cm) slices. These should be made across fish and at an angle.

Two

If using a knife on larger fish a considerable amount of force may be necessary to break through backbone. Discard head and tail or use to make a fish stock (see page 260).

easily start to cook on the defrost cycle. I like to partially defrost it in the microwave, then allow it to thaw fully in the refrigerator.

Do not thaw fish at room temperature, particularly during hot weather. If the edges have thawed and the center is still frozen, spoilage can begin before the entire package is thawed. Thawing in this way also allows for some moisture loss, resulting in dry fish.

BASIC COOKING TECHNIQUES

Broiling, grilling, and barbecuing

Broiling, grilling, or barbecuing fish produces very good results, but care is needed when cooking white-fleshed fish, as the intense heat can dry it out. Oily fish, such as tuna

and salmon, grill well, because their natural oils keep them moist.

To prevent the fish from drying out it can be marinated for 30 minutes, then drained (see pages 289 to 293 for marinade recipes). During cooking, baste the fish frequently with the reserved marinade or simply brush with olive oil — not only will this prevent drying, it will also add flavor.

Fillets, steaks, and small whole fish up to 4 lb (2 kg) broil, grill, or barbecue well. The broiler, grill, or barbecue must be preheated before adding the fish, and should be oiled to prevent sticking. Most fish should be cooked about 2 inches (5 cm) from the heat source, and larger whole fish about 4 inches (10 cm) from the heat so it cooks without burning.

Season fish well with salt and pepper.

BUTTERFLY OR BOOK FILLETS

'Butterfly', 'book', or 'one-piece' fillets are the two fillets from the one fish held together by the uncut flesh and skin from the back of the fish. Head, guts and backbone are removed. Mostly used on smaller fish like pilchards, garfish, and anchovies.

One

Three

1. Remove any fins. Remove the head, with a sharp knife, just behind the gills. Slit down length of fish along belly, leaving tail intact. Remove guts and rinse thoroughly.

2. Open fish out, skin down, on work surface; and holding tail with one hand pinch backbone; then gently pull bone up and out towards head end and remove. Remove any remaining bones. Clean and rinse thoroughly.

3. The resulting fillet leaves tail intact while head, guts and bones are discarded.

Two

FILLETING A ROUND FISH

One

Two

Three

1. With a sharp knife, cut the fish crosswise, half way through just behind the gills. In the same manner, cut all the way around edge of fish.

2. Keeping knife against backbone, lift fillet by carefully slicing down length of fish, until flesh is free of backbone.

3. Turn and repeat process on other side.

BONING

One

Scale and wash fish (see page 10). Head may be removed or left. Using a sharp knife, slit fish down belly to tail; gut and rinse thoroughly.

Two

With a firm hand, cut with short strokes down one side of fish lifting flesh away from rib bones. Take care not to pierce skin. Turn and repeat on other side.

Three

Spread fish flat on work surface, skin side down. Using kitchen shears or a sharp, sturdy knife, cut away backbone.

Four

Trimming one side at a time, remove all rib bones. Discard ribs and backbone or use to make fish stock (see page 260).

Cook 2 to 3 minutes per side for fillets, 3 to 4 minutes per side for steaks, 4 to 5 minutes per side for small whole fish, or until fish becomes opaque and starts to flake when tested. Baste fish regularly throughout cooking. Turn fish only once, halfway through cooking, to prevent it from breaking. For whole fish use a hinged rack, which will make turning easy.

Wrapping fish in foil hastens the cooking time so care must be taken not to overcook. Foil wrapping is recommended for stuffed fish or packages which have added ingredients like butters, vegetables, and other seafood.

Serve plain fish with either savory butters, mayonnaise, or freshly squeezed lemon juice. Suggested recipes from this book include: Barbecued Tuna with Marinated Vegetables (see page 165), Barbecued Baby Octopus (see page 133), Whole Fish with Fennel Seed and Garlic (see page 185), and cooked fish accompanied by Russian Mayonnaise (see page 264), Herb Butter (see page 261), or Garlic Avocado Sauce (see page 268).

Panfrying

Panfried fish should be golden, slightly crisp on the outside, and moist inside when done. The seasoned fish should be cooked in a shallow layer (about 3 tablespoons) of hot oil or butter (a combination works well). Butter is preferred for flavor and a golden color, although olive oil can also be used. Clarified butter (ghee) gives the best results; because the milk solids have been removed, it can be heated to a higher temperature than butter, without burning. The butter must be hot enough to brown the fish and retain its juices. If the heat is too low, the result will be a steamed effect.

Whole fish should be scored before cooking to enable it to cook evenly and for seasonings to permeate. Make 2 to 4 deep diagonal cuts on each side of the fish, from backbone to belly.

Over medium heat, melt enough butter to cover the base of a frying pan and heat until the butter is hot and just bubbling. Dust fish in flour, shaking off excess, then add to the pan and cook for 2 to 3 minutes per side for fillets, 3 to 4 minutes per side for steaks, 4 to 5 minutes per side for small whole fish (up to 8 oz/250 g each), turning fish only once.

The fish can be covered with a variety of ingredients, such as flour, polenta, finely chopped nuts, or breadcrumbs, which are used not only to protect the flesh from the intense heat of the fat, but also to provide a crisp and delicious coating.

An easy method of coating fish is to place coating ingredients in a freezer bag, shaking to mix well. Add fillets one at a time and shake bag, allowing coating to cover fish. Press coating on well; it will stick without egg because the fillets are generally quite moist. Should they be dry, dip first into beaten egg and then the coating to help the coating adhere.

Fillets, steaks, and small whole fish are all suitable for panfrying, as are shrimp (prawns), lobster, squid (calamari), and cuttlefish. Suggested recipes from this book include: Panfried Trout with Hot Vinaigrette (see page 193), Panfried Fish with Fennel Sauce (see page 145), and Fish with Wilted Arugula (see page 150), or serve panfried fish with

Turkish Almond Sauce (see page 274), Watercress Sauce (see page 274), or Skorthalia (see page 265).

Deep Frying

To deep fry is to fully immerse fish in hot oil. In most cases the fish is coated in breadcrumbs or batter, which protects it and results in beautifully moist flesh with flavor sealed in. Some recipes, like Thai Crispy Fish with Hot Sour Chili Sauce (see page 205), don't have a coating, just coarse salt rubbed into the flesh — the hot oil seals the skin and enables it to become crisp.

Correct oil temperature is important to obtain a crisp, golden result. Oil should be heated to 350°F (180°C). If you don't have a thermometer, drop crumbs or batter into the hot oil. If they sizzle immediately, the oil is hot enough; if they burn, turn down the heat and allow the oil to cool slightly. Do not overcrowd the pan with fish; this will lower the temperature of the oil, allowing the oil to seep into the coating, with soggy results. The fish is ready when it has turned golden. Drain excess oil on paper towels. Deep fried fish should be served immediately, while the coating is at its crispest.

Shellfish suitable for deep frying include squid (calamari), cuttlefish, scallops, and shrimp (prawns). Suggested recipes from this book include: Calamari Rings (see page 142), Fritto Misto (see page 144), Fish and Chips (see page 141), Deep Fried Chinese Fish (see page 88), and Fried Whitebait (see page 85).

Poaching

Poaching is a gentle cooking method that adds flavor and keeps fish moist. The fish is fully immersed in liquid, brought to boiling point, then heat is reduced and fish is simmered until tender. The liquid used can be court bouillon, lightly salted water, or fish or vegetable stock. Try chopped carrot, onion, and parsley with a few peppercorns in $1/2$ cup (4 fl oz/125 ml) dry white wine, then pour over enough water to cover fish – this should be enough for a 4 lb (2 kg) whole fish. After cooking, the poaching liquid can be used to make an accompanying sauce, such as velouté sauce (see recipe on page 277).

Fillets, steaks, and small whole fish can be poached in a small frying pan. Fish kettles are available for large whole fish; These are deep oval-shaped pots that have a perforated grid on the bottom. The grid can be lifted out to ease removal of the cooked fish.

Time the cooking of whole fish from when the poaching liquid reaches simmering point, allowing 6 minutes per 2 lb (1 kg). Drain fish on paper towels to keep it from weeping onto plates and into the sauce.

If serving cold, let the fish cool completely in poaching liquid and then refrigerate if desired. For the best flavor, remove the fish from the refrigerator at least 1 hour before serving and let stand at room temperature.

Suggested recipes from this book include: Chilled Poached Salmon (see page 178) and Poached Salmon in Orange, Honey and Wine (see page 177).

Shellfish suitable for poaching include lobster, crabs, mussels, cockles, clams, and squid (calamari).

Steaming

Fish is steamed over—not in—boiling liquid, and the result is extremely moist and tender. This method is mainly suited to white-fleshed fillets, steaks, or a whole fish. Plain water, stock, dry white wine, or court bouillon can be used, but the liquid should not be used to make an accompanying sauce as the flavor will be too intense from boiling. For still more flavor the fish can be laid on fresh herbs, vegetables, or even seaweed.

Fillets, steaks, and small whole fish can be steamed. Whole fish can be filled with chopped parsley and slices of lemon if desired. Fish must be placed in the steamer rack in a single layer; to allow for even cooking, do not overlap the fish.

Only a small amount of liquid is necessary for steaming — about 1 1/2 cups (12 fl oz/ 375 ml) liquid should suffice for four 7 oz (220 g) whole fish. The liquid should be ready and boiling before the rack is put in place. Be sure it remains at a rapid simmer throughout cooking.

Cover with a tight-fitting lid and steam, approximately 6 minutes per 2 lb (1 kg), until fish flakes when tested at the thickest part.

Shellfish suitable for steaming include mussels, crabs, scallops, and shrimp (prawns). Suggested recipes from this book include: Oven-Steamed Fish (see page 176) and Steamed Salmon Packages (see page 174).

Baking

Baked fish is extremely simple to prepare, and the fish remains moist and tender. Fillets, steaks, and whole fish are all suited to baking; whole fish can also be stuffed. Both oily and white-fleshed fish bake well on their own, lightly seasoned with a squeeze of lemon juice and with melted butter drizzled over the top, or with stuffings or special toppings. Extra flavor and moisture can be gained by the addition of herbs, garlic, shallots or other onions, oil, dry white wine, stock, or butter.

Fish should be baked at 350°F (180°C/ Gas 4) and covered with foil to keep fish from drying out. To brown, remove cover

When handling fish, octopus, squid, and cuttlefish it is a good idea to dip your fingers in salt first for a tighter grip

10 minutes before the end of cooking. As a guide, when baking whole fish allow 10 minutes per 1 lb (500 g).

Suggested recipes from this book include: Baked Citrus Fish (see page 168), Baked Fish Greek Style (see page 172), Baked Fish in Tahini (see page 169), and Baked Whole Fish With Lemon, Rosemary, and Honey (see page 170).

Microwaving

Cooking fish in the microwave oven gives moist, and tender results. Try the following hints for even cooking:

- fold tail of fillet under to give uniform depth; avoid stacking
- score whole fish (see page 39)
- to prevent eyes from bursting, pierce or remove.

Careful timing is essential, as seafood can overcook quickly. Because settings vary on different ovens, you should check your own oven guide for correct levels. However, these cooking times can be used as a guide:

- For cooking 1 lb (500 g) fillets, allow 5 minutes on 70% power (using a 600-watt microwave).
- For 1 lb (500 g) steaks, allow an additional 1 minute.
- For 1 lb (500 g) whole fish, allow 6 minutes on 70% power (using a 600-watt microwave).

An easy method is to place fish in a single layer in a microwave-proof dish. Season to taste with salt and pepper, sprinkle with chopped fresh herbs, dot with butter, and drizzle lemon juice over. Cover with plastic wrap and cook.

Testing fish for doneness
Fish can easily overcook and dry out, so the timing of cooking is vital, as is testing the fish for doneness.

Test whole fish at the thickest part, just behind the gills, by inserting a sharp knife or fork to the bone. The fish should flake easily yet still be pinkish at the bone. Remove the fish and let it stand for a few minutes before serving.

Fillets and steaks should flake easily but not fall apart when tested with a knife or fork. If it is dry and falls apart when tested the fish is overcooked.

The chart below gives an approximate guide to cooking times for panfrying, broiling, or barbecuing. Obviously the exact time depends on the size of whole fish and the thickness of fillets and steaks. Do not rely on these times exclusively — use them as a guide only, along with your own judgment. Testing the fish as described is the best way to check for doneness. Turn once only.

Fillets	2–3 minutes per side
Steaks	3–4 minutes per side
Whole fish	4–5 minutes per side

SHELLFISH
The variety of shellfish available is vast, ranging from tiny shrimp to giant crabs. However, many cooks shy away from cooking shellfish due to a lack of knowledge. You may be surprised at just how simple shellfish cookery is; a little time may be needed in the preparation, but the cooking is quick and easy.

Shellfish can be divided into two distinct groups:

1. Crustaceans
These are animals with an external shell that is jointed for movement. The group includes lobsters, crabs, shrimp (prawns), and crayfish.

2. Mollusks
These are divided into two groups:
(a) univalves and bivalves (meaning one or two shells) — animals protected by a hard shell. Examples of univalves include winkles, abalone, conch, and whelks; bivalves include mussels, scallops, and oysters.
(b) cephalopods — animals that carry their shells in the flesh of their bodies. Examples include the hard beak of the octopus, the long pen inside squid (calamari), and the cuttlebone inside cuttlefish.

CRUSTACEANS
Live crustaceans

Purchasing
When purchasing live crustaceans, look for the following:
- They should be active, not sluggish.
- They should have claws and limbs intact.
- They should not be foaming at the mouth, an indication that they are dying.
- They should be heavy for their size.

Storing
Live crustaceans should be stored in a cool spot, such as a large sink, covered with wet newspaper strips. They will survive for up to 18 hours.

Preparation

To kill live crustaceans, DO NOT drop them straight into boiling water. Not only is this cruel, it will also toughen and shrink the meat, and will often cause the claws to come away from the body. Perhaps the easiest and most humane method is to place them directly in the freezer for up to an hour which will gently freeze them to death — a far less painful or alarming process. The whole crustacean can then be boiled to cook it, or it can be segmented and used in stir-fries, sauces, or casseroles. Alternatively, the raw meat can be first extracted and then cooked in small pieces by sauteing or panfrying.

LOBSTERS AND CRABS

Purchasing

These can be purchased either alive or cooked. Some crabs can be purchased already killed but raw, but be sure to cook soon after purchase as they lose freshness quickly. Raw lobster tails can be purchased frozen.

Whether cooked or raw, lobsters and crabs should be heavy in relation to their size, and limbs should be intact with no sign of discoloration. Generally raw crustaceans should be green, blue or black; they turn bright orange when cooked. Properly cooked lobsters should have tails tightly curled.

Storing

Whether cooked or killed but still raw, lobsters and crabs should be kept in the coldest part of the refrigerator. Place on a plate or tray, cover well with plastic wrap or foil, and keep for up to 2 days. If raw, freeze for up to 2 months; if cooked, for up to 4 months. As the shells make packaging difficult, ice glazing is appropriate (see page 11).

HALVING A LOBSTER

One

Four

Two

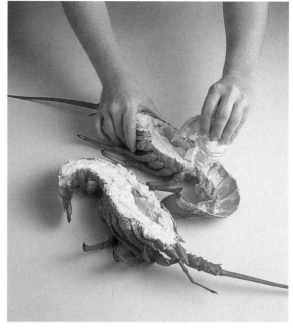

Three

Five

1. Place killed or cooked lobster on work surface underside up. With a sharp knife, pierce body in middle of chest. Cut down length of body through to tip of tail. Rotate and cut in opposite direction from shoulder right through the head.

2. Separate lobster halves to expose meat.

3. Remove and discard the intestinal thread running through tail and the liver which is green in raw lobster and yellow/orange when cooked.

4. Remove the claws and legs by twisting and pulling off. This may be done either before or after cutting lobster in half, or may even be left on for serving.

5. Crack claws with hammer, nutcracker, or shellfish cracker to remove meat.

CUTTING LOBSTER MEDALLIONS

One

Place lobster on work surface, underside up. Cut off tail as close as possible to the head.

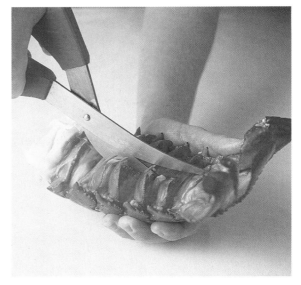

Two

Using kitchen shears, cut down the middle of the tail shell.

Three

Carefully prise the shell open and gently ease the flesh out in one piece.

Four

Slice the tail meat at approximately $^1/2$ in. (1.5 cm) intervals to create medallions.

Preparation

The same methods are used for extracting meat from crustaceans, whether they are raw or already cooked. The thing to remember is that cooked lobster or crab need only be combined into another dish by heating through gently until just warm. You should not "cook" it again as this will toughen it. For this reason, pre-cooked lobster and crab are best used in cold dishes.

Crabs need careful rinsing under cold water. If particularly dirty or muddy, they can be cleaned with a kitchen brush.

Cooking

Only raw lobsters or crabs need cooking, and only after they have been killed correctly (see page 22). A common method of cooking either crustacean is to plunge them whole into boiling salted water, allowing 8 minutes per 1 lb (500 g). After cooking, plunge into cold water to stop the cooking process. You can then extract the meat, but it should not be "cooked" again, only reheated gently if using in a recipe.

Broiling, Grilling, and Barbecuing

Raw lobster that has been split down the center or cut into medallions can be successfully barbecued, broiled, or grilled. It is important to baste the flesh often throughout cooking with marinade, oil, or melted butter (which may have the addition of chopped herbs or garlic to add flavor), to prevent drying out. Depending on the size of the lobster, cook for 5 to 8 minutes per side or until the flesh is opaque all the way through; check by inserting a knife into the thickest part .

Crabs are not recommended for this cooking method.

Panfrying

When panfrying lobster it is best to extract the raw meat from the shell and either cut into medallions or cube. To panfry, simply melt butter until hot and frothy, add seasonings, garlic, or herbs and fry for about 2 to 3 minutes, or until flesh is firm and opaque.

Crabs are not recommended for this form of cookery.

Deep Frying

Lobsters and crabs are not generally suited to deep frying.

Poaching

Only the meat of raw lobsters should be poached after it has been cut into medallions or cubes. Crabs which have been segmented are good to poach in soups, sauces and stews. Once again, be careful not to overcook or they will toughen — about 5 to 6 minutes for crab and lobster pieces, depending on size. See page 18 for further information on poaching.

Steaming

For steaming, lobster is best when flesh is removed from the shell and crabs are best segmented. Large shellfish will take 5 to 10 minutes to cook, smaller ones or pieces of shellfish 3 to 5 minutes. They are cooked when the shell turns orange and the flesh becomes firm and opaque. See page 18 for further steaming information.

Baking

The rule of not "cooking" an already cooked crustacean does not usually apply when it comes to baking. This is because the lobster

CRAB

One

Rinse killed or cooked crab thoroughly. Insert a knife in through the back section of the crab; pry off the top part of shell and discard.

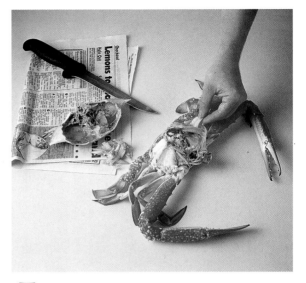

Two

Remove and discard white gills from either side of head. Rinse body, if desired, although this is not really necessary.

Three

Twist off legs and claws. These may be left intact or cracked with scissors, a nutcracker, or shellfish cracker if desired. cut body in half or quarters (if quite large).

Four

Meat is extracted with the point of a sharp knife.

or crab is mixed with other already prepared ingredients, as for Lobster Thermidor (see page 214), and then baked only to heat the dish through and to brown it.

SHRIMP

Purchasing

Shrimp (prawns) can be purchased raw — grey/white and translucent — or cooked — orange and opaque. They may be shelled or unshelled, fresh or frozen and vary in size from tiny (school prawns) to jumbo (king prawns). When buying them, look for tight shells with no sign of black discoloration along the belly and head. The flesh should be moist and firm with a sweet smell and no hint of ammonia.

Storing

Whether cooked or raw, shrimp should be stored with shells on, to keep from drying out. Place in a bowl, cover with a moist kitchen towel and refrigerate for up to two days.

Shrimp can be awkward to freeze, as their sharp feelers often pierce bags, allowing for freezer burn. I have found either of these two methods quite acceptable:

Place shrimp in a large plastic container, fill with water, then freeze. The water forms an ice block around the shrimp, preventing freezer burn. To thaw, simply run the ice block under cold water to loosen the shrimp (they will still be frozen), place them in a container, and return them to the refrigerator for thawing.

The other method is to place the shrimp in a single layer on a tray in the freezer and freeze until solid, usually about 1 hour. Then simply transfer them to a freezer bag, exclude all the air, seal, and label. The shrimp will be individually frozen, so you can remove as many at a time as you require.

Preparation

Shrimp that have been purchased ready peeled generally only need a quick rinse under cold water, then deveining. Raw shrimp with shells intact should be shelled under cold running water. Cooked shrimp can easily be shelled at the table and do not require rinsing, but make sure you have plenty of finger bowls available.

To shell raw or cooked shrimp, simply break off the head and remove the shell, leaving the tail fan intact for appearance if desired. Using a sharp knife, make a shallow cut down the back of the shrimp and remove the vein. Rinse only if raw. The flesh and vein can be pinched out of cooked shrimp using fingertips.

Cooking

Only raw shrimp need cooking. Do not cook shrimp that you have purchased already cooked, as they will dry out and toughen. Use these in dishes to be served cold, or serve plain with plenty of crusty bread, salad, and dipping sauces.

Shrimp will also toughen if cooked too long. Depending on size, shrimp generally need only 2 to 5 minutes of stir-frying, sauteing, broiling, grilling barbecuing, or deep frying. They can be cookedeither with or without their shells.

If you have caught your own shrimp or have raw shrimp that you just want to boil and serve chilled, simply bring a large pot of salted water to boil. Add shrimp and cook 2 to 5 minutes after the water has returned to boil. The shrimp should be orange, with curled tails and firm opaque flesh. Drain and plunge in cold water to stop the cooking process.

Broiling, Grilling, and Barbecuing

Peeled shrimp can easily dry out when cooked in this way so regular basting is essential. For easy handling, raw peeled shrimp can be threaded on to bamboo skewers that have been soaked in water to prevent burning. As with most cooking methods, shrimp require only about 2 to 5 minutes of broiling, grilling, or barbecuing.

Panfrying

Raw shrimp are best panfried for only 2 to 3 minutes. They work well in combination with other ingredients, particularly vegetables.

Deep Frying

When deep frying, raw peeled shrimp are usually coated with batter, breadcrumbs, or some other type of coating to protect them from the high temperature. Deep fry for the shortest possible time to prevent overcooking. If the oil is at the right temperature, a good indication of doneness will be a golden coating. See page 18 for further deep frying information.

Poaching

Raw peeled shrimp poach well and will generally take 3 to 5 minutes. See page 18 for further poaching information.

Steaming

Shrimp steam successfully and the general rules apply for guarding against overcooking and testing for doneness. See page 18 for further steaming information.

Baking

Shrimp, like lobster and crayfish, can be roasted in the oven for a short time on high heat.

Melted butter or olive oil adds flavor and results in a moist tender flesh.

FRESHWATER CRAYFISH

Freshwater crayfish are another type of crustacean which can be found worldwide. Species include swamp (crawfish) and signal crays in North America, the gray foot and red foot in Europe, and yabbies and marrons in Australia. They can be purchased cooked or alive. Look for a pleasant smell, and firm intact shells. If alive, they should be active, not sluggish.

Storing

If cooked, refrigerate in a large bowl covered with plastic wrap for up to 2 days, or freeze for up to 3 months. The crayfish can either be shelled or left whole for freezing. If left whole, they will be protected from freezer burn by their shells.

Preparation

The meat is mainly in the tail section. To extract meat from either a cooked or raw crayfish, simply twist off the head where it meets the body, then peel away the shell from the underside of the tail (you may need kitchen shears to do this), remove the tail meat. If a dark line of intestine exists (this is generally found in wild, not farmed, crayfish), pull away.

Cooking

Like other crustaceans, pre-cooked crayfish should not be cooked again, and are best used cold or reheated gently in a recipe.

The easiest way to cook raw crayfish is to place them in a large pot, cover with salted water, cover the pan, and bring to boil.

Cook for about 5 minutes or until the cray-fish are red and the tails are tightly curled. After cooking, plunge into cold water to stop the cooking process.

Live crayfish should be killed in the same manner as lobster and crab by freezing before use (see page 22).

Broiling, Grilling, and Barbecuing
Crayfish stay quite moist when cooked in their shell, although additional flavors from marinades and bastes will not be readily absorbed. If you shell crayfish, watch for dry-ing and overcooking. Crayfish are easier to handle when threaded onto a presoaked bamboo skewer and cooked for 4 to 6 min-utes or until the flesh is firm and opaque.

Poaching
Like shrimp, crayfish poach well in a variety of poaching liquids and take about 5 to 6 minutes for the flesh to become opaque, orange and firm. See page 18 for further poaching information.

Steaming
Crayfish can either be peeled or left unshelled for steaming and should take only about 3 to 5 minutes. See page 18 for further steaming information.

Baking
Uncooked crayfish work well roasted in the oven in the same manner as lobster and shrimp. Brushing with melted butter or olive oil, cook on a high heat for only a short time — the flesh will then be moist and firm but tender. If the crayfish is already cooked and incorporated into another dish, it should then only be gently reheated in the oven.

MOLLUSKS
Univalves
Also known as one-shelled gastropods, these mollusks have either an ear-shaped shell, as in the case of abalone, or else a thick, turreted or spiral shaped shell like those of the whelk or conch. Usually sold either in the shell or freshly shucked, the meat may be tough and require tenderizing by pounding before cooking. Univalves are best cooked by either frying, poaching, or steaming.

Bivalves
Purchasing
With the exception of oysters and scallops, most of these mollusks are sold alive in the shell. The shells should be tightly closed when purchased, an indication that they are still alive. If they do not close after tapping, dis-card, as they are dead – and there is no telling for how long. Shells should be uncracked and unbroken or the creatures will die quickly. They should have a pleasant sea smell.

Oysters are sold freshly shucked on the half shell, bottled in salt water, or alive in the shell. When buying them shucked on the half shell, look for plump, moist, shiny, creamy-colored flesh and clear liquor. If buying alive in the shell, look for tightly closed shells. If purchasing bottled oysters, observe the use-by date.

Scallops are available freshly shucked on the half shell, or as meat sold individually or in frozen blocks. Look for creamy-colored flesh without any dark markings. Some scallop vari-eties have roe intact. Do not purchase scallops that are sitting in a pool of water, as they will absorb quite a bit of this moisture, and may shrivel up to nothing on cooking.

OYSTER SHUCKING

One

Clean and scrub oyster shell to remove any dirt and grit. Holding oyster in palm of hand insert strong, short bladed knife, or oyster knife between the two shells at hinge point. Prising open, twist knife until hinge breaks and shells separate.

Two

To completely open shell, sever muscle attached to upper shell. Then run knife underneath oyster to fully release it from shell. Either remove oyster totally or replace on half shell, depending on intended use.

Storing

Place shells in a large bowl to collect any liquid, and cover with a damp kitchen towel. Store in the refrigerator for up to 24 hours; any longer and mollusks may die.

For scallops and oysters on the half shell, refrigerate in a single layer on a large plate or tray, covered with a damp cloth or paper towel. Store loose scallop meat in an airtight container in the refrigerator for up to 2 days.

To freeze mollusks, first steam them open: Place in a large pot with about 1/2 cup (4 fl oz/125 ml) water, cover, and bring to boil. Steam just until the mollusks open. Then cool and extract the meat. Place it in freezer bags, exclude air, seal, label and freeze for up to 3 months. Scallop meat can also be frozen in a freezer bag for up to 3 months. Do not freeze oysters.

Preparation

Oysters bought alive in shell will require shucking. Oysters and scallops on the half shell and bottled oysters require no preparation. Some species of scallop need the vein to be removed followed by light rinsing. The vein, which is similar to that of a shrimp, is on the side of the scallop's round of flesh.

Mollusks in the shell need thorough rinsing under cold water, sometimes scrubbing with a brush to remove mud and grit. Beards (the fibrous and hairlike fringe that attaches a mussel to the surface on which it grows) must be removed. A small, sharp knife makes this job easier. Some mollusks, such as cockles and clams, need soaking in cold water for up to 1 hour to purge them of sandy residue. The sand will settle at the bottom of the soaking container.

Cooking

With the exception of scallops on the half-shell, mollusks that are still in their shells must be alive when cooked. They should be cooked only until the shells open, a matter of a few minutes. If overcooked, they will toughen and shrink.

Mollusks can be poached, steamed, cooked in soups, sauces, and curries, barbecued, or stir-fried. If cooking in a sauce or other liquid, cover the pan to hasten cooking and trap moisture.

Oysters in the shell or freshly shucked are still alive but generally die within minutes of opening. All the cooking oysters need is a short heating, whether it is under the broiler (grill) with a topping, or in a deep fryer.

Broiling, Grilling, and Barbecuing

To cook most successfully in this manner, mollusks should be left in their shell. They only take a few minutes to open so it is best to be ready and waiting to remove them as soon as they open or they will overcook. A savory butter melted and added to the mollusks towards the end of the cooking time (when just opening) and at the end, will add flavor and moisture.

Panfrying

Mollusks can be panfried in butters or oils while still in the shell. The temperature needs to be quite high and maintained by continuous stirring after the mollusks are added to ensure they cook quickly. Remove from the heat as they open, which should take about 3 to 5 minutes, depending on size.

Poaching

Mollusks are perfect for poaching in soups, stews, and sauces and should be added in the last few minutes of cooking as they require only a short amount of cooking and are done when they are just open. They can also be poached in a variety of liquids (see page 18).

Steaming

Mollusks steam extremely well and only take a few minutes to open; remove as they open to prevent overcooking. They will remain moist and tender, and depending on the steaming liquid, extremely tasty. No sauce need be served with them, just a squeeze of lemon juice.

CEPHALOPODS

Squid (calamari), octopus, and cuttlefish are available worldwide, and if cooked correctly become moist and tender.

Purchasing

Octopus can be purchased as tiny babies or as large, fully grown specimens weighing up to 4 lb (2 kg) each. Cuttlefish can only be purchased whole. They require quite a bit of time to prepare, but their sweet and tender flesh makes it worthwhile. Squid can be purchased already cleaned and cut into rings, or left whole as tubes. They should have firm, resilient flesh and a pleasant sea smell.

Storing

Thoroughly clean octopus, squid, and cuttlefish before storage, as their high moisture content can cause them to seep when left standing and broken ink sacs can be messy. Refrigerate for up to 2 days in an airtight container or place in freezer bags, exclude all air, seal, label, and freeze for up to 4 months.

SQUID

One

Clean under running water. With salted fingers, hold the hood (body) and with the other hand reach in and take a firm grip of the head and tentacles. Gently pull tentacles away from body; tentacles may be used if cut from head. Discard head.

Two

Remove transparent quill from the hood (this is cartilage and pulls away easily); discard.

Three

Peel back the flaps and remove the skin and fins from the hood.

Four

Rinse well and leave whole or cut into rings or pieces.

Preparation

Octopus, squid, and cuttlefish should be washed well under cold running water before preparation. Take care when making incisions not to cut too deeply in case the intestines or ink sac are pierced. Once removed, the ink sac may be used in cooking and is often an ingredient in many European recipes. However, when these animals are netted they lose much of their ink so it usually has to be supplemented with additional ink from more animals when making up an ink sauce. Frozen ink can be bought commercially in some countries.

Cooking

The rule for squid and cuttlefish is very quick cooking: 2 to 3 minutes for small pieces, and a little longer if left whole.

Depending on size, octopus needs either short, quick cooking or long, slow, moist cooking. Whether simmered in sauces, soups, curries, casseroles, or water, large octopus requires up to $1^1/2$ hours to become tender. Small baby octopus may need only 40 minutes, simmering. The best way to check for tenderness is to cut off a small piece and taste it; if it is still tough, cook further.

Broiling, Grilling, and Barbecuing

Octopus, squid, and cuttlefish cook successfully by these methods although in this instance short cooking is vital to prevent toughening and drying out of the flesh — only 1 to 2 minutes for squid and cuttlefish and no longer than 5 minutes for octopus. Marinating works particularly well to add moisture. Small octopus can be cooked whole or segmented; squid can be cooked in rings, pieces, or whole tubes, and cuttlefish in pieces.

Panfrying

Squid and cuttlefish panfry well and take only about 2 to 3 minutes cooking Baby octopus are also suitable and take about 3 to 5 minutes. Toss well in pan juices. Large octopus are not suitable, even cut into pieces, as they need long slow cooking to tenderize.

Deep Frying

Octopus are not really suitable for deep frying. Squid and cuttlefish, however, coated in batter or crumbs are very tasty. Cook for the shortest possible time to prevent a tough, rubbery texture. If you begin with very hot oil, a light golden coating will be a good indication of doneness. See page 18 for further deep frying information.

Poaching

Poaching is ideal for octopus which requires long, slow cooking — up to 1 hour for small baby octopus, and 2 hours for large. The moist cooking process produces beautifully tender and succulent flesh. See page 18 for further poaching information.

Squid and cuttlefish can also be poached in soups, sauces, and stews for up to 1 hour to become very tender.

Baking

Squid and cuttlefish produce good results when baked with moist ingredients, like tomatoes. Squid can be stuffed for baking, then cut into rings for serving. To prevent drying, cover with foil and cook until tender and no longer translucent. Octopus is not recommended for baking as the length of time required for tender results is impractical.

CUTTLEFISH

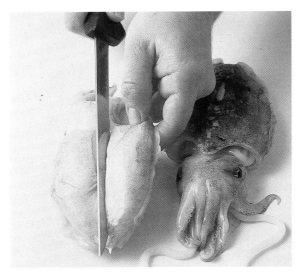

One

Place on work surface bone side down. With a sharp knife, make a cut down the length of the body, taking care not to cut too deeply, thereby piercing the intestines and ink sac.

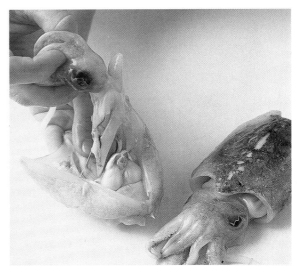

Two

Open body and firmly pull gut, head, and tentacles away and discard. Remove cuttlebone and discard.

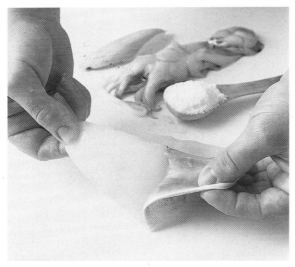

Three

Remaining are two separate fleshy pieces held together with skin. Pull firmly on the skin to strip away and then discard.

Four

The result is two pieces of cuttlefish, ready to be cooked whole, in strips, or honeycombed (see glossary, page 37).

OCTOPUS

One

Place octopus on work surface and cut off the head just below the eyes. If the octopus is small, there will not be much flesh on the head, so you can discard it.

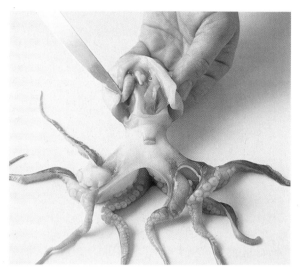

Two

Alternatively, make a shallow cut at the back along the length of the head, taking care not to cut too deeply, or you will pierce the intestines. Separate halves. Remove intestines and discard. Wash flesh.

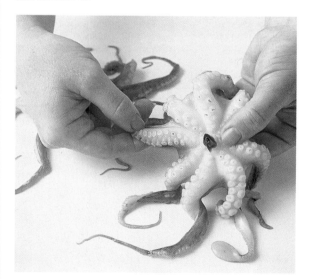

Three

Push thumb or finger up into the body section and push as if to turn inside out — the small black beak (mouth) should pop out, which is discarded.

Four

Rinse body and either keep whole, if it is small, or segment by cutting into pieces, using tentacles and head.

GLOSSARY

Almond Meal

Finely ground blanched almonds, used for coatings, in cakes and cookies, and as a thickener in curries and casseroles.

Arborio Rice

An Italian short–grain rice that has large, round grains and the ability to absorb sauce without becoming too soft and sticky.

Arugula

A crisp, nutty tasting salad green also known as rocket. Becoming increasingly popular not only as an addition to salad, but also cooked as a vegetable.

Asian Noodles

A fresh noodle, made from wheat and water, which needs refrigeration. Requires a very short cooking time, between 3 to 5 minutes. Readily available from Asian markets and some delicatessens.

Belgian Endive

An elongated, compact salad green, very crisp and sweet tasting, with slight bitterness; also known as chicory. It is suitable for cooking and can be sautéed and served as a vegetable accompaniment.

Blanch

To plunge food into boiling water for a very short time, then immediately into cold water to stop the cooking process. Blanching is done for a number of reasons — to partly cook food, especially vegetables; to reduce strong flavors; to loosen skin for easier peeling; and to remove excess fat.

Breadcrumbs

To make fresh breadcrumbs tear slices of bread, crusts removed, into small pieces and blend in a food processor or blender until crumbs are formed. Use while fresh in stuffings, puddings, and meat or fish loaves. About four slices of bread makes a cup of crumbs.

Bulghur Wheat

Also known as cracked wheat. The grains are boiled, then dried and cracked. When soaked in water it expands and becomes tender. Used extensively in Middle Eastern cookery, it is the basis for tabbouleh.

Chervil

A herb with fernlike feathery leaves and a delicate anise flavor.

Chinese Long Beans

Long, thin dark green beans, also known as snake beans, sold in bundles. They are generally chopped into smaller pieces, as they can be up to 12 in (30 cm) long.

Cilantro

Also known as coriander. A herb belonging to the parsley family, it has soft green foliage, which is used along with the roots. The leaves are used fresh and the seeds are made into ground coriander.

Clarified Butter (Ghee)

Pure butter fat with all the butter's nonfatty constituents removed. This is done by slowly heating the butter and skimming away the froth that rises to the top; what remains in the pan is the clarified butter. In cooking, clarified butter can be heated to a much higher temperature than butter without burning. It is readily available from Indian markets and delicatessens.

Coral Lettuce

A soft-leaf lettuce without a heart. The lacy leaves resemble coral and are variegated, with green leaves and red tips.

Cos Lettuce

Also known as romaine. An elongated head lettuce with crisp, bright green leaves, mild flavor and a firm, delicate heart.

Curry Paste

A smooth seasoning paste made by pounding together chilies, lemongrass, garlic, onion, shrimp paste, and other seasonings. Can be red or green (the milder of the two), depending on the type of chilies used. Available from most supermarkets in jars or packs.

Devein

To make a shallow cut along the back of certain crustaceans, such as shrimp, and remove the dark intestinal vein. To devein certain species of scallops, simply pinch vein, using fingertips and discard. The vein is easily located on the side of the scallop.

Emmenthal Cheese

A Swiss cow's milk cheese with large holes. Pale yellow, it has a sweet, nutty taste.

Escarole

A bitter green with curly green and white leaves, also known as curly endive. Can be cooked or used raw.

Fennel

A fleshy, anise-flavored herb of Italian origin, with crisp white stalks and bulb. The bulb is used as a salad ingredient or can be cooked as a vegetable.

Feta Cheese

A soft white cheese that is cured in brine. It has a somewhat salty flavor and can be used in salads or cooked dishes. Of Greek origin, it is now produced in many countries and, traditionally, is made from either sheep's or goat's milk.

Fish Sauce

A sauce used extensively in Thai cookery. A clear, watery, amber-colored liquid, it is made from salted and fermented fish. It is readily available bottled.

Focaccia

A soft Italian flat bread that is oiled and sprinkled with salt or various toppings.

Garlic, bruised

To bruise garlic simply place a clove on work surface and, with the flat blade of a knife, press down to gently squash clove. Peel and use as required.

Gorgonzola Cheese

A semisoft blue-veined cheese of Italian origin. It has a sharp taste and is creamy with a slightly crumbly texture.

Grape (Vine) Leaves

Sold loose in Middle Eastern markets, or, more commonly, covered with brine in jars. Featuring extensively in Middle Eastern cookery, the leaves are used as a wrapping for other foods, particularly rice mixtures.

Green or Red Oakleaf Lettuce

A soft-leaf lettuce without a heart. It has a delicate flavor.

Hoisin Sauce

A dark, sweet, spicy Chinese sauce made from soybeans and other flavorings such as vinegar, chili, and garlic. Used in stir-fried dishes combined with other ingredients, or used as a marinade or sauce.

Honeycomb

To score the flesh of squid or cuttlefish with a diamond grid of cuts. The process tenderizes the meat and allows for quick, even cooking.

Julienne

To cut vegetables or other ingredients into thin, even-sized strips.

Kaffir Lime Leaves

The dried leaves of the kaffir lime tree. The lime itself is dark green with warty skin and little juice; only the skin and the leaves are used. The fresh leaves are hard to find, but the dried leaves are inexpensive and are readily available from Asian food markets.

Lemongrass

A Thai herb that resembles tall, slim green reeds. It imparts a subtle lemon flavor due to the presence of citric oils. The whole stem can be used. The white, lower part of the stalk can be chopped or pounded. The green top may be bruised and used in cooking, then removed and discarded, as it can be woody.

Mesclun

A French term referring to a variety of greens combined for mixed salad. These include rocket, edible flower petals, sprouts, and varieties of lettuce.

Mirin

A sweet rice wine used in Japanese cookery. If mirin is not available, sweet or dry sherry may be substituted.

Mizuna

A soft, tender Japanese lettuce with small, deeply toothed leaves. Used as a salad green.

Olive Oil

An edible monosaturated oil made from olives. Olives are grown worldwide but the largest commercial production operates in the Mediterranean region, including Italy, Spain, and Greece. Once the olives are harvested they are crushed or pressed and the juice is collected. This juice is then allowed to settle and separate after which the oil component is removed. Extra virgin olive oil comes from the first pressing. It is the most expensive and is preferred when oil is a feature of the recipes as it is in dressings. The treatment of the pulp after this initial stage will determine what other types of oil are extracted, for example cold pressed, pure, unfiltered, or extrafine. Note that the term "light" olive oil refers to its flavor, not its fat content.

Olive Paste

A paste made of green or black olives pounded together with seasonings until smooth. Also known as tapenade.

Oyster Mushrooms

Moist, chewy mushrooms so named because they are said to resemble pale oyster shells.

Oyster Sauce

A thick Chinese sauce made with oysters. It is rich and salty in flavor.

Pasta

Pasta can be divided into two groups: dried or fresh. Dried pasta is the most widely available of pastas in packet form and comes in numerous shapes and textures, is made from durum wheat and water. It generally takes about 12 minutes to cook al dente — firm but tender. Fresh pasta, also available in a variety of shapes and forms, is made from soft flour, water, and sometimes egg. It takes less time to cook than dry pasta, about 6 minutes, depending on size.

The best method for cooking fresh or dry pasta is to bring a large pot of water to boil, add pasta and salt (if desired) and stir well. Return to boil and cook uncovered until al dente, stirring often.

Pecorino Cheese

A sharp-tasting hard Italian cheese, made from sheep's milk. Used for grating over pasta or in other cooked dishes. Can be substituted with parmesan cheese.

Radicchio

A salad green with beautiful deep red, cream-veined leaves. It forms a tight head and has crisp, slightly bitter leaves.

Rice

There are a couple of ways to successfully cook rice:

Boiling method. Bring a generous amount of water to boil. Add rice and salt to taste, stirring well. Return water to boil and cook uncovered about 10 to 12 minutes or until rice is firm but tender (do not overcook or rice will be soft and mushy). Drain well.

Absorption method. Used extensively in Asia, this is an extremely easy way to cook rice either by microwave or on a stovetop. Place required amount of rice in fine sieve or collander and wash under cold running water until water runs clear. Place rice into saucepan, or microwave-proof bowl, and cover with enough water to give a 1 in.(2.5 cm.) depth above rice. If cooking in saucepan, bring to a rapid boil and continue to boil until 'tunnels' appear in surface of rice. Turn off heat, cover pan with lid, and let stand for 10 minutes. If cooking in microwave, cook on high for about 12 minutes, stirring once. Remove bowl from oven, cover with plastic film, and let stand for 5 minutes. Fluff with a fork before serving.

Rocket – see Arugula

Score
To make deep cuts into a food to allow it to cook evenly, and for seasonings to permeate.

Seasoned Flour
To season $1/2$ cup ($1^1/2$ oz/45 g) all-purpose (plain) flour, add $1/4$ teaspoon salt and a good pinch of pepper. Place in a plastic bag, add fish pieces, and shake to coat.

Sesame Oil
A strongly flavored oil made from roasted sesame seeds. Widely used in Asian, particularly Chinese, cookery. Used sparingly, it adds a unique nutty flavor to cooked dishes and salad dressings.

Shrimp Paste
An extremely strong, fishy-smelling paste, sold in a hard, brown, compact slab. Made from dried shrimp and salt, it is used sparingly to enhance the flavor of food. Store in an airtight container in the refrigerator.

Shuck
To pry open oyster shells.

Sorrel
A green-leafed vegetable with a sour, sharp taste. The young leaves can be used as salad greens or cooked as a vegetable in stir-fries, soups and stews.

Sprouts
When a seed, grain, or pulse is germinated by soaking in water, the growth that results is known as a sprout. Sprouts are highly nutritious. Mung bean sprouts and alfalfa sprouts are the most common, although others like snowpea and mustard seed sprouts are becoming more popular.

Tahini
A creamy-colored paste made from sesame seeds. It can also be used as a dipping sauce.

Vinegar
The word vinegar means sour wine. It is used in pickling, preserving and in salad dressings. There are many varieties available, including:

Balsamic vinegar—an expensive Italian red wine vinegar, aged in barrels for up to 12 years. It has a slightly sweet, complex flavor.

Cider vinegar—made from apples, it has a mild sweet flavor and is yellowish in color.

Wine vinegar—made from red or white wine fermentation.

Wasabi
A pungent, bright green Asian horseradish, used in Japanese cookery. In Japan it is sold as a root, but in the West it is more commonly available in powdered or paste form.

Watercress
A sometimes bitter herb that grows in water and has small, pungent green leaves. The stem is discarded; only the leaves are used.

WHAT FISH IS THAT?
Identifying Your Fish

SPECIES NAME	UK	NORTH AMERICA	AUSTRALIA	NEW ZEALAND	CHARACTERISTICS	SOLD AS	SUITABLE TO
Anglerfish	Anglerfish, Monkfish	Anglerfish, Goosefish, Monkfish	*No Substitute*	Monkfish, Stargazer	Big ugly head. White, firm flesh. Often compared to lobster. Mild, sweet flavor.	Fillets	Bake, fry, poach, steam
Bluefish	*Substitute Mullet*	Bluefish	Tailor	*Substitute Mullet*	Oily, soft flesh. Fine texture.	Whole, Fillets	Bake, broil, barbeque, fry, grill
Bream	Black Bream	*Substitute Red Porgy*	Silver Bream, Yellowfin Bream, Black Bream	Black Bream	Large, flat fish. Firm, white flesh. Fine texture. Delicate flavor.	Whole	Bake, broil, barbeque, grill, fry, poach, steam
Brill	Brill	*Substitute Lemon Sole or Summer Flounder*	*Substitute Flounder or Common Sole*	Brill	Delicate flavor. Firm flesh.	Whole, Fillets	Broil, grill, barbeque, fry, poach, steam
Dory	John Dory	John Dory *Substitute Winter Flounder or Lemon Sole*	John Dory, Mirror Dory	John Dory	Fine texture. Delicate flavor. Firm, white flesh. Boneless. Mirror Dory resembles John as it is fine, white, and moist.	Whole, Fillets	Bake, broil, barbeque, fry, poach, grill, steam
Flounder	Forbay Sole	Winter Flounder, Lemon Sole (Common Flounder), Summer Flounder (Northern Fluke)	Flounder	Tinplate, Dab	Small, flat fish. Firm, white flesh. Sweet delicate flavor. Few bones.	Whole, Fillets	Bake, broil, barbeque, grill, fry, poach, steam
Garfish	Gar-Fish	Gar, *Substitute Small Red Mullet*	Garfish, Snub-Nosed Garfish	Piper	Fine texture. Sweet delicate flavor. Small soft bones.	Whole	Bake, broil, barbeque, grill, fry
Grenadier	Grenadier	Grenadier, Rat Tail	Blue Grenadier	Whip Tail, Rat Tail	Soft flesh. Fine texture.	Fillets Steaks	Bake, broil, barbeque, grill, fry
Gurnard	Grey Gurnard, Red Gurnard	Sea Robin *Substitute Rockfish*	Red Gurnard, Spotted Gurnard, Latchet	Gurnard	Dry, firm, white flesh. Medium flake.	Whole, Fillets	Bake, fry, poach, steam

SPECIES NAME	UK	NORTH AMERICA	AUSTRALIA	NEW ZEALAND	CHARACTERISTICS	SOLD AS	SUITABLE TO
Halibut	Halibut	Atlantic Halibut, Northern Pacific Halibut	*Substitute Mirror Dory, John Dory, or Flounder*	*Substitute Brill, Tinplate, or John Dory*	Large, flat fish. Firm, white flesh. Mild flavor.	Whole, Fillets	Bake, broil, barbeque, fry, grill, poach, steam
Herring	North Sea Herring, Baltic Herring	Herring	Sea Herring, Freshwater Herring	Herring	Fine texture. Oily, distinct flavor.	Whole, Fillets	Bake, broil, barbeque, cure, fry, grill
Jewfish	Meagre	Croaker, Drumfish	Jewfish, Mulloway	*Substitute Kingfish or Yellowtail*	Dry, firm flesh. Large flake. Mild flavor.	Whole, Fillets, Steaks	Bake, fry, poach, steam
Mackerel	Spanish	Mackerel	Spanish Mackerel, Slimy Mackerel	Blue Mackerel	Rich, oily flavor. Fine firm texture.	Whole, Fillets	Barbeque, broil, grill, fry
Mullet	Grey Mullet	Striped Mullet	Sea Mullet	Mullet	Oily, fine flesh.	Whole, Fillets	Broil, grill, barbeque, fry
Plaice	Plaice	American Plaice, Sand Dab	*Substitute Flounder or Sole*	*Substitute New Zealand Sole or English Sole*	Small, flat fish. Fine, delicate flavor.	Whole, Fillets	Broil, fry, poach, steam
Pollack	Pollack, Saithe, Coley	Pollock	*Substitute Snapper or Bream*	*Substitute Snapper or Bream*	Firm, white flesh.	Whole, Fillets, Steaks	Bake, fry, poach, steam
Red Mullet	Red Mullet	Red Mullet, Goatfish	Red Mullet, Goatfish, Barbunya	Red Mullet	Largest no more than 16 in. (40 cm). Delicate mild flavor. Fine texture.	Whole	Bake, broil, barbeque, fry, grill, poach, steam
Rudderfish	Amberjack	Rudderfish	Kingfish	Kingfish, Yellowtail	Medium to large flake. Firm white flesh that can be dry.	Whole, Fillets, Steaks	Broil, grill, barbeque, fry, poach, steam
Salmon	Salmon	Pacific Salmon, Atlantic Salmon	Farmed Atlantic Salmon	King Salmon	Oily, firm flesh. Delicate flavor and texture.	Whole, Fillets, Steaks	Broil, grill, barbeque, fry, poach, steam
Sardine (juvenile), Pilchard (adult)	Sardine, Pilchard	Sardine, Pilchard	Sardine, Pilchard	Sardine Pilchard	Oily, soft flesh. Fine texture. Edible bones.	Whole	Bake, broil, barbeque, fry, grill
Scorpionfish	Scorpionfish	Scorpionfish	Ocean Perch	Ocean Perch	Delicate flavor. Fine white flesh. Bony.	Whole, Fillets	Bake, broil, barbeque, fry, grill, poach

SPECIES NAME	UK	NORTH AMERICA	AUSTRALIA	NEW ZEALAND	CHARACTERISTICS	SOLD AS	SUITABLE TO
Sea Bream	Sea Bream	Red Porgy	Morwong, Sea Bream	Tarakihi	Firm, white flesh. Fine texture. Bony.	Whole, Fillets	Bake, broil, grill, barbeque, poach, steam
Skate	Skate, Ray	Skate	Skate	Skate	Soft, sweet, tasty. Remove skin before cooking. No bones, made up of cartilage.	Many varieties, although only wings are eaten.	Broil, grill, barbeque, fry, poach, steam
Snapper	*Substitute Black Bream*	*Substitute Red Porgy*	Snapper	Snapper, Bream	Firm, white flesh. Medium flake.	Whole, Fillets, Steaks	Bake, fry, poach, steam
Sole	Lemon sole, Dover sole	Lemon Sole	Lemon sole, Common Sole	New Zealand Sole, English Sole	Small, flat fish. Fine, firm flesh.	Whole, Fillets	Broil, grill, barbeque, fry, poach, steam
Trout	Brown Trout, Lake Trout, Sea Trout, Salmon Trout	Lake Trout, Brown Trout, Rainbow Trout, Brook Trout, Sea Trout	Brown Trout, Rainbow Trout	Brown Trout, Rainbow Trout	Soft, white, moist flesh. Fine bones.	Whole	Broil, grill, barbeque, fry
Tuna	Tuna, Bluefin, Tunny	Yellowfin, Bluefin	Yellowfin tuna, Southern Bluefin	Yellowfin, Southern Bluefin	Firm, oily but dry flesh. Large flake.	Steaks	Broil, fry, poach, steam
Turbot	Turbot	*Substitute Atlantic Halibut, Northern Pacific Halibut*	*Substitute Flounder, Sole, John Dory or Mirror Dory*	Turbot	Large, flat fish. White, firm flesh. Moist and tender.	Whole, Fillets	Bake, broil, grill, barbeque, fry
Whiting (Northern hemisphere only)	Whiting, Blue Whiting	Blue Whiting			Fine flesh. Delicate flavor.	Whole, Fillets	Broil, grill, barbeque, fry, poach
Whiting (Southern hemisphere only)			King George (also Spotted Whiting), School Whiting (also Red Spot) Sand Whiting (also Silver Whiting)	Southern Blue Whiting	Delicate fine flesh and flavor. Can be bony.	Whole, Fillets	Broil, grill, barbeque, fry, poach, steam
Whitebait	White Bait	Whitebait	Whitebait	New Zealand Whitebait	Tiny, silvery Eaten whole	Whole	Bake, deep fry

WHAT SHELLFISH IS THAT?

SPECIES NAME	CHARACTERISTICS	PURCHASE	AVAILABLE	SUITABLE TO
1. CRUSTACEANS				
CRABS Many species available worldwide: shore, blue, stone, rock, spanner, mud, mangrove. Caught in bays, harbors, mangroves, creeks, and streams.	Grow to a maximum size of 10 in. (25 cm). When alive or raw, range from green, blue or black. When cooked, they become bright orange. They have a rich sweet taste, and flake can vary from small and coarse to large flakes.	Raw, live or cooked	All year	Bake, boil, poach, steam
FLAT LOBSTERS Different to lobsters but related. Found worldwide, they have a flattened broad body, without claws, and are small compared to lobsters. Also known as slipper lobster, shovel nosed lobster, and locust lobster.	Grow to a maximum size of 6 in. (15 cm). When alive or raw they are an orange brown and become an orange red when cooked. They have white, sweet and mild tasting flesh, which is found in the tail section, with medium flake texture.	Raw, live or cooked	All year	Boil, broil, grill, barbecue, panfry, poach, steam
FRESHWATER CRAYFISH Small crustaceans that look like tiny clawed lobsters. Found worldwide in lakes, dams, rivers, creeks, and streams, but are also farmed. Also known as swamp, signal, and marron.	Many different species available. They can grow to weigh 12 lbs (6 kg), although the average grow to weigh between 1-3 oz (30-100 g) each. When alive or raw, range from brown to blue, and on cooking become bright orange or red. They have sweet, mild-tasting flesh.	Raw, live or cooked	All year	Boil, broil, grill, barbecue, panfry, poach, steam
LOBSTERS Found worldwide, known as spiny lobsters, rock lobsters and clawed lobsters. Caught in coastal waters, bays, tropical waters; also farmed.	Grow to a maximum length of 2 feet (60 cm). When alive or raw, they range from yellow, orange, green, blue to almost black. When cooked, they become bright orange to red. Meat is found in the tail section and claws. It has white, sweet meat with a firm texture and large flakes.	Raw, live or cooked	All year	Bake, boil, broil, grill, panfry, poach, steam

What Shellfish Is That?

SPECIES NAME	CHARACTERISTICS	PURCHASE	AVAILABLE	SUITABLE TO
SHRIMP Also known as prawns. The most well known and popular crustacean. Available worldwide, they come in many different sizes, depending on species. Caught in coastal waters, rivers, and estuaries; also farmed.	Range in size from tiny shrimp to large jumbo shrimp (king prawns), which can grow up to 10 in. (25 cm). Raw, they range from creamy yellow, pale pink, green, grey, olive brown and blue and become bright orange to red when cooked. They are moist and tender, with a sweet, succulent flesh.	Raw or cooked, peeled or unpeeled	All year	Bake, barbecue, boil, broil, grill, deep fry, panfry, poach, steam
SCAMPI Member of the lobster family. Found worldwide, if not in the wild, then farmed. Also known as Dublin bay prawn or langoustine.	Grow to a maximum length of 8 in. (20 cm). They resemble a small clawed lobster, with a sweet, mild taste and a fine, coarse texture.	Raw or cooked in the shell	All year	Bake, boil, deep fry, panfry, poach, steam
2. CEPHALOPODS				
CUTTLEFISH Has a thick oval shaped body and ten tentacles. Has an internal shell, known as a cuttlebone. Flesh is very similar to squid. Found worldwide in coastal waters.	Grow to a maximum length of 10 in. (25 cm). They are usually quite dark, with shades of pink, grey and brown. When cooked, the flesh is white, tender if not overcooked and can be very sweet. An ink sac can be found in the intestines and can be used in cooking.	Raw	All year	Bake, barbecue, deep fry, panfry, poach, stir fry,
SQUID Also known as calamari. Has a long, slender body, with side fins and ten tentacles. They have an internal transparent backbone, known as a quill. Many species available worldwide, they are caught in bays, estuaries and coastal waters.	Grow to a maximum length of 2 feet (60 cm), although baby squid, known as bottle squid can be as small as 1½ in. (4 cm). The raw squid varies from mottled pink to grey. When cooked, the flesh becomes very white and if not overcooked, quite tender. It has a sweet, mild taste. An ink sac can be found in the intestines.	Raw and whole, or cleaned and left in hoods or cut into rings	All year	Broil, grill, barbecue, deep fry, panfry, poach, steam,

WHAT SHELLFISH IS THAT?

SPECIES NAME	CHARACTERISTICS	PURCHASE	AVAILABLE	SUITABLE TO
OCTOPUS Has a soft oval shaped body, with an internal beak, and eight legs. Found worldwide in coastal waters.	Grow to a maximum length of 40 in. (1 m), although size ranges from baby octopus, which might weigh only 1 1/2 oz (50 g) each to large adults, weighing up to 6 lbs (3 kg) each. When raw, octopus is brownish grey. Upon cooking, the flesh changes to a beautiful reddish brown. Octopus can be very tender if cooked correctly, and has a mild sweet tasting flesh. Small baby octopus are often tenderized prior to selling — if the flesh is firm and legs are curled close to the head it indicates that the octopus is tenderized. Untenderized flesh is soft and limp.	Raw, some may be gutted	All year	Broil, grill, barbecue, panfry, poach
3. MOLLUSKS These are classified as invertebrates with a shell which is made up of one or two pieces, hence the name uni- or bi- valve. Clams, cockles, mussels, oysters, and scallops are all examples of bivalves. Conch, winkles, limpets, and abalone are examples of univalves. Found worldwide.	Mollusks come in many shapes and sizes, and range in size from tiny shells no more than 1 in. (2.5 cm) to large shells 4 in. (10 cm) round. When alive, they should have tightly closed shells, upon cooking their shells open. Some mollusks, such as clams and cockles, need soaking prior to cooking to rid them of sandy residue.	Raw and live in the shell	All year	Bake, barbecue, panfry, poach, steam
OYSTERS Many species found world-wide. Most commonly farmed, and found in estuaries and sea shores.	Oysters vary in size and shape depending on their species. When sold they are graded according to size. Their flesh is plump and creamy.	Raw and live in the shell, freshly shucked on the half shell, in jars shelled and topped with salted water	All year	Bake, deep fry, broil, grill
SCALLOPS Many species found world-wide. Mostly caught by trawling or dredging.	Scallops vary in size and shape depending on their species. Raw flesh is white and plump, some species have orange roe intact.	Raw and live in shell, freshly shucked on half shell, or shelled meat	All year	Bake, broil, grill, panfry, poach, steam

FIRST COURSES

Shrimp, Tomato, and Roasted Garlic on Focaccia (page 104)

BRANDADE

SERVES 8

This Provençal specialty is perfect used as a spread on crusty breads. It makes a wonderful appetizer served with predinner drinks.
Dried salted cod is known as morue in France, baccalà in Italy, and bacalao in Spain. It needs to be soaked in fresh water for 24 hours, then drained and cooked.

10 oz (300 g) salted cod, soaked in water to cover, changing frequently, for 24 hours

3/4 cup (6 fl oz/180 ml) olive oil

3/4 cup (6 oz/180 g) mashed potato

3 cloves garlic, chopped

salt and freshly ground pepper

Place drained cod in large saucepan and cover with water. Bring to boil, then simmer 5 minutes or until cod flakes when tested. Drain and cool. Discard skin and bones.

Place cod in food processor or blender with some of the oil and puree. Add remaining oil, potato, garlic, and salt and pepper to taste and process until well combined.

Can be made up to 2 days in advance and stored in fridge. Serve at room temperature or chilled.

TARAMASALATA

MAKES 2 CUPS (16 FL OZ/500 ML)

Taramasalata is a Greek paste made from fresh or smoked cod roe. It is processed to form a smooth spread with oil, lemon juice, and garlic and is used as a dip or spread with crackers, bread, or crudités.

7 oz (220 g) fresh or smoked mullet or cod roe

1/2 cup (4 fl oz/125 ml) extra virgin olive oil

1/4 cup (2 fl oz/60 ml) lemon juice

1/2 cup (1 oz/30 g) fresh breadcrumbs (see page 36)

2 cloves garlic, chopped

salt and freshly ground pepper

If using fresh roe, place in saucepan cover with water, and bring to boil over medium heat. Cook 2 to 3 minutes or until tender. Drain.

Remove skin from poached or smoked roe by making a shallow cut at one end of the roe, then gradually peel away skin. Place roe in food processor or blender and puree. Add oil, lemon juice, breadcrumbs, garlic, and salt and pepper and process until well combined.

BUCKWHEAT BLINI WITH SMOKED SALMON

SERVES 6

Blini are small yeast pancakes. They can be made up to an hour before serving. Try any variety of smoked fish as a topping. Oysters and sashimi also make unusual toppings.

1/3 oz (10 g) compressed yeast or 1 teaspoon active dry yeast

1/2 teaspoon sugar

1 cup (8 fl oz/250 ml) warm milk

1/2 cup (2 oz/60 g) buckwheat flour

1/2 cup (2 oz/60 g) all-purpose (plain) flour

1 teaspoon salt

1 egg, beaten

2 tablespoons butter

sour cream, to serve

4 oz (125 g) smoked salmon, cut into strips

salmon roe, to serve

chopped chives, to serve

Place yeast in small bowl with sugar. Pour in 1/4 cup (2 fl oz/60 ml) of the milk and mix well. Cover with cloth and let stand in a warm place for about 10 minutes or until frothy and nearly tripled in volume.

Combine flours and salt in large bowl. Add remaining milk, yeast mixture, and egg and mix to form smooth batter. Cover with cloth and let stand in a warm place for about 15 minutes or until light and fluffy.

Heat butter in frying pan over medium heat. Add small spoonfuls of mixture and cook until bubbles begin to appear on the surface. Turn and cook a further 1 to 2 minutes or until golden.

To serve, place small spoonful of sour cream on blini and top with salmon, roe, and chives.

Buckwheat Blini with Smoked Salmon

RED MULLET, OLIVE PASTE, AND ONION BRUSCHETTA

SERVES 4 TO 6

Green olive paste is made by pureeing olives, spices, and olive oil. It is readily available in supermarkets and delicatessens.

3 tablespoons olive oil
1 tablespoon butter
1 onion, thinly sliced
2 teaspoons chopped fresh thyme
8 thick slices Italian bread, toasted
green olive paste
8 oz (250 g) red mullet fillets
thyme sprigs for garnish

Heat 2 tablespoons oil and butter in large frying pan over medium heat. Add onion and cook slowly until tender, golden, and transparent, about 15 minutes. Add thyme and set aside.

Spread bread with generous layer of olive paste and keep warm.

Heat remaining 1 tablespoon oil in frying pan over medium heat and fry fillets 1 to 2 minutes per side or until opaque and just beginning to flake. Place on bread, top with onion and thyme sprigs. Serve immediately.

CEVICHE

SERVES 4 TO 6

This famous Mexican dish is quick to make and very refreshing. The seafood isn't actually cooked, although the acid from the lime juice gives it a cooked appearance and texture. Lemon juice can be substituted.

1 lb (500 g) white-fleshed fish fillets, skinned and chopped
1/2 cup (4 fl oz/125 ml) lime juice
1 cup (4 oz/125 g) peeled, seeded, and chopped tomato
2 tablespoons chopped onion
2 tablespoons chopped cilantro (fresh coriander leaves)
1 red chili, seeded and chopped
1 clove garlic, chopped
2 teaspoons chopped fresh oregano
1/3 cup (3 fl oz/90 ml) olive oil

Place fish and lime juice in glass bowl. Cover and marinate in refrigerator for as long as possible or at least 1 hour. Drain if very watery.

Just before serving add tomato, onion, cilantro, chili, garlic, oregano, and oil and mix well. Serve chilled.

FISH CAKES WITH CUCUMBER RELISH

SERVES 6

These Thai cakes can be made a day in advance and stored in the refrigerator until ready to fry. They also freeze very well, and can be stored this way for up to 4 months.

3 tablespoons seeded and chopped cucumber

3 tablespoons finely chopped carrot

5 tablespoons chopped cilantro (fresh coriander leaves)

1 red chili, seeded and chopped

1/4 cup (2 fl oz/60 ml) white vinegar

1/2 cup (4 fl oz/125 ml) boiling water

1/4 cup (2 oz/60 g) sugar

7 oz (220 g) white-fleshed or oily fish fillets, skinned and chopped

14 oz (440 g) uncooked shrimp (prawns), peeled and deveined

1 tablespoon green curry paste

1/4 cup (2 fl oz/60 ml) vegetable oil

cilantro (fresh coriander) sprigs

Combine cucumber, carrot, 2 tablespoons cilantro, chili, vinegar, water, and sugar in small bowl and mix well. Let stand 15 minutes before serving.

Combine fish and shrimp in food processor and grind (mince) finely. Add 3 tablespoons cilantro and curry paste and blend well. Divide mixture into 12 parts and form into patties using wet hands.

Heat oil in frying pan over medium heat. Add patties and cook 1 to 2 minutes per side. Drain on paper towels.

To serve, divide hot patties among six plates. Spoon a small amount of cucumber relish over patties and garnish with cilantro.

Following pages: Fish Cakes with Cucumber Relish (page 53), Steamed Shrimp Buns (page 56), and Sushi (page 56)

STEAMED SHRIMP BUNS

SERVES 6

1¹/2 cups (6 oz/180 g) self-rising flour

1¹/2 tablespoons butter

¹/3 cup (3 fl oz/90 ml) warm water

¹/2 teaspoon rice vinegar

1 tablespoon hoisin sauce

1 tablespoon oyster sauce

1 tablespoon soy sauce

¹/2 teaspoon sesame oil

1 teaspoon cornstarch (cornflour)

1 tablespoon water

¹/2 cup (3 oz/90 g) chopped cooked shrimp (prawns)

2 tablespoons chopped scallions (spring onions/shallots)

Combine flour and butter in food processor and blend until mixture resembles fine breadcrumbs. Gradually add water and vinegar, and mix until soft dough forms. Wrap dough in plastic and let stand while preparing filling.

Combine sauces, oil, cornstarch, and water in small saucepan and bring to boil, stirring until thickened. Remove from heat and add shrimp and scallions.

Divide dough into 6 pieces and roll each into 4 in. (10 cm) circle. Place a portion of filling in middle. Brush edges of dough with water, bring edges up, and twist firmly to enclose filling. Arrange buns twisted side up on steamer rack and steam 20 minutes.

Serve hot.

SUSHI

SERVES 6 TO 8

Wasabi is green horseradish, used extensively in Japanese cooking. It is available in powdered or prepared form and is extremely hot, so use it sparingly.

1¹/2 cups (10 oz/300 g) short-grain rice

2 cups (16 fl oz/500 ml) water

2 tablespoons rice vinegar

2 tablespoons sugar

2 teaspoons salt

6 sheets dried seaweed

prepared wasabi

8 oz (250 g) sashimi-quality tuna, cut into strips

1 small cucumber, halved, seeded, and cut into strips

soy sauce

Wash rice until water runs clear. Place in colander and drain for 30 minutes. Place rice and water in saucepan over high heat and bring to boil. Boil uncovered until tunnels begin to appear on surface. Turn heat as low as possible, cover, and cook 10 minutes without stirring or lifting lid. Combine vinegar, sugar, and salt. Stir into rice and mix well. Spread out on tray, cover with wet cloth, and let cool.

Spread layer of rice about ¹/2 in. (1 cm) thick over seaweed. Using tip of knife, spread small line of wasabi over rice at one end of sheet; lay tuna and cucumber over the wasabi.

Starting at end closest to tuna, begin rolling seaweed tightly. Using sharp knife, cut the roll into slices at 1 in. (2.5 cm) intervals. Arrange on plates and serve with soy sauce.

HOT SMOKED TROUT AND WALNUT SALAD

SERVES 4

Try a mixture of salad greens: arugula (rocket), Belgian endive (witloof), escarole (curly endive) and radicchio, for example. Hot smoked trout are available from most delicatessens and fish markets.

2 whole hot smoked trout, 10 oz (300 g) each, filleted

7 oz (220 g) mixed salad greens

3 tablespoons chopped chives

3 tablespoons chopped walnuts

2 tablespoons walnut oil

2 tablespoons olive oil

1 tablespoon balsamic vinegar

salt and freshly ground pepper

Place trout, greens, chives, and walnuts in large bowl. Combine oils, vinegar, and salt and pepper to taste. Pour over greens and mix well. Divide among four plates and serve.

SEAFOOD AND RICE SALAD WITH SESAME DRESSING

SERVES 4

1 lb (500 g) mussels, scrubbed, and debearded

8 oz (250 g) scallops, deveined if necessary

1 lb (500 g) cooked shrimp (prawns), peeled and deveined

1/2 cup (3 oz/90 g) short-grain rice, cooked

1/4 cup (2 fl oz/60 ml) white wine vinegar

2 tablespoons olive oil

2 teaspoons sesame oil

1 tablespoon tahini

1 tablespoon honey

1 teaspoon sesame seeds

2 cloves garlic, chopped

salt and freshly ground pepper

Steam open mussels (see page 31). Poach scallops (see page 31).

Combine mussels, scallops, shrimp, and rice in large bowl. Mix vinegar, oils, tahini, honey, seeds, garlic, and salt and pepper to taste in jar and shake well. Pour over salad just before serving and toss well.

MEDITERRANEAN SEAFOOD SALAD

This terrific salad is ideal for a light lunch or first course. It can be prepared a few hours ahead of time, refrigerated, and dressed just before serving. Freshly shucked oysters, freshwater crayfish, and poached squid could also be used — try a combination. Serve with crusty bread or focaccia.

1 red bell pepper (capsicum)

1 lb (500g) cooked shrimp (prawns), peeled and deveined

2 plum (egg) tomatoes, quartered

14 oz (440g) can artichoke hearts, drained and quartered

2 cups (3 oz/100 g) escarole (curly endive) leaves

1/3 cup (3 fl oz/90 ml) extra virgin olive oil

1/4 cup (2 fl oz/60 ml) lemon juice

2 tablespoons finely chopped onion

1 tablespoon chopped fresh oregano or 1/2 teaspoon dried

salt and freshly ground pepper

Place red pepper under preheated broiler (grill) until skin blackens and blisters, about 15 minutes. Let cool, then peel away skin and remove seeds. Slice pepper. Combine with shrimp, tomatoes, artichokes and escarole in large bowl.

Combine oil, lemon juice, onion, oregano, and salt and pepper to taste. Just before serving, pour dressing over salad and toss well. Pile high on plates and serve.

GREEK OCTOPUS SALAD

For a succulent result, be sure the octopus is simmered long enough to tenderize it. Small baby octopus may only need 30 minutes cooking, whereas large octopus may take up to 1 hour. The best way to check is to cut off a small piece and taste it! If still tough, continue to cook until tender.

2 lb (1 kg) baby octopus, cleaned

1 purple (Spanish) onion, thinly sliced

2 stalks celery, chopped

1 red bell pepper (capsicum), chopped

1/3 cup (3 fl oz/90 ml) extra virgin olive oil

1/4 cup (2 fl oz/60 ml) lemon juice

1 clove garlic, chopped

2 teaspoons chopped fresh oregano or 1/2 teaspoon dried

1/4 teaspoon salt

freshly ground pepper

Place octopus in large saucepan and cover with water. Bring to boil and simmer 30 minutes or until tender. Drain and cool.

Place octopus in large bowl with onion, celery, and red pepper. Pour in oil, juice, garlic, oregano, and salt and pepper and mix well. Marinate salad for at least 30 minutes in refrigerator before serving.

Mediterranean Seafood Salad

SEAFOOD AND NOODLE SALAD

SERVES 6

1 lb (500 g) cuttlefish, cleaned and honeycombed (see page 34)

1 lb (500 g) fish fillets, skinned and chopped to bite size

4 oz (125 g) scallops, deveined if necessary

1 lb (500 g) mussels, scrubbed and debearded (see page 31)

1 lb (500 g) fresh Asian noodles

2 cloves garlic, chopped

2 tablespoons chopped cilantro (fresh coriander leaves)

2 tablespoons chopped lemongrass

1 red chili, seeded and chopped

1/3 cup (3 fl oz/90 ml) thin coconut cream

1/3 cup (3 fl oz/90 ml) lime juice

2 tablespoons fish sauce

1 tablespoon sugar

Place 2 cups (16 fl oz/500 ml) water in frying pan and bring to boil over high heat. Add cuttlefish. When water returns to boil, simmer 1 to 2 minutes until tender. Remove and drain. Add fish and scallops to same water, and cook 1 to 2 minutes until tender. Remove and drain. Place mussels in pan with 1/2 cup (4 fl oz/125 ml) water, cover, and bring to boil. Simmer until mussels open, 2 to 3 minutes; discard any that do not open. Remove and drain. Remove mussels from shells, discard shells. Combine all seafood in large bowl.

Cook noodles in boiling water until tender. Drain well and add to seafood. Combine garlic, cilantro, lemongrass, chili, coconut cream, lime juice, fish sauce, and sugar in small bowl and mix well. Just before serving, pour over seafood and noodles and toss well.

SEAFOOD CAESAR SALAD

SERVES 4

Croutons are small cubes of crispy fried bread, served with soups and salads. To make croutons, simply slice day-old bread into 1/3 in. (1 cm) cubes. Heat enough oil to cover base of frying pan, add bread and fry all sides until crispy and golden.

1 lb (500 g) cooked jumbo shrimp (large prawns), peeled and deveined

2 bacon strips (rashers), chopped and fried until crisp

1 romaine (cos) lettuce, torn into small pieces

1/3 cup (3 fl oz/90 ml) extra virgin olive oil

1/4 cup (2 fl oz/ 60 ml) white wine vinegar

6 anchovy fillets, halved

1 hard-cooked (boiled) egg, finely chopped

1/4 teaspoon salt

1 cup (2 oz/60 g) croutons

parmesan cheese shavings

Place shrimp, bacon, and lettuce in salad bowl. Combine oil, vinegar, anchovy fillets, egg, and salt and mix well. Pour over salad just before serving and toss well. Top with croutons and parmesan shavings.

FISH AND PEANUT SALAD

SERVES 4

1 lb (500 g) white-fleshed fish fillets

1/2 cup (4 fl oz/125 ml) water

3 oz (90 g) green beans, steamed until tender crisp

3 oz (90 g) mizuna or red oakleaf lettuce

3 oz (90 g) mung bean sprouts

3 tablespoons chopped scallions (spring onions/shallots)

2 tablespoons peanut oil

2 tablespoons white vinegar

1 1/2 tablespoons peanut butter

2 teaspoons sesame oil

2 tablespoons chopped peanuts

3 tablespoons chopped fresh mint leaves

Skin fish fillets and cut into small pieces. Place fish and water in frying pan, cover, and poach until fish is tender, about 3 minutes (see page 18). Drain.

Place fish in large bowl with beans, lettuce, sprouts, and scallions. Combine peanut oil, vinegar, peanut butter, and sesame oil and mix well. Pour over fish. Divide fish among four plates and sprinkle with peanuts and mint leaves. Serve.

SHELLFISH WITH ARUGULA

SERVES 4

12 cooked slipper lobsters or shrimp (large prawns)

1 purple (Spanish) onion, thinly sliced

7 oz (220 g) arugula (rocket), stems trimmed

1/4 cup (2 fl oz/60 ml) extra virgin olive oil

1 tablespoon balsamic vinegar

1 teaspoon dijon mustard

salt and freshly ground pepper

Extract meat from lobsters (see pages 22 to 25) and place in bowl with onion and arugula. Combine oil, vinegar, mustard, and salt and pepper to taste and mix well. Pour over salad and toss.

Pile salad onto chilled plates and serve.

CRAYFISH AND MESCLUN SALAD WITH PESTO DRESSING

SERVES 4

This delicious salad can be made with shrimp (prawns) if desired. The pesto dressing can be made ahead of time and stored in an airtight container in the refrigerator for 3 days.

2 lb (1 kg) cooked freshwater crayfish (see page 25)

6 oz (185 g) mesclun (see glossary)

3/4 cup (2 oz/60 g) bean sprouts

1/2 cup (11/2 oz/45 g) chopped fresh basil

1/3 cup (3 fl oz/90 ml) extra virgin olive oil

1 clove garlic, chopped

2 tablespoons grated parmesan cheese

2 tablespoons lemon juice

1 tablespoon pine nuts

salt and freshly ground pepper

Shell crayfish and discard shells. Place crayfish in bowl with mesclun and bean sprouts.

Combine basil, oil, garlic, parmesan, juice, pine nuts, and salt and pepper in food processor or blender and blend until nearly smooth. Pour over salad and toss well. Serve immediately.

Crayfish and Mesclun Salad with Pesto Dressing

SHELLFISH, WATERCRESS, AND AVOCADO SALAD

SERVES 4

Serve with rye bread and butter. Shrimp (large prawns) are a suitable alternative.

1½ lb (750 g) cooked lobster tails (see page 25)

1 large avocado, peeled and sliced

2 cups (3 oz/90 g) watercress

⅓ cup (3 fl oz/90 ml) olive oil

¼ cup (2 fl oz/60 ml) tarragon vinegar

1 teaspoon dijon mustard

1 clove garlic, chopped

salt and freshly ground pepper

Remove flesh from lobster tails (see pages 22 to 25) Place in a bowl with avocado and watercress. Blend oil, vinegar, mustard, garlic, and salt and pepper. Add to lobster and avocado and mix well.

OYSTERS, SHRIMP, AND AVOCADO WITH TOMATO DRESSING

SERVES 4

2 ripe tomatoes, peeled, seeded, and chopped

1 small onion, chopped

1 clove garlic, chopped

⅓ cup (3 fl oz/90 ml) olive oil

2 tablespoons tarragon vinegar

2 teaspoons chopped fresh tarragon

salt

12 freshly shucked oysters

12 cooked shrimp (prawns), peeled and deveined

1 avocado, sliced

freshly ground pepper

Combine tomatoes, onion, garlic, and oil in saucepan and bring to boil over medium heat. Simmer for 15 minutes or until thick. Pour into food processor with vinegar, tarragon, and salt to taste and blend until smooth. Chill.

Arrange oysters, shrimp, and avocado on four small plates. Drizzle with tomato puree and sprinkle with pepper. Serve.

64

CRAB, FISH, AND BEAN SALAD

SERVES 4

2 zucchini (courgettes)

10 oz (300 g) white-fleshed fish fillets, poached (see page 18) and cut into bite size pieces

6 oz (185 g) cooked crabmeat (see pages 25 to 26)

10 oz (300 g) Chinese long (snake) beans, blanched (see glossary)

1/3 cup (3 fl oz/80 ml) olive oil

2 tablespoons lemon juice

1/4 teaspoon salt

1 tablespoon chopped chives

1 tablespoon chopped fresh parsley

1/2 teaspoon black olive paste (see glossary)

Using a vegetable peeler slice along the length of the zucchini to obtain long, thin strips. Bring a saucepan of water to boil and plunge in strips for about 2 seconds or until bright green. Refresh by plunging quickly in cold water to stop the cooking process.

Arrange fish, crab, beans, and zucchini on individual plates. For dressing, combine oil, juice, salt, chives, parsley, and olive paste, mixing well. Spoon dressing over salad just prior to serving.

SEAFOOD PLATE WITH GREEN MAYONNAISE

SERVES 4

French bread makes an excellent accompaniment to this dish. Any variety of chilled cooked seafood can be used; for preparation instructions, see pages 21 to 35. Green mayonnaise can be made 2 days in advance and stored in a jar in the refrigerator.

12 cooked jumbo shrimp (large prawns), peeled and deveined

12 oysters on the half shell

2 small cooked crabs, segmented

8 cooked freshwater crayfish, meat removed from tails

1/3 cup (3 fl oz/80 ml) good quality whole-egg mayonnaise

1/3 cup (3 fl oz/80 ml) sour cream

1 clove garlic, chopped

3 tablespoons chopped fresh parsley

2 tablespoons chopped fresh dill

2 tablespoons chopped chives

1 tablespoon lemon juice

Arrange shrimp, oysters, crabs, and crayfish on platter.

Combine mayonnaise, sour cream, garlic, parsley, dill, chives, and lemon juice in food processor and blend until smooth. Transfer mixture to bowl for use as a dipping sauce, or spoon directly over seafood.

MINCED FISH WRAPPED IN LETTUCE

SERVES 6

Similar to Sang Choy Bow, this Thai-inspired dish is equally delicious hot or cold.

1 lb (500 g) white-fleshed or oily fish fillets, skinned and ground (minced)

2 tablespoons lemon juice

1 tablespoon fish sauce

1 tablespoon water

2 tablespoons finely chopped scallions (spring onions/shallots)

2 tablespoons chopped cilantro (fresh coriander leaves)

1/3 cup (1 1/2 oz/45 g) chopped celery

2 tablespoons sweet chili sauce

freshly ground pepper

6 iceberg lettuce leaves

Combine fish, lemon juice, fish sauce, and water in frying pan or wok over high heat and bring to boil. Break up fish using a wooden spoon and simmer 2 to 3 minutes.

Place fish in bowl with scallions, cilantro, celery, and chili sauce and season to taste with pepper. Mix well. Divide mixture among lettuce leaves and serve.

OCTOPUS AND VEGETABLE JULIENNE

SERVES 4 TO 6

Julienne is a French term for the cooking technique where ingredients are cut into thin, even-sized strips or "matchsticks". Squid (calamari), cuttlefish, and cooked shrimp (prawns) are also very good in this recipe.

2 lb (1 kg) octopus, cleaned

1 carrot, peeled and julienned

2 stalks celery, julienned

1 zucchini (courgette), julienned

1 red bell pepper (capsicum), julienned

1 small onion, thinly sliced

2 tablespoons peanut oil

1 tablespoon sesame oil

2 tablespoons lemon juice

1 tablespoon honey

salt and freshly ground pepper

1 teaspoon sesame seeds

Cut octopus into small pieces. Place in saucepan with water to cover and bring to boil. Simmer 30 minutes or until tender. Drain and cool.

Combine octopus, carrot, celery, zucchini, pepper, and onion in large bowl. Combine oils, juice, honey, salt and pepper, and seeds and pour over octopus mixture. Mix well. Marinate 15 minutes before piling high onto individual plates.

Minced Fish Wrapped in Lettuce

Octopus and Watercress with Warm Herb Dressing

SERVES 4 TO 6

Substitute shrimp (prawns), scallops, cuttlefish, or squid (calamari) if you like.

2 lb (1 kg) baby octopus, cleaned

2 cups (3 oz/90 g) watercress

3 tablespoons chopped chives

1/4 cup (2 fl oz/60 ml) extra virgin olive oil

1 clove garlic, chopped

2 tablespoons balsamic vinegar

1 tablespoon chopped fresh dill

1 tablespoon chopped fresh parsley

Place octopus in large saucepan with enough water to cover and bring to boil. Simmer 30 minutes or until tender. Drain and cool.

Combine octopus, watercress, and chives in large bowl.

Combine oil, garlic, vinegar, and herbs in small saucepan and warm over low heat. Pour over octopus. Serve piled high on plates.

Indian Spiced Shrimp

SERVES 4

These shrimp can be threaded onto skewers if desired. Or you may substitute fish pieces, scallops, or squid (calamari).

7 oz (220 g) plain yogurt

2 red chilies, seeded and chopped

2 cloves garlic, chopped

2 tablespoons chopped cilantro (fresh coriander leaves)

1 teaspoon garam masala

1 teaspoon turmeric

1 teaspoon grated lemon rind

2 tablespoons lemon juice

2 lb (1 kg) uncooked shrimp (prawns), peeled and deveined

Combine yogurt, chilies, garlic, cilantro, garam masala, turmeric, rind, and juice in large bowl. Add shrimp and mix well. Marinate 30 minutes, or overnight in refrigerator if time allows.

Drain excess marinade from shrimp and reserve. Heat frying pan, broiler (grill), or barbecue. Cook shrimp 1 to 2 minutes per side, basting frequently with marinade. Serve hot.

GREEK SEAFOOD KEBABS

SERVES 4

Soak bamboo skewers in water for 30 minutes before using to prevent burning.

1/2 cup (4 fl oz/125 ml) olive oil

1/4 cup (2 fl oz/60 ml) lemon juice

1 onion, finely chopped

2 tablespoons chopped fresh parsley

2 teaspoons chopped fresh oregano or 1/2 teaspoon dried

8 oz (250 g) white-fleshed fish fillets, cut into cubes

12 uncooked shrimp (prawns), peeled and deveined

12 scallops, deveined if necessary

Combine oil, juice, onion, parsley, oregano, fish, shrimp, and scallops in large bowl and mix well. Marinate in refrigerator for 1 hour, or longer if time permits.

Drain excess marinade from seafood and reserve. Thread seafood alternately onto bamboo skewers.

Broil (grill), barbecue, or panfry kebabs 1 to 2 minutes per side, basting with reserved marinade. Serve immediately.

SCALLOP AND SHRIMP SAUTÉ

SERVES 4

This recipe can be prepared well in advance and allowed to marinate in the refrigerator until ready to sauté. A variety of fish or shellfish can be substituted, and steamed rice or noodles can be served as an accompaniment.

1 clove garlic, chopped

1 teaspoon chopped fresh ginger

1 tablespoon sake or mirin

2 tablespoons soy sauce

12 uncooked jumbo shrimp (large prawns), peeled and deveined

16 scallops, deveined if necessary

1 tablespoon vegetable oil

3 tablespoons chopped scallions (spring onions/shallots)

Combine garlic, ginger, sake, soy sauce, shrimp, and scallops and mix well. Marinate in refrigerator 30 minutes, or longer if time permits. Drain.

Heat oil in wok or frying pan. Add shrimp and scallops and sauté 1 to 2 minutes or until tender and no longer translucent. Add scallions and serve.

STIR-FRIED SEAFOOD WITH NOODLES

8 oz (250 g) soft Asian noodles
1 tablespoon peanut oil
2 teaspoons sesame oil
1 tablespoon chopped lemongrass
3 cloves garlic, chopped
1 red chili, seeded and chopped
8 oz (250 g) uncooked shrimp (prawns), peeled and deveined
8 oz (250 g) fish fillets, skinned and cut into small pieces
8 oz (250 g) scallops, deveined if necessary
2 tablespoons fish sauce
2 tablespoons chopped cilantro (fresh coriander leaves)
1 tablespoon sweet chili sauce

Cook noodles in boiling salted water 5 minutes. Drain.

Heat oils in frying pan over medium heat. Add lemongrass, garlic, and chili and cook until fragrant, about 1 minute. Add shrimp and fish and cook 3 to 5 minutes until tender and no longer translucent. Stir in noodles, scallops, fish sauce, cilantro, and chili sauce and cook, stirring well, until noodles are heated through and scallops are tender, about 3 to 4 minutes. Serve immediately.

STIR-FRIED CUTTLEFISH WITH CARAWAY SEEDS

Try substituting shrimp (prawns), squid (calamari), or fish fillets in this recipe. Serve with lemon wedges if desired.

2 lb (1 kg) cuttlefish, cleaned and honeycombed (see page 34)
1 clove garlic, chopped
1 teaspoon chopped fresh ginger
1 tablespoon brown sugar
1 tablespoon peanut oil
1 tablespoon lemon juice
1 teaspoon caraway seeds

Combine cuttlefish, garlic, ginger, sugar, oil, lemon juice, and seeds in bowl and mix well. Marinate in refrigerator 30 minutes, or longer if time permits.

Heat frying pan or wok over high heat. Add drained cuttlefish and stir-fry 2 to 3 minutes or until tender. Serve.

Stir-Fried Seafood with Noodles

CRAB IN RED CURRY

SERVES 4

This Thai curry makes a good base for any seafood. Try substituting 1½ lbs (750 g) chopped skinless fish fillets for the crab. Serve curry with steamed rice.

1 tablespoon peanut oil

1 tablespoon red curry paste

2 cups (16 fl oz/500 ml) thin coconut cream

6 kaffir lime leaves

1 tablespoon fish sauce

1 tablespoon sugar

3 tablespoons chopped cilantro (fresh coriander leaves)

3 tablespoons chopped fresh basil

3 lb (1.5 kg) uncooked crabs, segmented (see page 26)

Heat oil in saucepan over medium heat. Add curry paste and cook 1 minute. Stir in coconut cream, lime leaves, fish sauce, sugar, cilantro, and basil and bring to boil. Simmer 10 minutes. Add crab, cover, and cook 15 minutes or until crab is cooked through.

MUSSELS IN TOMATO CHILI SAUCE

SERVES 4

This basic tomato sauce recipe can be used to simmer a variety of seafood, including crabs, shrimp (prawns), or even small whole fish. Serve with lots of crusty Italian bread.

1 tablespoon olive oil

1 clove garlic, chopped

1 red chili, seeded and chopped

14 oz (440 g) can peeled tomatoes, chopped

2 tablespoons tomato paste

½ cup (4 fl oz/125 ml) red wine

2 teaspoons chopped fresh oregano or ½ teaspoon dried

salt and freshly ground pepper

1½ lb (750 g) mussels, scrubbed and debearded

Heat oil in large frying pan over medium heat. Add garlic and chili and sauté until fragrant. Add in tomatoes, tomato paste, wine, and oregano, and salt and pepper and bring to boil. Simmer 15 to 20 minutes or until thickened. Add mussels and return to boil. Simmer, covered, about 2 to 3 minutes, just until mussels open; discard any that do not open. Serve immediately.

INSALATA DI FRUTTI DI MARE

SERVES 4 TO 6

This classic Italian salad is great to serve during the summer months — use any variety of fresh seafood in season. It makes an ideal light lunch served with crusty bread and lots of tossed salad.

1 lb (500 g) cooked jumbo shrimp (large prawns), peeled and deveined

1 lb (500 g) squid (calamari), cleaned and cut into rings

8 oz (250 g) mussels, scrubbed and debearded

1/3 cup (3 fl oz/90 ml) olive oil

1/4 cup (2 fl oz/60 ml) lemon juice

1 clove garlic, chopped

1 tablespoon capers

1 tablespoon chopped fresh parsley

salt and freshly ground pepper

Place shrimp in bowl. Place squid in saucepan with 1/2 cup (4 fl oz/125 ml) water and bring to boil. Simmer 2 minutes or until tender; drain. Place mussels in saucepan with 1/4 cup (2 fl oz/60 ml) water, cover, and bring to boil. Simmer just until mussels open, 2 to 3 minutes; discard any mussels that do not open. Drain mussels and remove from shells; discard shells. Add mussels and squid to shrimp.

Combine oil, juice, garlic, capers, parsley, and salt and pepper to taste and mix well. Pour over seafood and toss. Marinate in refrigerator for 30 minutes before serving. Serve chilled.

MIXED SEAFOOD WITH WILD RICE

SERVES 4

Wild rice is not actually rice, but a type of aquatic grass native to America and now also grown in Canada, Japan, and China. It is chewy, with a nutty, earthy flavor, and takes about 40 minutes to cook.

3 tablespoons butter

2 cloves garlic, chopped

8 oz (250 g) white-fleshed fish fillets, skinned and chopped

7 oz (220 g) uncooked shrimp (prawns), peeled and deveined

3 oz (90 g) scallops, deveined if necessary

1/2 teaspoon ground coriander

1/2 teaspoon ground cumin

1/2 teaspoon ground fenugreek

1/4 teaspoon chili powder

1/4 teaspoon turmeric

1/2 cup (4 fl oz/125 ml) fish stock (see page 260)

2 tablespoons light whipping cream

salt and freshly ground pepper

3 oz (90 g) wild rice, cooked according to package instructions

Melt butter in frying pan over medium heat. Add garlic and sauté until fragrant. Add fish and shrimp and cook 3 to 5 minutes until no longer translucent. Stir in scallops and sauté 1 minute. Remove seafood and keep warm.

Stir coriander, cumin, fenugreek, chili powder, and turmeric into same frying pan and cook over medium heat 1 minute. Pour in stock and cream and bring to boil, stirring constantly. Simmer until thickened and reduced.

Return seafood to sauce and heat through. Season with salt and pepper. Serve with wild rice.

Mixed Seafood with Wild Rice

PASTA WITH PESTO AND SEAFOOD

SERVES 4

The pesto for this delicious first course can be made ahead and stored in an airtight container in the refrigerator for up to 3 days. This is also an ideal main dish if served with salad and crusty bread.

1/2 cup (2/3 oz/20 g) chopped fresh basil

1/4 cup (1 oz/30 g) grated parmesan cheese

1/4 cup (2 fl oz/60 ml) extra virgin olive oil

1/4 cup (1 oz/30 g) pine nuts

1/4 teaspoon salt

1/4 teaspoon freshly ground pepper

7 oz (220 g) penne pasta

1 tablespoon olive oil, for cooking

1 clove garlic, chopped

8 oz (250 g) uncooked shrimp (prawns), peeled and deveined

8 oz (250 g) squid (calamari), cleaned and cut into rings

8 oz (250 g) scallops, deveined if necessary

chopped pine nuts, for serving (optional)

shaved parmesan cheese, for serving (optional)

Combine basil, grated parmesan, extra virgin oil, pine nuts, salt, and pepper in food processor or blender and blend until smooth.

Cook pasta following directions on package. Before draining, reserve 1/4 cup (2 fl oz/60 ml) cooking water.

Meanwhile, heat remaining 1 tablespoon oil in frying pan over medium heat. Add garlic and sauté until fragrant. Add shrimp and squid and cook 3 to 5 minutes until tender and no longer translucent. Add scallops and cook a further 1 minute.

To serve, toss pasta, reserved water, seafood, and pesto together, mixing well. Divide among four plates and serve sprinkled with chopped pine nuts and shaved parmesan if desired.

SPAGHETTI CON VONGOLE

SERVES 4

Vongole is the Italian name for small clams which are tasty and very tender if not overcooked. Be certain to soak them in cold water for 30 minutes to remove grit and sand.

1/3 cup (3 fl oz/90 ml) olive oil

2 cloves garlic, chopped

2 cups (8 oz/250 g) chopped tomato

1 lb (500 g) vongole, washed well

1/4 cup (2 fl oz/60 ml) dry white wine

2 tablespoons chopped fresh basil

salt and freshly ground pepper

8 oz (250 g) spaghetti, cooked according to package instructions

Heat oil in saucepan over medium heat. Add garlic and sauté until fragrant. Stir in tomato and bring to boil, then simmer 5 minutes. Add vongole and wine, basil and salt and pepper. Simmer, covered, about 2 to 3 minutes until vongole open; discard any that do not open.

Toss spaghetti with sauce and serve immediately.

LINGUINE WITH MIXED SHELLS

SERVES 4

Mussels, clams, and cockles are all suitable for this recipe. Really sandy mollusks need soaking prior to cooking; soak for up to 1 hour to remove grittiness.

1/4 cup (2 fl oz/60 ml) olive oil

1 onion, chopped

2 cloves garlic, chopped

1 red chili, seeded and finely chopped

14 oz (440 g) can peeled tomatoes, chopped

3 tablespoons chopped fresh parsley

3 tablespoons tomato paste

1/4 cup (2 fl oz/60 ml) red wine

salt and freshly ground pepper

1 lb (500 g) mixed bivalves, scrubbed, debearded and soaked if necessary

8 oz (250 g) linguine, cooked according to package instructions

Heat oil in large saucepan over medium heat. Add onion and cook 4 minutes or until tender. Stir in garlic and chili and cook 1 minute. Add tomatoes, parsley, tomato paste, wine, and salt and pepper to taste and bring to boil. Cover and simmer 30 minutes or until sauce has thickened.

Add seafood, stir well, cover, and simmer about 2 to 3 minutes until all shells have opened; discard any that do not open.

Pour over linguine, toss well, and serve.

SPAGHETTI AND SQUID IN GARLIC AND CHILI OIL

SERVES 4

It is important to allow the garlic to infuse slowly in the oil, as this gives a wonderful flavor. See glossary for advice on bruising garlic. Try substituting mussels, shrimp (prawns), or cuttlefish for the squid.

1/3 cup (3 fl oz/90 ml) extra virgin olive oil

3 whole cloves garlic, peeled and bruised

1 1/2 lb (750 g) squid (calamari), cleaned and finely chopped

2 red chilies, seeded and chopped

3 tablespoons chopped fresh parsley

salt and freshly ground pepper

8 oz (250 g) spaghetti, cooked according to package instructions

Place oil and garlic in a saucepan and cook slowly over low heat until golden, about 5 minutes. Remove and discard garlic.

Add squid and cook 2 to 3 minutes or until tender. (The squid will exude quite a bit of liquid; this makes up the sauce.) Stir in chilies, parsley, and salt and pepper to taste.

Toss hot cooked spaghetti with sauce and serve immediately.

PASTA SALAD WITH SHRIMP, SMOKED SALMON, AND RADICCHIO

SERVES 4 TO 6

This recipe can be prepared several hours in advance, covered, and refrigerated. Add dressing just prior to serving. The dressing can be made ahead and refrigerated for up to 3 days. For added flavor, add 3 tablespoons chopped mixed fresh herbs.

8 oz (250 g) short pasta

1 lb (500 g) cooked shrimp (prawns), peeled and deveined

4 oz (125 g) smoked salmon, sliced

1/3 cup (1/2 oz/15 g) chopped chives

4 oz (125 g) radicchio, shredded

1/2 cup (4 fl oz/125 ml) extra virgin olive oil

1 egg yolk

2 tablespoons lemon juice

2 teaspoons dijon mustard

salt and freshly ground pepper

Cook pasta according to package instuctions; allow to cool completely.

Combine pasta with shrimp, salmon, chives, and radicchio in large bowl.

Combine oil, yolk, juice, mustard, and salt and pepper to taste in food processor or blender and blend until thick and creamy. Pour over salad and toss well.

To serve, pile high on plates.

Pasta with Shrimp, Smoked Salmon, and Radicchio

Spaghetti Marinara

SERVES 4 TO 6

A hearty first course; try it with a variety of seafoods in season. Larger portions can be served as a main course accompanied by crusty Italian bread and salad. See page 37 for advice on bruising garlic.

1/4 cup (2 fl oz/60 ml) olive oil

3 whole cloves garlic, peeled and bruised

14-oz (440 g) can tomatoes, chopped

2 tablespoons tomato paste

2 tablespoons chopped fresh parsley

1/4 teaspoon salt

1/4 teaspoon pepper

8 oz (250 g) baby octopus, cleaned

4 oz (125 g) white-fleshed fish fillets, skinned and cubed

10 oz (300 g) uncooked shrimp (prawns), peeled and deveined

8 oz (250 g) scallops, deveined if necessary

8 oz (250 g) mussels, scrubbed and debearded

8 oz (250 g) spaghetti, cooked according to package instructions

Place oil and whole garlic in large saucepan over low heat and cook slowly until garlic is golden, about 5 minutes. Discard garlic.

Add tomatoes, tomato paste, parsley, salt and pepper, and simmer, covered, 20 minutes.

Add octopus, fish, and shrimp and simmer 3 to 5 minutes until tender and no longer translucent. Stir in scallops and mussels and simmer, covered, for a further 2 to 3 minutes until mussels open; discard any that do not open.

Toss hot cooked spaghetti with sauce and serve immediately.

SPAGHETTI IN CREAMY SEAFOOD SAUCE

SERVES 4

2 tablespoons butter

2 cloves garlic, chopped

12 large uncooked shrimp (prawns), peeled and deveined

8 oz (250 g) squid (calamari), cleaned and cut into rings

8 oz (250 g) scallops, deveined if necessary

1/2 cup (4 fl oz/125 ml) dry white wine

1 cup (8 fl oz/250 ml) light whipping cream

salt and freshly ground pepper

3 tablespoons chopped fresh parsley

2 tablespoons chopped scallions (spring onions/shallots)

8 oz (250 g) spaghetti, cooked according to package instructions

Melt butter in large saucepan over medium heat. Add garlic and sauté until fragrant. Add shrimp and squid and sauté 3 to 5 minutes until tender and no longer translucent. Add scallops and sauté 1 minute. Remove seafood with slotted spoon and keep warm.

Add wine to juices in saucepan and boil rapidly until reduced by half. Reduce heat, pour in cream, season to taste with salt and pepper, and simmer until sauce is thick and creamy. Add parsley, scallions, and seafood and cook over medium heat just until seafood is heated through.

Toss hot cooked spaghetti with sauce and serve immediately.

Following pages: Mushrooms Stuffed with Fish, Pancetta, and Gorgonzola (page 84), Fish and Cashew Kebabs with Cucumber Yoghurt (page 85), Fried Whitebait (page 85)

MUSHROOMS STUFFED WITH FISH, PANCETTA, AND GORGONZOLA

SERVES 6

These mushrooms can be prepared a day ahead and kept covered in the refrigerator until baking time. The dish also makes an excellent light lunch with plenty of tossed salad.

6 cups mushrooms, about 1 lb (500 g)

4 tablespoons olive oil

1 onion, finely chopped

1/3 cup (1 1/2 oz/45 g) chopped pancetta

8 oz (250 g) white-fleshed or oily fish fillets, skinned and ground (minced)

1/3 cup (1 1/2 oz/45 g) crumbled gorgonzola cheese

2 teaspoons chopped fresh marjoram

salt and freshly ground pepper

Remove stalks from mushrooms and chop these finely; reserve mushroom cups.

Heat 2 tablespoons oil in frying pan over medium heat. Add onion and chopped mushroom stalks and sauté until tender, 2 to 3 minutes. Remove from heat and transfer to bowl; cool slightly. Add pancetta, fish, gorgonzola, marjoram, and salt and pepper and mix well.

Preheat oven to 350°F (180°C/Gas 4). Brush outsides of mushroom cups with remaining 2 tablespoons oil. Pack fish mixture into mushroom cups. Arrange in greased baking dish and bake 20 minutes or until golden. Serve hot.

FISH AND CASHEW KEBABS WITH CUCUMBER YOGURT

SERVES 4

To prevent bamboo skewers from burning, soak in water for about 30 minutes before threading on food. Four skewers required.

1 lb (500 g) white-fleshed or oily fish fillets, skinned and ground (minced)

1 small onion, chopped

2 tablespoons chopped cilantro (fresh coriander leaves)

1/3 cup (1 1/2 oz/45 g) chopped cashews

1/2 teaspoon ground cumin

1/4 teaspoon paprika

1/4 teaspoon ground ginger

7 oz (220 g) plain yogurt

2 tablespoons chopped fresh mint

1/2 cup (2 oz/60 g) peeled, seeded, and chopped cucumber

2 tablespoons sweet chili sauce

olive or vegetable oil

Combine fish, onion, cilantro, cashews, cumin, paprika, and ginger in bowl and mix well. Shape mixture into 8 long ovals using wet hands. Thread onto soaked bamboo skewers, allowing 2 per skewer.

Combine yogurt, mint, cucumber, and chili sauce and mix well. Refrigerate until ready for use.

Heat broiler (grill) or barbecue plate and cook kebabs for 5 to 6 minutes, turning frequently and basting with a little oil to prevent them from drying out. Serve hot with chilled yogurt sauce.

FRIED WHITEBAIT

SERVES 4 TO 6

Whitebait are very tiny fish that are cooked whole without removing head or innards. For preparation, just rinse under cold water and pat dry. This method of cooking is popular in Mediterranean countries, and tastes great. A dipping sauce is not really required, although homemade mayonnaise would make a good accompaniment (see pages 262 to 264).

1 lb (500 g) whitebait

seasoned flour (see glossary)

vegetable oil for deep frying

Dust whitebait with flour and shake off excess.

Heat oil in large saucepan over medium heat until very hot (flour should sizzle if dropped into the oil). Add whitebait and cook 1 minute or until crisp and golden. Drain on paper towels and serve hot.

FISH, BASIL, AND RED PEPPER TERRINE

SERVES 6

2 red bell peppers (capsicums)

2 teaspoons unflavored gelatin

2 tablespoons water

1 lb (500 g) white-fleshed fish fillets, skinned and poached (see page 18)

1/2 cup (4 fl oz/125 ml) crème fraîche

1/2 cup (4 fl oz/125 ml) plain yogurt

1/3 cup (2/3 oz/20 g) finely chopped fresh basil

salt and freshly ground pepper

2 tablespoons chopped chives

toast, to serve

Place peppers under preheated broiler (grill) and cook until skin blisters and becomes black, about 15 to 20 minutes, turning to blacken all sides. Cool, then peel, seed, and cut into quarters.

Sprinkle gelatin over water in cup and let stand briefly until water is absorbed. Combine fish, crème fraîche, and yogurt in food processor or blender and puree. Transfer to bowl. Fold in basil, salt and pepper to taste, and softened gelatin and mix well. Rinse out 8 in. x 4 in. (20 cm x 10 cm) size loaf pan with water; drain but do not dry. Pour half of mixture into pan, lay peppers on top in single layer, then pour in remaining fish mixture. Cover and refrigerate several hours or overnight.

Turn out of pan and slice. Serve chilled with toast.

FISH AND PARSLEY MOUSSELINE

SERVES 6

8 oz (250 g) white-fleshed fish fillets, skinned

1/2 cup (1 oz/30 g) chopped fresh parsley

1/4 teaspoon salt

1 egg white

1 cup (8 fl oz/250 ml) light whipping cream

toast, to serve

Combine fish and parsley in food processor and puree until smooth. With motor running, add salt, egg white, and mix well. Gradually add cream until well incorporated.

Preheat oven to 325°F (170°C/Gas 3). Divide mixture among six 1/4-cup (2 fl oz/60 ml) greased individual molds. Arrange molds in baking dish and pour in enough hot water to come halfway up sides of molds. Cover with foil and bake 20 minutes or until a knife inserted in mousseline comes out clean. Unmold by inverting on board and gently tapping. Serve hot or cold with toast.

Fish, Basil, and Red Pepper Terrine

SPICY BATTERED FISH

SERVES 4

¹/₄ teaspoon ground ginger

¹/₂ teaspoon ground cumin

¹/₂ teaspoon turmeric

¹/₂ teaspoon ground coriander

1 clove garlic, chopped

1 teaspoon chili sauce

2 tablespoons soy sauce

1 tablespoon lemon juice

1 lb (500 g) firm white-fleshed fish fillets, skinned and cut into small pieces

¹/₂ cup (2 oz/60 g) all-purpose (plain) flour

¹/₂ cup (4 fl oz/125 ml) water

1 egg white, beaten to soft peaks

vegetable oil for deep frying

lemon wedges, to serve

Combine ginger, cumin, turmeric, coriander, garlic, sauces, and juice in large bowl and mix well. Add fish and marinate 30 minutes, or longer if time permits. Drain fish on paper towels.

Combine flour and water in bowl, mixing well to form smooth batter. Fold in egg white. Drop pieces of fish into batter. Heat oil in deep pan; test temperature by dropping a small amount of batter into oil. If it sizzles immediately the oil temperature is correct; if it burns immediately, turn down heat slightly and allow to cool a little. Fry fish 1 to 2 minutes or until crisp and golden. Drain on paper towels. Serve hot with lemon wedges.

DEEP-FRIED CHINESE FISH

SERVES 4

The batter in this dish is unusual as the fish is marinated in it before deep frying. It is very thin, more like a coating than a crispy batter, and the end result is a very succulent piece of fish.

¹/₃ cup (1¹/₂ oz/45 g) cornstarch (cornflour)

1 tablespoon lemon juice

1 tablespoon soy sauce

1 tablespoon oyster sauce

1 tablespoon sherry

1 clove garlic, chopped

1 egg white, lightly beaten

¹/₄ teaspoon five spice powder

1 lb (500 g) white-fleshed or oily fish fillets, skinned and cut into small pieces

vegetable oil for deep frying

lemon wedges, to serve

Place cornstarch, juice, sauces, sherry, garlic, egg white, and spice powder in a bowl and mix well. Add fish and marinate 1 hour, or longer if possible.

Heat oil in deep pan until hot; test temperature by dropping a small amount of batter into oil. If it sizzles immediately, the oil temperature is correct; if it burns immediately, turn down heat slightly and allow to cool a little. Drain excess marinade from fish and drop fish into oil, cooking until golden. Drain on paper towels. Serve with lemon wedges.

Coconut Shrimp with Fruity Mayonnaise

SERVES 4

These are really wonderful — crisp on the outside, moist and tender inside. Do not overcook, as the coconut will burn. To check oil for the correct temperature, drop in a few crumbs; if they sizzle immediately, the oil is ready. For a quick version, mix 1 cup (8 fl oz/250 ml) commercial whole egg mayonnaise with the chutney and chili sauce.

1 cup (2 oz/60 g) fresh breadcrumbs (see page 36)

1 cup (3 oz/90 g) unsweetened shredded coconut

1 1/2 lb (750 g) uncooked large shrimp (prawns), peeled and deveined

1 egg, beaten

1 egg yolk

2 tablespoons lemon juice

salt and freshly ground pepper

3/4 cup (6 fl oz/180 ml) olive oil

1/4 cup (2 fl oz/60 ml) mango chutney

1 teaspoon mild or hot chili sauce

oil for deep frying

Combine breadcrumbs and coconut in bowl. Dip shrimp into egg, then into breadcrumb mixture, pressing firmly to help coating adhere. Chill 15 minutes to allow coating to set.

Combine yolk, lemon juice, and salt and pepper in food processor or blender and blend until smooth. With motor running, gradually add oil, mixing until totally incorporated. Add chutney and chili sauce and mix well.

Heat oil in large saucepan over medium heat until hot. Add shrimp and cook 3 to 5 minutes or until tender and golden. Drain on paper towels and serve with the mayonnaise.

WHOLE FISH IN GRAPE LEAVES

SERVES 4

This dish can be prepared a day in advance and stored in the refrigerator, covered, until ready for baking. Red mullet is recommended as it is widely used in the Mediterranean. Sardines make an interesting alternative.

1/2 cup (3 oz/90 g) cooked short-grain rice

1/2 cup (2 oz/60 g) chopped tomatoes

1/4 cup (11/2 oz/45 g) crumbled feta cheese

2 tablespoons chopped black olives

2 tablespoons extra virgin olive oil

salt and freshly ground pepper

4 small whole fish, 6 oz (180 g) each, scaled and cleaned

4 oz (125 g) grape (vine) leaves

2 tablespoons olive oil

Combine rice, tomatoes, cheese, olives, extra virgin oil, and salt and pepper to taste in bowl and mix well. Divide mixture into four and pack into cavity of each fish, pressing well.

Lay 1 to 2 grape leaves, depending on size of fish, out flat and place fish on top. Fold leaves over fish, enclosing body but exposing tail and face. More leaves may be needed to obtain a neat and fully enclosed package.

Preheat oven to 350°F (180°C/Gas 4). Brush packages with oil and arrange in oiled baking dish. Cover and bake about 20 minutes; the fish is cooked when opaque and beginning to flake when tested with a knife at thickest part. Serve, with leaves.

RED MULLET BAKED WITH GARLIC AND HERBS

SERVES 4

This delicious and simple dish can be marinated up to a day in advance and placed in the oven just prior to serving. Sardines, or any white-fleshed or oily fish fillets and steaks or cutlets can be used as alternatives.

2 lb (1 kg) whole red mullet, scaled and cleaned

1/4 cup (2 fl oz/60 ml) lemon juice

1 tablespoon chopped fresh tarragon

1 tablespoon chopped chives

1 tablespoon chopped fresh chervil

2 cloves garlic, chopped

2 tablespoons melted butter

salt and freshly ground pepper

Place fish in greased baking dish. Combine juice, herbs, garlic, and butter and mix well. Season fish well with salt and pepper and pour herb mixture over. Marinate in refrigerator at least 30 minutes.

Preheat oven to 350°F (180°C/Gas 4). Cover and bake 20 minutes or just until fish is opaque and beginning to flake when tested with a knife at the thickest part. Serve at once.

Whole Fish in Grape Leaves

WHOLE FISH IN EGGPLANT AND TOMATO SAUCE

Any small whole fish would be suited to this recipe, including red mullet, garfish, and sardines. Serve with lots of crusty bread to soak up the sauce.

1/4 cup (2 fl oz/60 ml) olive oil

10 oz (300 g) eggplant (aubergine), chopped

2 cloves garlic, chopped

14 oz (440 g) can peeled tomatoes, chopped

3/4 cup (6 fl oz/180 ml) red wine

1/4 teaspoon salt

1/4 teaspoon freshly ground pepper

2 teaspoons chopped fresh oregano or 1 teaspoon dried

2 bay leaves

6 small whole fish, 4 oz (125 g) each, scaled and cleaned

Heat oil in frying pan over medium heat. Add eggplant and sauté 5 minutes or until tender. Add garlic, tomatoes, wine, salt, pepper, oregano, and bay leaves and bring to boil. Simmer uncovered 20 minutes, adding a little water if sauce becomes too thick.

Add fish to sauce and simmer, covered 15 to 20 minutes or until fish is opaque and beginning to flake when tested with a knife at the thickest part.

TONNO E FAGIOLI

SERVES 4

This northern Italian dish is light and tasty. It can be made several hours in advance and kept in the refrigerator. Serve with lots of good Italian bread to soak up the oil.

1/2 cup (3 oz/90 g) dried cannellini beans or 14 oz (440 g) can

10 oz (300 g) tuna steaks, poached or steamed (see page 18)

1 onion, thinly sliced

1/3 cup (3 fl oz/80 ml) extra virgin olive oil

1 tablespoon water

salt and freshly ground pepper

1 teaspoon fresh thyme

If using dried beans, soak beans in plenty of cold water overnight. Drain. Place beans in large saucepan and cover with water. Bring to boil. Simmer until tender, about 30 minutes. Drain, cool, and transfer to bowl.

Flake tuna into small pieces and add to bowl with cooked or canned beans. Stir in onion, oil, water, salt and pepper, and thyme. Serve chilled.

Tuna Tapenade with Fusilli

SERVES 4

Tapenade is a paste made from olives, capers, anchovies, and oil. It can be used as a spread on crusty bread or as a dip with crackers. Store in an airtight container in the refrigerator for up to 1 week. Fusilli is a pasta made from short lengths with a slight twist.

7 oz (220 g) tuna steak, poached (see page 18)

10 oz (300 g) pitted black olives

2 cloves garlic, chopped

2 oz (60 g) capers

2 oz (60 g) anchovies

1/3 cup (3 fl oz/90 ml) extra virgin olive oil

8 oz (250 g) fusilli or any shaped pasta

2 teaspoons fresh thyme

salt and freshly ground pepper

Cook pasta according to package instructions. Drain, reserving 1/3 cup (3 fl oz/90 ml) cooking water.

Meanwhile, break cooked tuna up into bite-size pieces and set aside.

Combine olives, garlic, capers, anchovies, and oil in food processor and blend until smooth.

Place hot pasta in large bowl and add reserved water, tuna, tapenade, thyme, and salt and pepper to taste. Toss well and serve.

Tuna and Egg Salad

SERVES 4

13 oz (400 g) tuna steak, poached and cooled (see page 18)

2 hard-cooked (boiled) eggs, quartered

4 anchovy fillets

1 tablespoon capers

1 tablespoon chopped fresh parsley

2 tablespoons mayonnaise

1 tablespoon extra virgin olive oil

2 tablespoons lemon juice

salt and freshly ground pepper

parmesan cheese shavings

Break cooked tuna up into small pieces and place in medium bowl. Add eggs and anchovies. Combine capers, parsley, mayonnaise, oil, juice, and salt and pepper. Pour over salad and mix well. Divide salad among four plates. Top with parmesan and serve.

SARDINE AND OLIVE TART

SERVES 4 TO 6

This tasty dish is more like a pizza than a pie. Almost any type of seafood may be substituted for the sardines in this recipe.

1/2 oz (15 g) compressed yeast or 2 teaspoons active dry yeast

1 teaspoon sugar

1 cup (8 fl oz/250 ml) warm water

2 cups (8 oz/250 g) all-purpose (plain) flour

1 teaspoon salt

about 4 tablespoons olive oil

1 large onion, sliced

6 sardines, cleaned and butterflied (see page 13)

1/3 cup (2 oz/60 g) chopped black olives

2 tablespoons chopped fresh parsley

2 teaspoons chopped fresh oregano

salt and freshly ground pepper

Combine yeast, sugar, and 1/4 cup (2 fl oz/60 ml) of the warm water in small bowl and mix well. Cover with cloth and let stand in a warm place for 10 minutes or until frothy, creamy, and nearly tripled in volume.

Combine flour and salt in large bowl. Make a well in middle and pour in yeast mixture, remaining water, and 2 tablespoons oil. Mix well, adding more water if necessary, to make a firm dough. Turn out onto well-floured surface and knead 10 minutes, or until dough is smooth and elastic and springs back when indented with a finger. Place dough in oiled large bowl, brush with more oil, cover loosely with plastic wrap and then a cloth, and let rise in a warm place for about 30 to 40 minutes or until doubled.

Heat 2 tablespoons oil in frying pan over medium heat. Add onion and cook slowly until tender and golden, about 15 minutes. Cool.

Preheat oven to 450°F (230°C/Gas 8). Punch down dough. Turn out onto lightly floured surface and knead 2 minutes or until smooth and elastic. Using a floured rolling pin, roll dough out into 15 in. (38 cm) round and place on well-oiled baking sheet.

Spread onion, sardines, olives, parsley, and oregano over dough. Season to taste with salt and pepper. Bake 10 to 15 minutes or until golden. Serve hot.

Sardine and Olive Tart

SARDINES WITH ROSEMARY

SERVES 4

Try these marinated sardines without the breadcrumb topping; after the initial marinating time, just barbecue or broil (grill) for 1 to 2 minutes per side. For best results, marinate overnight and baste with marinade during cooking.

1½ lb (750 g) sardines, cleaned

1 tablespoon chopped fresh rosemary or 1 teaspoon dried

2 garlic cloves, chopped

juice of 1 lemon

1 cup (2 oz/60 g) fresh breadcrumbs (see glossary)

¼ cup (1 oz/30 g) grated parmesan cheese

¼ cup (2 fl oz/60 ml) olive oil

2 tablespoons chopped fresh parsley

Arrange sardines in single layer in baking dish. Combine rosemary, garlic, and lemon juice and pour over fish. Marinate 30 minutes in refrigerator.

Preheat oven to 350°F (180°C/Gas 4). Combine breadcrumbs, parmesan, oil, and parsley and sprinkle over fish. Bake 20 minutes or until golden. Serve hot.

PEPPERED TERIYAKI SALMON

SERVES 4

Teriyaki is a Japanese dish in which food is marinated, then either broiled (grilled) or panfried. *Teri* means glaze and *yaki* means to cook. Mirin is sweet rice wine; it adds flavor and gives the characteristic glaze to teriyaki.

4 salmon steaks, about 4 oz (125 g) each

2 tablespoons sake or sherry

2 tablespoons mirin

2 tablespoons soy sauce

2 tablespoons sugar

2 cloves garlic, chopped

1 teaspoon cracked peppercorns

3 tablespoons peanut oil

lemon wedges, for serving (optional)

Place fish in glass dish. Combine sake, mirin, soy sauce, sugar, garlic, and peppercorns. Pour mixture over fish to coat thoroughly. Marinate 1 hour, or longer if time permits in refrigerator.

Heat oil in frying pan or wok over medium heat. Drain fish and cook 3 to 4 minutes per side, or just until fish is beginning to flake when tested. Serve with lemon wedges, if desired.

MARINATED SKATE

SERVES 4

Skate is a large flat fish which belongs to the same family as rays. The fins of the skate are the only part used for cooking. It needs to be skinned and cut into smaller pieces before being poached, panfried or steamed. If skate is unavailable, try any firm white-fleshed fish fillet or steak or cutlet.

1 lb (500 g) skate, skinned

seasoned flour (see glossary)

oil for shallow frying

1/3 cup (3 fl oz/80 ml) olive oil

2 cloves garlic, chopped

1 red chili, seeded and chopped

2 tablespoons balsamic vinegar

1/3 cup (1 1/2 oz/45 g) pine nuts, finely chopped

Dust skate with flour until well coated, shaking off excess. Heat enough oil to cover base of frying pan over medium heat. Add skate and fry 2 to 3 minutes per side. Transfer to glass dish.

Heat olive oil in saucepan over medium heat. Add garlic and chili and sauté until fragrant. Add vinegar and nuts and bring to boil. Remove from heat and immediately pour over skate. Cover and marinate 10 to 15 minutes. Serve hot, or let cool and serve at room temperature.

SPANISH MARINATED FISH

SERVES 4

This excellent Caribbean dish, also known as escabeche, is preparared a day ahead. It can be served with crusty bread as a first course or for light lunch, add vegetables or a salad. Try small whole fish, such as red mullet, as a substitute for the fillets.

1 lb (500 g) white-fleshed fish fillets, skinned

seasoned flour (see glossary)

3/4 cup (6 fl oz/180 ml) olive oil

1 onion, chopped

2 cloves garlic, chopped

1/4 cup (2 fl oz/60 ml) lemon juice

3 tablespoons chopped fresh parsley

grated rind of 2 oranges

1 small red chili, seeded and chopped

2 teaspoons paprika

Cut fish into small pieces and dust in flour.

Heat 1/4 cup (2 fl oz/60 ml) oil in frying pan over medium heat and fry fish 2 to 3 minutes per side or until opaque and just beginning to flake when tested. Place fish in glass dish.

Combine remaining olive oil, onion, garlic, juice, parsley, rind, chili, and paprika in food processor and puree until smooth. Pour over fish, cover, and refrigerate overnight. Allow to return to room temperature before serving.

HERB-FRIED SARDINES WITH MUSTARD MAYONNAISE

SERVES 4

Sardines can be coated with breadcrumbs and frozen for up to 4 months if desired. Just thaw and fry as usual. For an alternative quick mayonnaise, mix 3/4 cup (6 fl oz/180 ml) commercial whole-egg mayonnaise with 1 tablespoon mustard.

3 cups (6 oz/180 g) fresh breadcrumbs (see glossary)

3 tablespoons chopped mixed fresh herbs (parsley, chervil, chives)

1 lb (500 g) sardines, cut into "book" fillets (see page 13)

1 egg, beaten

1 egg yolk

2 tablespoons lemon juice

1 tablespoon seeded mustard

salt and freshly ground pepper

3/4 cup (6 fl oz/180 ml) olive oil

oil for frying

Combine breadcrumbs and herbs. Dip butterflied sardines in beaten egg, then in breadcrumb mixture, pressing firmly to allow crumbs to adhere. Chill while preparing mayonnaise.

To make mayonnaise, combine yolk, juice, mustard, and salt and pepper to taste in food processor bowl and blend well. With motor running, gradually pour in oil and process until mayonnaise is thick and creamy.

Heat oil in frying pan over medium heat. Add sardines and fry 1 minute on each side or until golden. Drain on paper towels. Serve hot with mayonnaise.

Herb-Fried Sardines with Mustard Mayonnaise

GARLIC BUTTERED SHRIMP

SERVES 4

Serve with lots of crusty bread to soak up the garlic butter.

3 tablespoons butter

2 tablespoons olive oil

3 cloves garlic, chopped

1¹/2 lb (750 g) uncooked shrimp (prawns), peeled and deveined

2 tablespoons lemon juice

2 tablespoons chopped fresh parsley

Melt butter with oil in frying pan over medium heat. Add garlic and cook until fragrant. Add shrimp and sauté 3 to 5 minutes or until tender and no longer translucent. Stir in lemon juice and parsley and heat through.

BUTTERED SHRIMP WITH SPAGHETTI

SERVES 4

Try substituting squid (calamari), lobster, or cuttlefish pieces for the shrimp (prawns).

7 tablespoons butter

1 lb (500 g) uncooked shrimp (prawns), peeled and deveined

2 cloves garlic, chopped

¹/3 cup (¹/2 oz/15 g) chopped chives

salt and freshly ground pepper

8 oz (250 g) spaghetti, cooked according to package instructions

Melt 1 tablespoon butter in frying pan over medium heat. Add shrimp and cook 3 to 5 minutes until tender and no longer translucent. Remove and keep warm.

Add garlic to pan and cook over medium heat 1 minute. Add remaining 6 tablespoons butter, chives, and salt and pepper to taste and cook until butter has melted. Add shrimp and stir just until heated through.

Pour shrimp mixture over hot spaghetti, and serve.

SHRIMP AND FETA IN RICH TOMATO SAUCE

SERVES 4

This is a delicious dish of Greek origin. It can be prepared ahead of time, covered, and refrigerated until ready for baking. Also works well cooked as individual serves in small ramekins or soufflé dishes.

2 tablespoons olive oil

12 uncooked jumbo shrimp (large prawns), peeled and deveined

2 tablespoons butter

1/3 cup (1 1/2 oz/45 g) finely chopped red bell pepper (capsicum)

1 onion, chopped

1 clove garlic, chopped

3 bay leaves

14 oz (440 g) can peeled tomatoes

1 tablespoon tomato paste

2 teaspoons chopped fresh oregano or 1/2 teaspoon dried

1 tablespoon chopped fresh parsley

salt and freshly ground pepper

1/2 cup (4 oz/125 g) black olives

1/3 cup (3 fl oz/90 ml) dry white wine

1 tablespoon worcestershire sauce

1/3 cup (2 oz/60 g) crumbled feta cheese

Heat oil in frying pan over medium heat. Add shrimp and cook 3 to 5 minutes or until tender and no longer translucent. Transfer to baking dish.

Add butter to frying pan and sauté bell pepper, onion, and garlic until tender, about 4 minutes. Add bay leaves, tomatoes, tomato paste, oregano, parsley, and salt and pepper. Simmer, covered, 15 minutes. Stir in olives, wine, and worcestershire sauce.

Preheat oven to 350°F (180°C/Gas 4). Pour tomato sauce over shrimp and sprinkle with cheese. Bake until cheese is melted, about 10 minutes. Serve hot.

Following pages: Shrimp, Tomato, and Basil with Parmesan Risotto (page 104), Shrimp and Asparagus Fettuccine (page 105), Marinated Shrimp and Mushrooms with Radicchio (page 105)

SHRIMP, TOMATO, AND BASIL WITH PARMESAN RISOTTO

SERVES 4

3 cups (24 fl oz/750 ml) hot fish stock (see page 260)

4 tablespoon butter

1 onion, chopped

1 cup (5 oz/150 g) arborio rice (see glossary)

salt and freshly ground pepper

1/3 cup (1 1/2 oz/45 g) grated parmesan cheese

2 tablespoons olive oil

1 lb (500 g) uncooked shrimp (prawns), peeled and deveined

1 clove garlic, chopped

1/2 cup (4 fl oz/125 ml) dry white wine

1/2 cup (4 fl oz/125 ml) light whipping cream

1/2 cup (2 oz/60 g) peeled and chopped tomato

3 tablespoons chopped fresh basil

Place stock in a small saucepan and bring to boil. Melt 2 tablespoons butter in large saucepan over medium heat. Add onion and sauté until tender, about 4 minutes. Add rice and stir to coat with butter. Pour in half the boiling stock, stir well, and simmer, covered, until most of stock has been absorbed. Pour in remaining boiling stock and season to taste with salt and pepper. Simmer, stirring occasionally, until all liquid has been absorbed. Stir in parmesan and remaining 2 tablespoons butter.

Meanwhile, heat oil in large saucepan. Add shrimp and sauté 3 to 5 minutes or until tender and no longer translucent. Remove from pan. Add garlic, wine, and cream to saucepan and simmer uncovered until sauce is thick and creamy. Add tomato, basil, and shrimp and stir well.

Place a small amount of risotto on individual plates and top with shrimp mixture. Serve immediately.

SHRIMP, TOMATO, AND ROASTED GARLIC ON FOCACCIA

SERVES 4

1 head garlic, unpeeled

1 loaf focaccia, toasted and cut into 4 pieces

1 cup (4 oz/125 g) peeled, seeded, and finely diced tomato

1/3 cup (3 fl oz/90 ml) extra virgin olive oil

2 teaspoons chopped fresh oregano or 1/2 teaspoon dried

salt and freshly ground pepper

1 lb (500 g) cooked jumbo shrimp (large prawns), peeled, deveined and chilled

Preheat oven to 400°F (200°C/Gas 6). Place garlic head on baking sheet and roast 30 minutes. Test for doneness by pressing outer cloves gently; they should yield to pressure. Cut top from garlic and squeeze flesh out onto plate. Spread over focaccia.

Combine tomato, oil, oregano, and salt and pepper to taste in small bowl and mix well. Let stand for a while at room temperature for flavors to develop.

Place chilled shrimp on bread, top with tomato mixture, and serve.

SHRIMP AND ASPARAGUS FETTUCCINE

SERVES 4

1/4 cup (2 fl oz/60 ml) olive oil

2 cloves garlic, chopped

1 cup (4 oz/125 g) chopped asparagus

1/2 cup (2 oz/60 g) finely chopped red bell pepper (capsicum)

1 lb (500 g) uncooked shrimp (prawns), peeled and deveined

salt and freshly ground pepper

2 tablespoons butter

2 tablespoons sherry

1 teaspoon fresh thyme or 1/4 teaspoon dried

8 oz (250 g) fettuccine, cooked according to package instructions

Place oil and garlic in frying pan over medium heat and sauté until fragrant. Add asparagus and bell pepper and cook 1 to 2 minutes or until tender. Stir in shrimp and salt and pepper and sauté a further 3 to 5 minutes until shrimp are tender and no longer translucent. Add butter, sherry, and thyme and stir until butter has melted.

Pour sauce over hot fettuccine and toss well. Serve at once.

MARINATED SHRIMP AND MUSHROOMS WITH RADICCHIO

SERVES 4

1 lb (500 g) cooked shrimp (prawns), peeled and deveined

8 oz (250 g) button mushrooms, halved

1/3 cup (3 fl oz/80 ml) extra virgin olive oil

1/4 cup (2 fl oz/60 ml) red wine vinegar

2 teaspoons creamed horseradish

salt and freshly ground pepper

3 plum (egg) tomatoes, quartered

1 small purple (Spanish) onion, thinly sliced

1 small head radicchio, torn

Place shrimp and mushrooms in bowl. Combine oil, vinegar, horseradish, and salt and pepper to taste and pour over. Marinate 15 minutes, or longer if time permits. Add tomatoes, onion, and radicchio and toss well. Divide among four plates, piling high, and serve.

BRAISED SHRIMP AND LEEKS

SERVES 4

3 tablespoons butter

1 lb (500 g) uncooked shrimp
(prawns), peeled and deveined

2 leeks, halved lengthwise

3/4 cup (3 oz/90 g) peeled, seeded,
and chopped tomato

2 teaspoons chopped fresh
oregano or 1/2 teaspoon dried

freshly ground pepper

1 tablespoon dry white wine

1 tablespoon lemon juice

crusty bread, to serve

Melt 1 tablespoon butter in frying pan or wok over medium heat. Add shrimp and sauté 3 to 5 minutes or until tender and no longer translucent. Remove and keep warm.

Melt remaining 2 tablespoons butter over medium heat. Add leeks and sauté until tender, 2 to 3 minutes. Add tomato, oregano, pepper to taste, wine, juice, and shrimp and cook 2 minutes or until heated through. Serve immediately.

PANFRIED SHRIMP WITH HOT TOMATO DRESSING

SERVES 4

A deliciously different way of serving shrimp (prawns), dressed in a light hot vinaigrette and topped with shaved parmesan cheese. It's quick and easy to make, so prepare just prior to serving.

2 teaspoons olive oil

1 1/2 lb (750 g) uncooked shrimp
(prawns), peeled and deveined

1/4 cup (2 fl oz/60 ml) extra virgin
olive oil

2 tablespoons balsamic vinegar

1/4 cup (1 oz/30 g) peeled, seeded,
and finely chopped tomato

2 tablespoons chopped fresh basil

freshly ground pepper

parmesan cheese shavings,
to serve

crusty bread, to serve

Heat oil in frying pan over medium heat. Add shrimp and sauté 3 to 5 minutes or until tender and no longer translucent.

Combine oil, vinegar, tomato, basil, and pepper. Stir into shrimp and heat through. Serve immediately with parmesan shavings and bread.

Braised Shrimp and Leeks

WARM VIETNAMESE SHRIMP SALAD

SERVES 4

This crunchy salad is also terrific cold — just dress the shrimp and refrigerate until ready to serve.

5 tablespoons vegetable oil

1 clove garlic, chopped

1½ lb (750 g) uncooked shrimp (prawns), peeled and deveined

1 small onion, thinly sliced

2 tablespoons chopped fresh mint

¼ cup (1 oz/30 g) chopped peanuts

1 tablespoon sesame seeds

2 tablespoons lemon juice

1 tablespoon soy sauce

2 teaspoons sugar

Place 1 tablespoon oil and garlic in frying pan and sauté until fragrant. Add shrimp and stir-fry 3 to 5 minutes until tender and no longer translucent

Transfer shrimp to bowl and add onion, mint, peanuts, and seeds. Combine remaining 4 tablespoons oil, juice, soy sauce, and sugar. Pour over salad and toss well. Divide among four plates, piling shrimp in the middle. Serve warm.

BUTTERED LOBSTER WITH ORANGE BRANDY

SERVES 4

This is a delicately-flavored dish that is equally as good when made with shrimp (prawns) or crayfish. Serve with steamed rice.

2 lb (1 kg) uncooked lobster tails

3 tablespoons butter

1 tablespoon brandy

1 tablespoon orange juice

1 teaspoon grated orange rind

1 tablespoon chopped chives

1 tablespoon chopped fresh dill

1 teaspoon seeded mustard

salt and freshly ground pepper

Extract meat from lobster tails and cut into medallions (see pages 22 to 25).

Heat butter in frying pan over medium heat until frothy. Add lobster and sauté just until tender, about 3 minutes. Add brandy, juice, rind, chives, dill, mustard, and salt and pepper to taste. Simmer until heated through, stirring well. Serve immediately.

LOBSTER IN MUSHROOM AND MUSTARD SAUCE

SERVES 4

This easy first course is fast to make yet has a beautifully flavored sauce with a touch of mustard. Serve it with wild rice. Shrimp (prawns), scallops, and white-fleshed fish fillets make good substitutes for the lobster.

2 lb (1 kg) uncooked lobster tails

2 tablespoons butter

1 1/2 cups (5 oz/155 g) sliced button mushrooms

1/2 cup (4 fl oz/125 ml) light whipping cream

1 teaspoon dijon mustard

salt and freshly ground pepper

Extract meat from lobster tails and chop into small pieces (see pages 22 to 25).

Melt butter in frying pan over medium heat, add lobster and cook until tender, about 3 to 5 minutes. Remove and keep warm. Add mushrooms to frying pan and cook until tender, about 5 minutes. Add cream, mustard, and salt and pepper and mix well. Bring to boil and simmer until sauce thickens slightly. Return lobster and heat through. Serve immediately.

LOBSTER MEDALLIONS WITH TOMATO AND BASIL DRESSING

SERVES 4

This extremely simple recipe can be prepared well in advance. Have the lobster cut and ready to be placed onto plates. Make the dressing up to 1 hour in advance, and spoon over just before serving. Shrimp (prawns), crayfish, scampi, or panfried fish fillets can be substituted for the lobster.

1 1/2 lb (750 g) cooked lobster

1/3 cup (3 fl oz/80 ml) extra virgin olive oil

2 tablespoons lemon juice

1/3 cup (1 1/2 oz/45 g) peeled and finely diced tomato

1 tablespoon finely chopped fresh basil

1/4 teaspoon cracked pepper

salt

Extract meat from lobster and cut into medallions (see pages 22 to 25). Divide lobster medallions among four plates.

Combine oil, juice, tomato, basil, pepper, and salt to taste and mix well. Chill.

Spoon dressing over lobster and serve.

LOBSTER QUENELLES WITH RED PEPPER COULIS

SERVES 4

These egg-shaped dumplings are extremely light and delicious, but very rich. Serve one or two as a first course; the red pepper sauce makes an unusual accompaniment. Shrimp (prawns), crayfish and white-fleshed fish fillets make good substitutes — just use 8 oz (250 g), not including shell weight.

2 red bell peppers (capsicums)

1/4 cup (2 fl oz/60 ml) extra virgin olive oil

freshly ground pepper

1 lb (500 g) uncooked lobster tail

1 cup (8 fl oz/250 ml) light whipping cream

1 egg white

1/2 teaspoon salt

2 tablespoons chopped chives

Broil (grill) bell pepper until skin blisters and blackens; let cool. Peel away skin and remove seeds. Place peppers in food processor and puree until smooth. Add oil and pepper and mix well. Set aside.

Extract meat from lobster tail (see page 24) and cut into small pieces. Place in food processor and puree until smooth. With motor running, gradually add cream, egg white, salt, and chives and blend well. Mixture should be firm enough to mold; if not, chill 15 minutes.

Pour about 1 in. (2.5 cm) water into frying pan and bring to boil. Turn down to simmer. Using wetted tablespoons, mold quenelle mixture into egg shapes and drop into water. Simmer 1 to 2 minutes per side; do not allow water to boil or quenelles will fall apart. Drain quenelles on paper towels and serve with a small amount of the red pepper coulis at room temperature.

Lobster Quenelles with Red Pepper Coulis

CRAB AND CHEESE SOUFFLÉ

SERVES 6

This is a simple and great-tasting soufflé that must be served as soon as it comes out of the oven. If preferred, 6 individual soufflés can be made, using 1 cup (8 fl oz/250 ml) soufflé dishes and baking for 15 to 20 minutes. Any cooked seafood can be substituted for the crab.

3 tablespoons butter

2 tablespoons all-purpose (plain) flour

1 cup (8 fl oz/ 250 ml) milk

1/3 cup (1 1/2 oz/45 g) grated pecorino cheese

1/2 cup (2 oz/ 60 g) peeled, seeded, and chopped tomato

2 teaspoons chopped fresh oregano or 1/2 teaspoon dried

3 scallions (spring onions/shallots), chopped

1 tablespoon chopped fresh parsley

7 oz (220 g) cooked crabmeat

4 eggs, separated

salt and freshly ground pepper

Melt butter in saucepan over medium heat. Add flour and cook 1 minute. Remove from heat and gradually stir in milk. Return to heat and bring to boil, stirring constantly until sauce thickens. Remove from heat and add pecorino, tomato, oregano, scallions, parsley, crab, egg yolks, and salt and pepper to taste. Mix well.

Preheat oven to 375°F (190°C/Gas 5). Grease an 8 in. (20 cm) soufflé dish. Beat egg whites in a bowl until soft peaks form. Fold into crab mixture and pour into prepared dish. Bake 35 to 40 minutes or until golden. Serve immediately.

CRAB AND SHRIMP BABY OMELETTES WITH SPICY TOMATO SALSA

SERVES 4

The shrimp and crab combination tastes great in these omelettes, but if you wish to substitute other seafood, try scallops, ground (minced) fish, or finely chopped squid (calamari).

4 tablespoons olive oil

1 onion, chopped

1 clove garlic, chopped

1 red chili, seeded and chopped

1 teaspoon ground cumin

1 teaspoon ground coriander

14 oz (440 g) can peeled tomatoes

4 eggs, lightly beaten

8 oz (250 g) uncooked shrimp (prawns), chopped

3 oz (90 g) cooked crabmeat

2 scallions (spring onions/ shallots), finely chopped

3 tablespoons chopped cilantro (fresh coriander leaves)

1/4 teaspoon salt

1/4 teaspoon freshly ground pepper

Combine 2 tablespoons oil, onion, garlic, chili, cumin, coriander and tomatoes, in saucepan and bring to boil over medium heat. Simmer 15 minutes. Transfer to food processor and blend until smooth. Set aside and keep warm.

Combine eggs, shrimp, crabmeat, scallions, 2 tablespoons cilantro, salt, and pepper in bowl and mix well.

Heat remaining 2 tablespoons oil in frying pan over medium heat until hot. Drop in seafood mixture by tablespoonfuls, forming eight baby omelettes, and cook 2 minutes. Turn and cook a further 1 to 2 minutes. Divide omelettes among four plates and spoon salsa over. Sprinkle with remaining 1 tablespoon cilantro. Serve hot.

Following pages: Crab in Black Bean Sauce (page 116), Crab in Chili Oyster Sauce (page 116), Crab and Shrimp Baby Omelettes with Spicy Tomato Salsa (page 113)

CRAB IN BLACK BEAN SAUCE

When serving crabs in the shell, it's important to have the claws cracked to allow your guests easy eating. Claws are easily cracked using a nutcracker or meat mallet. Make sure you have lots of finger bowls and hand towels available. Serve the crabs with steamed rice.

1 tablespoon peanut oil

3 tablespoons chopped scallions (spring onions/shallots)

2 cloves garlic, chopped

1 teaspoon chopped fresh ginger

1/3 cup (3 fl oz/90 ml) black bean sauce

1/2 cup (4 fl oz/125 ml) fish stock (see page 260)

1 tablespoon sherry (optional)

3 lb (1.5 kg) uncooked crab, segmented and claws cracked (see page 26)

Heat oil in frying pan or wok over medium heat. Add scallions, garlic, and ginger and sauté until fragrant, about 1 minute. Pour in sauce, stock, and sherry and bring to boil. Simmer until slightly thickened, about 4 minutes. Add crab and stir well. Cover and cook 10 to 15 minutes or until crab is cooked through — to test, crack a shell and see if flesh is tender.

CRAB IN CHILI OYSTER SAUCE

See the notes in the recipe above about serving crab. Serve with steamed Jasmine rice or Asian noodles.

2 tablespoons peanut oil

2 red chilies, seeded and finely chopped

2 cloves garlic, chopped

1 tablespoon chopped fresh ginger

1/4 cup (2 fl oz/60 ml) oyster sauce

1/2 cup (4 fl oz/125 ml) fish stock (see page 260)

2 tablespoons sweet chili sauce

2 lb (1 kg) uncooked crab, segmented (see page 26)

4 scallions (spring onions/shallots), chopped

Heat oil in large frying pan over medium heat. Add chilies, garlic, and ginger and sauté until fragrant, about 1 minute. Add oyster sauce, stock, and sweet chili sauce and bring to boil. Simmer until slightly thickened, about 4 minutes.

Add crab and scallions and stir to coat with sauce. Simmer, covered, 15 to 20 minutes or until crab is cooked through — to test, crack a shell and see if flesh is tender.

WARM SCALLOP SALAD

SERVES 4

Serve this simple but special salad with buttered brown bread.

3 oz (90 g) Belgian endive (witloof), sliced, or green oakleaf lettuce

2 oz (60 g) snow pea (mange tout) sprouts

2 oz (60 g) macadamia nuts, halved

8 oz (250 g) scallops, deveined if necessary

1/4 cup (2 fl oz/60 ml) water

1/4 cup (2 fl oz/60 ml) macadamia nut oil

2 tablespoons tarragon vinegar

1 clove garlic, chopped

2 teaspoons seeded mustard

salt and freshly ground pepper

Combine endive, sprouts, and nuts in large bowl.

Place scallops and water in saucepan over medium heat and simmer 1 to 2 minutes or until scallops are just tender. Drain and add to salad.

Combine oil, vinegar, garlic, mustard, and salt and pepper to taste. Pour over salad and toss well. Divide among four plates and pile high.

FARFALLE WITH SPINACH AND SCALLOPS

SERVES 4

Farfalle, or butterfly-shaped pasta, is easy to eat using just a fork, but another variety of pasta can be used.

2 tablespoons olive oil

1 onion, finely chopped

2 cups (3 oz/90 g) finely chopped fresh spinach

1/2 cup (4 fl oz/125 ml) light whipping cream

8 oz (250 g) scallops, deveined if necessary

1/4 teaspoon nutmeg

salt

8 oz (250 g) farfalle pasta, cooked according to package instructions

Heat oil in saucepan over medium heat. Add onion and cook 1 to 2 minutes or until tender. Add spinach and cook 2 minutes. Pour in cream and simmer until sauce has thickened slightly.

Add scallops, nutmeg, and salt to taste and simmer a further 2 minutes or until scallops are tender.

Toss sauce with hot farfalle and serve.

SCALLOPS AND SNOW PEAS IN OYSTER SAUCE

SERVES 4

This sauce works equally well with broccoli and shrimp (prawns). Serve with boiled or steamed rice.

1 tablespoon peanut oil

1 clove garlic, chopped

1 teaspoon chopped fresh ginger

4 oz (125 g) snow peas (mange-tout)

10 oz (300 g) scallops, deveined if necessary

2 tablespoons oyster sauce

2 tablespoons fish stock (see page 260)

1 tablespoon soy sauce

1 teaspoon cornstarch (cornflour)

Place oil, garlic and ginger in frying pan or wok over medium heat and sauté until fragrant, about 1 minute. Stir in snow peas and fry 1 minute or until tender but still crisp. Add scallops and sauté 1 minute.

Combine oyster sauce, stock, soy sauce, and cornstarch. Add to pan and bring to boil. Simmer until thickened.

SCALLOPS ON THE SHELL WITH BASIL BUTTER SAUCE

SERVES 4

This recipe could also be used with oysters on the half shell.

24 scallops on the half shell

3 tablespoons butter

2 cloves garlic, chopped

3 tablespoons finely chopped leek

3 tablespoons finely chopped fresh basil

salt and freshly ground pepper

Preheat broiler (grill) on high. Arrange scallops on a tray.

Melt butter in frying pan over medium heat. Add garlic and leek and sauté 1 minute or until tender. Remove from heat and stir in basil.

Divide sauce evenly among scallops; season with salt and pepper. Place under broiler (grill) for 1 to 2 minutes or until scallops are opaque. Serve immediately.

Scallops on the Shell with Basil Butter Sauce

SCALLOPS AND MUSHROOMS IN CHERVIL CREAM SAUCE

SERVES 4

This light creamy sauce is best accompanied by boiled white rice.

2 tablespoons butter

2 cloves garlic, chopped

2 cups (8 oz/250 g) sliced brown mushrooms

1/2 cup (4 fl oz/125 ml) fish stock (see page 260)

1/4 cup (2 fl oz/60 ml) light whipping cream

salt and freshly ground pepper

13 oz (400 g) scallops, deveined if necessary

1 tablespoon chopped fresh chervil

Melt butter in frying pan over medium heat. Add garlic and mushrooms and sauté over low heat 5 minutes. Add stock, cream, and salt and pepper to taste, increase heat, and boil until the sauce thickens slightly. Add scallops and chervil and simmer 1 to 2 minutes or until scallops are tender.

SCALLOPS WITH CREAMED SPINACH AND BASIL

SERVES 4

2 tablespoons butter

2 cloves garlic, chopped

2 cups (3 oz/90 g) finely chopped fresh spinach

1 cup (1 1/2 oz/45 g) chopped fresh basil

1/2 cup (4 fl oz/125 ml) light whipping cream

1/4 teaspoon salt

8 oz (250 g) scallops, deveined if necessary

1/2 cup (3 oz/90 g) short-grain rice, cooked

Melt butter in saucepan over medium heat. Add garlic, spinach, and basil and sauté 1 to 2 minutes or until tender. Add cream and salt and simmer, covered, 2 minutes.

Transfer spinach mixture to food processor or blender and puree until smooth. Return puree to saucepan and bring to boil over medium heat. Add scallops and simmer 1 to 2 minutes until scallops are tender. Add rice and mix well. Serve at once.

SCALLOPS AND ASPARAGUS WITH BUTTERED BREADCRUMBS

SERVES 4

Shrimp (prawns), scampi, or slipper lobsters can be substituted for scallops in this recipe.

13 oz (400 g) asparagus

2 hard-cooked (boiled) eggs, finely chopped

5 tablespoons butter

8 oz (250 g) scallops, deveined if necessary

1/2 cup (1 oz/30 g) fresh breadcrumbs (see glossary)

2 tablespoons chopped fresh parsley

1 tablespoon chopped chives

freshly ground pepper

Steam, microwave or blanch asparagus until tender. Divide among warmed plates and sprinkle with egg.

Melt 2 tablespoons butter in frying pan over medium heat. Add scallops and sauté 1 to 2 minutes or until tender. Arrange over asparagus and egg.

Melt remaining 3 tablespoons butter in same pan, add breadcrumbs, and stir until coated. Sprinkle crumbs over scallops. Sprinkle with parsley, chives, and pepper. Serve immediately.

OYSTERS WITH SOUR CREAM AND CHEESE

SERVES 4

This delicious topping is also suited to scallops and mussels on the half shell. Scallops do not require cooking prior to broiling, although mussels should first be steamed open (see page 121), then topped with sour cream mixture and broiled (grilled).

1/3 cup (3 fl oz/80 ml) sour cream

2 tablespoons grated cheddar cheese

1 tablespoon chopped chives

1 teaspoon grated lemon rind

freshly ground pepper

24 freshly shucked oysters on the half shell

Preheat broiler (grill) on high. Combine sour cream, cheddar, chives, rind, and pepper to taste in small bowl and mix well. Divide mixture evenly among oysters. Broil (grill) until hot and golden. Serve immediately.

PARMESAN AND CHIVE SOUFFLÉ OYSTERS

SERVES 4

The cheese mixture can be made in advance, without the egg white, and stored in the refrigerator. Just prior to serving, beat egg white, fold it through the cheese mixture, and proceed according to the recipe.

2 tablespoons butter

1½ tablespoons all-purpose (plain) flour

½ cup (4 fl oz/125 ml) milk

1 teaspoon prepared mustard

salt and freshly ground pepper

2 tablespoons grated parmesan cheese

2 tablespoons chopped chives

2 eggs, separated

24 freshly shucked oysters on the half shell

Melt butter in small saucepan over medium heat. Add flour and cook 1 minute, stirring constantly. Remove from heat and gradually stir in milk. Return to medium heat and stir until sauce boils and thickens. Remove from heat and add mustard, salt and pepper to taste, parmesan, chives, and egg yolks. Cool slightly.

Preheat broiler (grill). Place oysters on the tray. Place egg whites in large bowl and beat until soft peaks form. Fold into cheese mixture until well combined. Cover each oyster with mixture and broil (grill) until puffy and golden. Serve immediately.

OYSTERS AND SCALLOPS KILPATRICK

SERVES 4

12 oysters on the half shell

12 scallops on the half shell

4 bacon strips (rashers), finely chopped

4 scallions (spring onions/shallots), finely chopped

⅓ cup (3 fl oz/80 ml) worcestershire sauce

Preheat broiler (grill). Arrange oysters and scallops on the tray. Sprinkle with bacon and scallions. Drizzle ½ teaspoon worcestershire sauce over each. Broil (grill) on high just until bacon begins to sizzle. Serve immediately.

Parmesan and Chive Soufflé Oysters

OYSTERS WITH BLUE CHEESE DRESSING

SERVES 4

Dressing can be made in advance and stored in an airtight container in the refrigerator for up to 3 days.

24 freshly shucked oysters on
the half shell

$^1/_3$ cup (2 oz/60 g) crumbled
blue cheese

$^1/_4$ cup (2 fl oz/60 ml) lemon juice

2 tablespoons olive oil

salt and freshly ground pepper

chopped chives

Divide oysters among four small plates; chill. Combine cheese, juice, oil, and salt and pepper in food processor and blend until smooth. Spoon dressing over chilled oysters and sprinkle with chives. Serve at once.

OYSTERS WITH EGG AND CAPER SAUCE

SERVES 4

Dressing can be made in advance and stored in an airtight container in the refrigerator up to 3 days.

24 freshly shucked oysters on
the half shell

$^1/_4$ cup (2 fl oz/60 ml) extra virgin
olive oil

2 tablespoons lemon juice

grated rind of 1 lemon

1 teaspoon chopped capers

1 teaspoon chopped chives

1 teaspoon chopped fresh dill

1 hard-cooked (boiled) egg yolk

salt and freshly ground pepper

Divide oysters among four small plates; chill. Combine oil, juice, rind, capers, chives, dill, yolk, and salt and pepper to taste in food processor and blend until well combined. Chill if time permits. Spoon a small amount of dressing over oysters and serve.

OYSTERS WITH HORSERADISH CREAM

SERVES 4

This cream makes a delicious dipping sauce for any cold seafood. It stores well in an airtight container in the refrigerator for up to 3 days.

24 freshly shucked oysters on the half shell

1/3 cup (3 fl oz/90 ml) lightly whipped cream

1 tablespoon creamed horseradish

1 tablespoon chopped chives

freshly ground pepper

Divide oysters among four small plates. Combine cream, horseradish, chives, and pepper in small bowl and mix well. Place teaspoonsful of mixture onto oysters and chill before serving.

MARINATED MUSSELS AND FENNEL

SERVES 4

3 lb (1.5 kg) mussels, scrubbed and debearded

1/2 cup (4 fl oz/125 ml) water

2 scallions (spring onions/ shallots), chopped

1 teaspoon fennel seeds

1 fennel bulb, thinly sliced

2 teaspoons dijon mustard

1/3 cup (3 fl oz/90 ml) olive oil

1/4 cup (2 fl oz/60 ml) lemon juice

salt and freshly ground pepper

crusty bread, to serve

Place mussels in large saucepan with water, cover, and bring to boil. Simmer just until mussels open, 2 to 3 minutes; discard any that do not open. Remove mussels from shells. Discard shells.

Combine mussels, scallions, seeds, and fennel in bowl. Combine mustard, oil, juice, and salt and pepper to taste. Pour over mussels and mix well. Marinate at least 30 minutes before serving with bread.

BAKED MUSSELS

SERVES 4

Mussels can be prepared and filled a day ahead and stored covered in the refrigerator. Cook just before serving.

1 cup (2 oz/60 g) fresh breadcrumbs (see glossary)

2 tablespoons grated parmesan cheese

2 tablespoons lemon juice

2 tablespoons finely chopped fresh parsley

2 cloves garlic, chopped

1/4 cup (2 fl oz/60 ml) olive oil

salt and freshly ground pepper

1 1/2 lb (750 g) mussels, scrubbed and debearded

1/2 cup (4 fl oz/125 ml) water

Combine breadcrumbs, parmesan, juice, parsley, garlic, oil, and salt and pepper in bowl and mix well.

Place mussels and water in large saucepan over high heat and bring to boil. Cook just until mussels open, about 2 to 3 minutes; discard any that do not open. Separate shells, discarding one half. Loosen mussel from remaining shell and replace in shell.

Place teaspoonfuls of breadcrumb mixture over mussels and cook under hot broiler (grill) until golden. Serve immediately.

MUSSELS STEAMED IN WINE

SERVES 4 TO 6

1 tablespoon olive oil

2 cloves garlic, chopped

1/2 cup (4 fl oz/125 ml) dry white wine

1/2 cup (4 fl oz/125 ml) fish stock (see page 260)

2 scallions (spring onions/shallots), chopped

3 tablespoons chopped fresh parsley

2 lb (1 kg) mussels, scrubbed and debearded

crusty bread, to serve

Heat oil in large saucepan over medium heat. Add garlic and sauté until fragrant. Add wine, stock, scallions, parsley, and mussels, cover, and bring to boil. Simmer just until mussels open, about 2 to 3 minutes; discard any that do not open. Serve immediately with bread.

Mussels Steamed in Wine

Buttered Garlic and Mussel Rice

SERVES 4 TO 6

2 lb (1 kg) mussels, scrubbed and debearded

1/2 cup (4 fl oz/125 ml) dry white wine

1 scallion (spring onion/ shallot), halved

3 tablespoons butter

1 onion, chopped

2 cloves garlic, chopped

1 cup (6 oz/180 g) short-grain rice

2 cups (16 fl oz/500 ml) fish stock (see page 260)

salt and freshly ground pepper

2 tablespoons chopped fresh dill

Combine mussels, wine, and scallion in a large saucepan, cover, and bring to boil over high heat. Simmer just until mussels open, about 2 to 3 minutes; discard any that do not open. Reserve 1 cup cooking liquid. Remove mussels from shells and reserve; discard shells.

Melt butter in large saucepan over medium heat. Add onion and sauté until tender. Add garlic and rice and stir until all rice grains are well coated with butter.

Pour in fish stock, reserved liquid, and salt and pepper to taste. Cover, and cook, stirring occasionally, until liquid has been absorbed by rice, about 15 to 20 minutes. Five minutes before end of cooking time, add dill and reserved mussels.

STUFFED AND POACHED MUSSELS

SERVES 4

This unusual way of preparing mussels was taught to me by my father, who is Italian and a great cook. A little effort is needed, but it's really worth it!

1¹/₂ lb (750 g) mussels, scrubbed and debearded

³/₄ cup (1¹/₂ oz/45 g) fresh breadcrumbs (see glossary)

2 tablespoons grated parmesan cheese

2 cloves garlic, chopped

4 tablespoons chopped fresh parsley

3 tablespoons lemon juice

1 tablespoon mayonnaise

4 oz (125 g) canned tuna in oil, undrained

salt and freshly ground pepper

¹/₂ cup (4 fl oz/125 ml) dry white wine

¹/₂ cup (4 fl oz/125 ml) fish stock (see page 260)

2 tablespoons olive oil

crusty bread, to serve

Hold one mussel firmly and force tip of sharp knife into straight edge of mussel. Run knife tip around edge of shell until curve of mussel is reached. Pry shell open but do not separate the two halves. Repeat with remaining mussels.

Combine breadcrumbs, parmesan, half of garlic, 1 tablespoon parsley, 1 tablespoon lemon juice, mayonnaise, tuna, and salt and pepper in bowl and mix well. Divide stuffing among mussels, placing a small amount on one half of shell. Press shells closed and tie each mussel with wet kitchen twine.

Pack mussels into large saucepan and pour in wine, stock, oil, remaining 3 tablespoons parsley, and remaining 2 tablespoons lemon juice. Bring to boil, then turn down heat and simmer 10 minutes.

To serve, cut twine from mussels. Place mussels in soup bowls, pour cooking liquid over, and accompany with plenty of crusty bread.

PENNE WITH MUSSELS AND CHILI TOMATO SAUCE

SERVES 6

1/4 cup (2 fl oz/60 ml) olive oil

1 clove garlic, chopped

1 red chili, seeded and chopped

1/4 cup (2 fl oz/60 ml) dry white wine

2 lb (1 kg) mussels, scrubbed and debearded

14 oz (440 g) can peeled tomatoes, chopped

2 tablespoons tomato paste

salt and freshly ground pepper

3 tablespoons chopped fresh basil

3 tablespoons light whipping cream

13 oz (400 g) penne pasta, cooked to package instructions

Place oil, garlic, and chili in large saucepan over medium heat and sauté until fragrant, about 1 minute. Add wine and mussels and cook, covered, over high heat just until mussels open, about 2 to 3 minutes; discard any that do not open. Reserve cooking liquid. Remove mussels from shells; discard shells.

In same saucepan, combine reserved cooking liquid, tomatoes, tomato paste, and salt and pepper to taste and bring to boil. Simmer, covered, 30 minutes or until sauce has thickened slightly.

Add basil, cream, and reserved mussels to sauce and heat through; do not boil or mussels will overcook and toughen.

Pour sauce over hot penne, toss well and serve.

Penne with Mussels and Chili Tomato Sauce

MUSSELS WITH GARLIC, CHILI, AND COCONUT CREAM

SERVES 4

A slightly sweet, spicy sauce is used to steam the mussels. Other bivalves, such as clams or cockles, can be substituted. Serve with rice or noodles.

1 tablespoon peanut oil

2 to 3 cloves garlic, chopped

2 red chilies, seeded and chopped

1/4 cup (2 fl oz/60 ml) thin coconut cream

2 tablespoons water

1 tablespoon fish sauce

1 teaspoon sugar

2 tablespoons chopped cilantro (fresh coriander leaves)

1 lb (500 g) mussels, scrubbed and debearded

Place oil, garlic, and chili in frying pan over medium heat and sauté until fragrant, about 1 minute. Stir in coconut cream, water, fish sauce, sugar, and cilantro and bring to boil. Add mussels, cover, and simmer just until mussels open, 2 to 3 minutes; discard any that do not open. Serve immediately.

MIXED MOLLUSKS IN RICH WINE SAUCE

SERVES 4

This flavorful dish makes a delicious starter for any meal. Be sure to have fingerbowls and extra napkins at the table. Clams, mussels, and cockles are ideal in this recipe.

4 tablespoons butter

2 cloves garlic, chopped

1/3 cup (3 fl oz/80 ml) dry white wine

1/4 teaspoon cracked pepper

salt

2 tablespoons chopped fresh parsley

1 1/2 lb (750 g) mixed bivalves, scrubbed, debearded and soaked if necessary

crusty bread, to serve

Melt butter in frying pan over medium heat. Add garlic and sauté until fragrant, about 1 minute. Add wine, pepper, salt, parsley, and seafood, cover, and bring to boil. Simmer just until shells open, about 2 to 3 minutes; discard any that do not open. Serve immediately with bread.

BARBECUED BABY OCTOPUS

SERVES 4

Small baby octopus are ideal for barbecuing and will be very tender if not overcooked. Large octopus is not suited to the barbecue, as it needs long, slow, moist cooking to tenderize it.

2 lb (1 kg) baby octopus, cleaned

1/3 cup (3 fl oz/90 ml) olive oil

1/4 cup (2 fl oz/60 ml) lemon juice

2 cloves garlic, chopped

2 tablespoons chopped fresh parsley

2 teaspoons chopped fresh rosemary or 1 teaspoon dried

lemon wedges, to serve

Place octopus in large bowl with oil, juice, garlic, parsley and rosemary and mix well. Marinate at least 1 hour, or overnight if time allows.

Drain octopus, reserving marinade. Place on preheated barbecue, or under broiler (grill) and cook until tender, about 5 minutes, basting frequently with reserved marinade; do not overcook, or octopus will toughen. Test by cutting off a small piece and tasting; if tender remove immediately. Serve with lemon wedges.

OCTOPUS IN PEANUT SAUCE

SERVES 4

Serve with steamed rice or Asian noodles to make the most of this tasty sauce. You can use this sauce with other seafood too, such as squid (calamari), or cuttlefish.

1/2 cup (4 fl oz/125 ml) thin coconut cream

1/4 cup (2 fl oz/60 ml) water

3 tablespoons crunchy peanut butter

1/4 teaspoon chili powder

1/2 teaspoon ground cumin

1/2 teaspoon ground coriander

1/2 teaspoon curry powder

1 1/2 lb (750 g) baby octopus, or one large, cleaned

Combine coconut cream, water, peanut butter, chili powder, cumin, coriander, and curry in saucepan and bring to boil over medium heat. Add octopus, cover, and simmer, stirring occasionally, 30 minutes or until octopus is tender. Serve hot.

CUTTLEFISH WITH TOMATO AND ONION

SERVES 4

For an equally simple first course, substitute squid (calamari) for the cuttlefish or try shrimp (prawns) panfried in a small amount of olive oil. Serve with toasted crusty bread.

1 cup (8 fl oz/250 ml) water

2 lb (1 kg) cuttlefish, cleaned and honeycombed (see page 34)

2 tomatoes, thinly sliced

1 small purple (Spanish) onion, thinly sliced

1/3 cup (3 fl oz/90 ml) extra virgin olive oil

2 teaspoons chopped fresh oregano or 1/2 teaspoon dried

salt and freshly ground pepper

Bring water to boil in saucepan over high heat. Add cuttlefish and simmer 1 to 2 minutes or until tender. Drain and cool.

Divide tomatoes and onion among four plates. Top with cuttlefish. Drizzle with oil and sprinkle with oregano, salt and pepper. Let stand 5 minutes before serving.

WARM CUTTLEFISH AND ARUGULA SALAD

SERVES 4

Substitute squid (calamari), shrimp (prawns), or scallops for the cuttlefish if you wish.

1 cup (8 fl oz/250 ml) water

2 lb (1 kg) cuttlefish, cleaned and honeycombed (see page 34)

2 cups (4 oz/125 g) arugula (rocket), trimmed and washed

1/3 cup (3 fl oz/90 ml) olive oil

1/4 cup (2 fl oz/60 ml) lemon juice

1 teaspoon grated lemon rind

1 teaspoon chopped fresh ginger

1/4 teaspoon salt

1/4 teaspoon crushed peppercorns

Place water in saucepan over high heat and bring to boil. Add cuttlefish and simmer 1 to 2 minutes or until tender. Drain well.

Place in large bowl and cool slightly. Add arugula.

Combine oil, juice, rind, ginger, salt and pepper in screwtop jar and shake well. Pour dressing over salad, mixing well. Divide among small plates and serve warm.

Cuttlefish with Tomato and Onion

CUTTLEFISH WITH PEAS AND POTATO

This dish can be made with squid (calamari) instead of cuttlefish if desired.

1 tablespoon olive oil

1 onion, chopped

2 bacon strips (rashers), chopped

2 lb (1 kg) cuttlefish, cleaned and honeycombed (see page 34)

8 oz (250 g) peas

2 large potatoes, peeled and chopped

3/4 cup (6 fl oz/180 ml) fish stock (see page 260)

salt and freshly ground pepper

Heat oil in large saucepan over medium heat. Add onion and bacon and sauté 2 to 3 minutes or until onion is tender. Add cuttlefish and sauté 2 minutes. Stir in peas, potatoes, stock, and salt and pepper to taste and bring to boil. Cover and simmer 20 minutes or until potatoes are tender. Serve hot.

SQUID AND PEAS IN MINT AND COCONUT CREAM

SERVES 4

Serve this delicately flavored dish with rice to soak up the sauce.

1 tablespoon peanut oil

1 clove garlic, chopped

1 red chili, seeded and chopped

1 1/2 lb (750 g) squid (calamari), cleaned and honeycombed (see page 32)

1/2 cup (4 fl oz/125 ml) thin coconut cream

1 cup (7 oz/220 g) peas

3 tablespoons chopped fresh mint

salt and freshly ground pepper

Place oil, garlic, and chili in large saucepan over medium heat and sauté until fragrant, about 1 minute. Add squid and sauté 2 to 3 minutes until opaque. Add coconut cream, peas, mint, and salt and pepper and simmer 15 minutes or until squid is tender. Serve immediately.

SPICY INDIAN SQUID FRITTERS

SERVES 6

Wonderfully crisp squid rings with a difference. Serve with plain yoghurt mixed with cilantro (fresh coriander leaves) or basil or choose one of the mayonnaises in the sauces section (see pages 262 to 266) to accompany it, along with lemon wedges.

1/2 cup (2 oz/60 g) all-purpose (plain) flour

1 teaspoon ground cumin

1/2 teaspoon ground coriander

1/2 teaspoon garam masala

1/2 teaspoon chili powder

1/2 teaspoon ground cardamom

10 oz (300 g) plain yogurt

1/2 cup (4 fl oz/ 125 ml) water

11/2 lb (750 g) squid (calamari), cleaned and cut into rings

vegetable oil for deep frying

Sift flour, cumin, coriander, garam masala, chili powder and cardamom into large bowl. Pour in yogurt and water and mix to form smooth batter. Add squid and mix well.

Heat oil in deep pan. Test by dropping a small amount of batter into oil — if it sizzles immediately the temperature is correct; if it burns immediately, reduce heat and allow to cool a little. Drain excess batter from squid and drop into oil. Fry 1 to 2 minutes or until golden. Drain on paper towels. Serve hot.

SQUID AND SPINACH WITH RICE

SERVES 4 TO 6

A great combination and a hearty starter! Also suitable in large portions for a light lunch.

2 tablespoons olive oil

1 onion, chopped

1 lb (500 g) squid (calamari), cleaned and diced

3 cups (5 oz/155 g) chopped fresh spinach

1 tomato, chopped

1 cup (5 oz/155 g) short-grain rice

3 cups (24 fl/750 ml) fish stock (see page 260)

1/4 teaspoon turmeric

salt and freshly ground pepper

Heat oil in saucepan over medium heat. Add onion and sauté 2 minutes or until tender. Stir in squid and spinach and cook 3 to 5 minutes until squid becomes white and tender; mixture will be runny.

Stir in tomato, rice, half the stock, turmeric, and salt and pepper to taste. Cover and bring to boil, then simmer, stirring occasionally, until all liquid has been absorbed. Stir in remaining stock and simmer until rice is tender, 15 to 20 minutes. Serve hot.

MAIN COURSES

Lobster Medallions with Chervil and Asparagus (page 213)

FISH AND CHIPS

This batter is one of my favorites — it is crisp, light, and golden. Cooking the perfect traditional English "Fish and Chips" can be tricky. It is important to coordinate the cooking so everything is ready to be cooked without interruption. Have the oil heating, the batter made, and an oven preheated to a low temperature to keep the fish warm while the chips are cooking. While fish is in the oven, place it on a cake rack to allow hot air to circulate around the pieces, keeping them crisp.

For the best chips, cook potatoes twice — once over low heat to cook them through, and then a second time to make them crisp and golden. Traditional English chips are not in slices but are rather finger-sized sticks of potato.

Serve with garlic and herb mayonnaise (see page 262), tartare sauce (see page 266) and lemon wedges

1 cup (4 oz/125 g) all-purpose (plain) flour

1 teaspoon salt

1 teaspoon baking (bicarbonate) soda

1½ cups (12 fl oz/375 ml) buttermilk

1 egg white, beaten to soft peaks

vegetable oil for deep frying

4 potatoes, peeled and cut into uniform "fingers"

4 white-fleshed fish fillets, 5 oz (150 g) each, skinned and halved

Sift flour, salt, and soda into large bowl. Make a well in middle and gradually add buttermilk, mixing to form smooth batter. Fold in egg white.

Heat oil to 325°F (170°C). Add potatoes, in two or more batches if necessary, and fry until tender and just starting to brown — they will be fried again later. Drain well and cool.

Preheat oven to 275°F (140°C/Gas 1). Reheat oil to 350°F (180°C). Pat fish dry with paper towel. Dip into batter, allowing excess to drain. Plunge fish into oil and cook until crisp and golden, about 1 to 2 minutes depending on size of pieces. Drain on paper towels. Keep warm in oven.

Reheat oil to 375°F (190°C). Return potatoes to oil and cook 1 to 2 minutes or until crisp and golden. Drain on paper towels and serve immediately.

CALAMARI RINGS

SERVES 4

Calamari rings should be crisp and golden. To achieve this, the oil must be at the correct temperature before adding the squid. To test, sprinkle in a few breadcrumbs into hot oil; they should start to sizzle immediately but not burn. Do not overcrowd the pan with squid, as this will lower the temperature of the oil and give soggy results.

2 lb (1 kg) squid (calamari), cleaned and cut into rings

seasoned flour

2 eggs, beaten

1¹/₂ cups (6 oz/180 g) dry breadcrumbs

oil for deep frying

tartare sauce (see page 266), to serve

lemon wedges, to serve

Dust squid with flour, shaking off excess. Dip into egg and then breadcrumbs, pressing firmly. Chill 30 minutes.

Heat oil in deep pan over medium heat until hot. Add squid in batches cook until crisp and golden, about 1 to 2 minutes. Drain well on paper towels and keep warm. Serve with tartare sauce and lemon wedges.

CRUMBED FISH WITH WARM SPINACH DRESSING

SERVES 4

1 lb (500 g) white-fleshed or oily fish fillets, skinned

1 egg, beaten

1¹/₂ cups (3 oz/90 g) fresh breadcrumbs (see glossary)

2 tablespoons chopped chives

2 tablespoons olive oil

1 cup (2 oz/60 g) finely chopped fresh spinach

2 tablespoons cider vinegar

1 clove garlic, chopped

¹/₃ cup (3 fl oz/90 ml) light whipping cream

¹/₄ cup (2 fl oz/60 ml) olive oil, for frying

Dip fillets in egg, allowing excess to drain off. Combine breadcrumbs and chives in shallow bowl and dip fish into mixture, pressing firmly. Chill 30 minutes.

Combine 2 tablespoons oil, spinach, vinegar, garlic, and cream in food processor or blender and blend until smooth. Transfer to saucepan and heat through over low heat until just warm.

Heat ¹/₄ cup oil in frying pan over medium heat. Add fillets and cook 2 to 3 minutes per side or until fish is opaque and beginning to flake when tested. To serve, place on plates and spoon dressing over.

Calamari Rings

CRISPY GOLDEN FISH WITH CHUTNEY MAYONNAISE

SERVES 4

The chutney mixture is easily prepared with commercial mayonnaise. Try to use good quality ingredients for the best result. Any unused portion can be stored in a jar, refrigerated, and used when needed.

1 cup (8 fl oz/250 ml) whole egg mayonnaise

2 tablespoons fruit chutney

3 teaspoons curry powder

1/2 cup (2 oz/60 g) all-purpose (plain) flour

1/4 teaspoon salt

1 lb (500 g) white-fleshed or oily fish fillets, skinned

2 tablespoons olive oil

Combine mayonnaise, chutney, and 1 teaspoon curry powder in a small bowl and mix well.

Combine flour, remaining 2 teaspoons curry powder, and salt in plastic bag and shake well to combine. Add fillets and shake bag to coat with flour. Remove fillets and dust off any excess flour.

Heat oil in frying pan over medium heat until hot. Add fillets and cook 2 to 3 minutes per side or until fish is opaque and is beginning to flake when tested.

Serve hot fish with mayonnaise.

FRITTO MISTO

SERVES 4 TO 6

Fritto misto is an Italian dish that consists of battered mixed seafood. It takes quite a bit of time to cook, so if you can, have two deep fryers going at the same time. Keep cooked seafood warm in the oven. Serve with lemon wedges, tartare sauce (see page 266) and red pepper mayonnaise (see page 264).

2 cups (8 oz/250 g) all-purpose (plain) flour

2 cups (16 fl oz/500 ml) club soda (sparkling soda water)

1/2 cup (4 fl oz/125 ml) lemon juice

vegetable oil for deep frying

1 lb (500 g) uncooked shrimp (prawns), peeled and deveined

4 small squid (calamari), cleaned and cut into rings

4 oz (125 g) scallops, deveined if necessary

4 white-fleshed fish fillets, about 3 oz (90 g) each, skinned

6 oz (185 g) whitebait (optional)

8 garfish, scaled and cleaned (optional)

Place flour in large bowl and make a well in middle. Gradually add soda and juice, mixing well to form smooth batter.

Preheat oven to 275°F (140°C/Gas 1). Heat oil in large saucepan or deep fryer until hot. Dip seafood into batter, allowing excess to drain. Drop in batches into oil and cook until crisp and golden, about 2 to 5 minutes depending on seafood. Drain on paper towels and keep warm in oven. Continue until all seafood has been cooked. Serve hot with choice of accompaniments.

PANFRIED FISH WITH RATATOUILLE

This already excellent sauce can be enriched even further by the addition of 1/4 cup (2 fl oz/60 ml) light whipping cream or sour cream.

3 tablespoons olive oil

1/2 cup (2 oz/60 g) chopped leek

2 cloves garlic, chopped

2 cups (10 oz/300 g) finely diced eggplant (aubergine)

3/4 cup (5 oz/150 g) finely diced zucchini (courgette)

1/2 cup (2 oz/60 g) chopped red bell pepper (capsicum)

1 cup (4 oz/125 g) chopped tomato

1/4 cup (2 fl oz/60 ml) red wine

salt and freshly ground pepper

4 white-fleshed or oily fish steaks (cutlets), about 8 oz (250 g) each

Heat 2 tablespoons oil in frying pan over medium heat. Add leek, garlic, eggplant, zucchini, and pepper and cook until tender, about 10 minutes. Stir in tomato, wine, and salt and pepper and bring to boil. Cover and simmer 15 minutes, stirring occasionally.

Heat remaining tablespoon oil in pan over medium heat. Add fish and season with salt and pepper. Cook 3 to 4 minutes per side or until fish is opaque and beginning to flake when tested.

To serve, place fish on plates and spoon sauce over.

PANFRIED FISH WITH FENNEL SAUCE

4 tablespoons butter

1 1/2 cups (5 oz/185 g) chopped fennel

1 teaspoon fennel seeds

4 white-fleshed or oily fish steaks (cutlets) about 8 oz (250 g) each

1/4 cup (2 fl oz/60 ml) fish stock (see page 260)

2 tablespoons sherry

Melt 2 tablespoons butter in frying pan over low heat. Add fennel and seeds and cook until fennel is tender, about 5 minutes. Remove and keep warm.

Add fish to pan and cook over medium heat 3 to 4 minutes per side or until fish is opaque and beginning to flake when tested. Remove and keep warm.

Return fennel to frying pan and place over high heat. Add stock, sherry, and remaining butter and bring to boil. Simmer until sauce boils, reduces slightly, and thickens. Pour over fish and serve.

SPANISH-STYLE FISH STEAKS

SERVES 4

4 white-fleshed or oily
fish steaks (cutlets), about
8 oz (250 g) each

1 purple (Spanish) onion, finely
chopped

1 clove garlic, chopped

2 teaspoons chopped fresh
oregano or 1/2 teaspoon dried

1/3 cup (3 fl oz/90 ml) olive oil

2 tablespoons lemon juice

2 tablespoons chopped capers

2 tablespoons chopped
black olives

2 tomatoes, sliced

salt and freshly ground pepper

Place fish and onion in greased baking dish. Combine garlic, oregano, oil, juice, capers, and olives and pour over fish. Marinate 30 minutes, or longer if time permits.

Preheat oven to 350°F (180°C/Gas 4). Lay tomato slices over fish and season with salt and pepper. Cover with foil and bake 15 to 20 minutes, or until fish is opaque and beginning to flake when tested.

FISH WITH GREEN PEPPERCORN SAUCE

SERVES 4

2 tablespoons butter

4 white-fleshed or oily
fish steaks (cutlets), about
8 oz (250 g) each

2 tablespoons green peppercorns

1/4 cup (2 fl oz/60 ml) fish stock
(see page 260)

1/4 cup (2 fl oz/60 ml)
dry white wine

1/4 cup (2 fl oz/60 ml) light
whipping cream

2 tablespoons chopped chives

Melt butter in frying pan over medium heat. Add fish and fry 3 to 4 minutes per side or until fish is opaque and beginning to flake when tested. Remove and keep warm.

Pour excess butter from pan. Add peppercorns, stock, wine, and cream to pan and bring to boil. Simmer until sauce thickens. Add chives, pour over fish, and serve.

Fish with Green Peppercorn Sauce

FISH WITH ONION BUTTER SAUCE

SERVES 4

This sauce is really excellent; it tastes sweet because the onions caramelize during the slow cooking process. It is also slightly tangy from the lemon juice.

3 tablespoons butter

2 tablespoons olive oil

2 onions, thinly sliced

4 white fleshed or oily fish steaks (cutlets), about 8 oz (250 g) each

1/4 cup (2 fl oz/60 ml) lemon juice

2 tablespoons chopped fresh parsley

1/4 teaspoon turmeric

Heat butter and oil in frying pan over medium heat. Add onions and cook over low heat until tender and golden, about 15 minutes. Remove and keep warm.

Return frying pan to medium heat. Add fish and cook 3 to 4 minutes per side or until fish is opaque and beginning to flake when tested. Place onto plates.

Return onions to frying pan. Add juice, parsley, and turmeric and heat through over high heat. Pour over fish and serve.

FISH WITH CITRUS BUTTER

SERVES 4

2 tablespoons olive oil

4 white fleshed or oily fish steaks (cutlets), about 8 oz (250 g) each

4 tablespoons butter

2 tablespoons lemon juice

2 tablespoons orange juice

grated rind of 1 lemon

grated rind of 1 orange

2 tablespoons orange marmalade

Heat oil in frying pan over medium heat. Add fish and cook 3 to 4 minutes per side or until fish is opaque and beginning to flake when tested. Remove and keep warm.

Melt butter in same frying pan until frothy. Add juices, grated rinds, and marmalade, stirring well. Heat through and pour over fish. Serve at once.

FISH IN BROWN BUTTER SAUCE

SERVES 4

This is an extremely simple sauce with a wonderful taste and texture. Make sure you don't burn the butter, as you will have to start again. Melt it just to the golden brown stage.

1/2 cup (4 oz/125 g) butter

1 lb (500 g) white-fleshed or oily fish fillets, skinned

1/4 cup (2 fl oz/60 ml) lemon juice

2 tablespoons chopped fresh parsley

2 tablespoons capers, halved

Melt 2 tablespoons butter in frying pan over medium heat. Add fillets and cook 2 to 3 minutes per side or until fish is opaque and just beginning to flake when tested. Remove and keep warm.

Add remaining butter to frying pan and cook over medium heat until golden with a nutty aroma, about 4 to 5 minutes. Remove from heat and add juice, parsley, and capers; butter will sizzle and foam. Pour over fish while still foaming and serve.

FISH IN HERB BUTTER SAUCE

SERVES 4

3 tablespoons butter

4 white-fleshed fish steaks (cutlets), about 8 oz (250 g) each

1/4 cup (2 fl oz/60 ml) lemon juice

1 tablespoon chopped fresh rosemary

1 tablespoon chopped fresh parsley

1 tablespoon chopped chives

2 tablespoons brandy

freshly ground pepper

Melt 1 tablespoon butter in frying pan over medium heat. Add fish and cook 3 to 4 minutes per side or until fish is opaque and beginning to flake when tested. Remove and keep warm.

Melt remaining butter in same frying pan over medium heat. Add juice, herbs, brandy, and pepper to taste and bring to boil. Pour over fish and serve.

FISH WITH WILTED ARUGULA

SERVES 4

1 tablespoon olive oil, for frying

4 white-fleshed or oily
fish steaks (cutlets), about
8 oz (250 g) each

salt and freshly ground pepper

1/3 cup (3 fl oz/90 ml) olive oil

7 oz (220 g) arugula (rocket),
stems trimmed, leaves cut in half

2 cloves garlic, chopped

2 tablespoons lemon juice

Heat 1 tablespoon oil in frying pan over medium heat. Add fish, season with salt and pepper and cook 3 to 4 minutes per side or until fish is opaque and beginning to flake when tested. Remove and keep warm.

Add 1/3 cup oil, arugula, garlic, and lemon juice to same frying pan. Season with salt and pepper and cook over medium heat until arugula has just wilted and is bright green.

To serve, place fish on plates and arrange arugula and juices over fish.

FISH WITH WATERCRESS SAUCE

SERVES 4

The sauce can be made several days ahead and stored in an airtight container in the refrigerator. It is served at room temperature.

2 cups (4 oz/125 g) watercress

1/2 teaspoon salt

freshly ground pepper

1/3 cup (3 fl oz/90 ml) fish stock
(see page 260)

1/3 cup (3 fl oz/90 ml) light
whipping cream

2 tablespoons butter

4 white-fleshed or oily
fish steaks (cutlets), about
8 oz (250 g) each

Combine watercress, salt, pepper, stock, and cream in food processor or blender and process until smooth.

Melt butter in frying pan over medium heat. Add fish, season with salt and pepper, and cook 3 to 4 minutes per side or until fish is opaque and beginning to flake when tested.

To serve, place fish on plates and spoon sauce over.

Fish with Wilted Arugula

FISH WITH PINE NUT SAUCE

SERVES 4

From Syria, this pine nut sauce is unusual and delicious. It can be served with all types of seafood.

2 tablespoons olive oil

4 tablespoons lemon juice

4 white fleshed or oily fish steaks (cutlets), about 8 oz (250 g) each

2/3 cup (3 oz/90 g) pine nuts

1/2 cup (4 fl oz/125 ml) olive oil, extra

1/2 cup (1 oz/30 g) fresh breadcrumbs (see glossary)

1 clove garlic, chopped

salt and freshly ground pepper

Combine oil and 2 tablespoons juice and pour over fish in a bowl. Marinate 30 minutes.

Combine pine nuts, 1/2 cup oil, breadcrumbs, garlic, remaining lemon juice, and salt and pepper in food processor or blender and process until nuts are finely chopped. Sauce should have a thick, flowing consistency; if too thick, thin with lemon juice and/or water.

Drain fish. Place frying pan over medium heat. Add fish and cook 3 to 4 minutes per side or until fish is opaque and beginning to flake when tested. Serve with pine nut sauce.

FISH IN CREAM CAPER SAUCE

SERVES 4

A rich, tangy recipe; serve only a small quantity of the sauce.

2 tablespoons butter

1 lb (500 g) white-fleshed or oily fish fillets, skinned

1 clove garlic, chopped

1/2 cup (4 fl oz/125 ml) light whipping cream

2 tablespoons chopped capers

salt and freshly ground pepper

grated rind of 1 lemon

1 tablespoon chopped fresh parsley

Melt butter in frying pan over medium heat. Add fillets and cook 2 to 3 minutes per side or until fish is opaque and beginning to flake when tested. Remove and keep warm.

Add garlic to pan and cook 1 minute. Add cream, capers, salt and pepper, rind, and parsley and bring to boil. Simmer until thickened. Add fillets and stir through to warm. Serve immediately.

FISH IN LEMON SAUCE

SERVES 4

1 lb (500 g) white-fleshed or oily fish fillets, skinned

seasoned flour (see glossary)

2 tablespoons butter

1/2 cup (2 oz/60 g) chopped red bell pepper (capsicum)

1/3 cup (1/2 oz/15 g) chopped scallions (spring onions/shallots)

2 teaspoons cornstarch (cornflour)

1 tablespoon water

1/3 cup (3 fl oz/90 ml) lemon juice

1 teaspoon grated lemon rind

1 tablespoon brown sugar

3/4 cup (6 fl oz/180 ml) fish stock (see page 260)

1/4 teaspoon turmeric

salt and freshly ground pepper

Dust fillets in flour, shaking off excess. Melt butter in frying pan over medium heat. Add fillets and cook 2 to 3 minutes per side or until fish is opaque and beginning to flake when tested. Remove and keep warm.

Add pepper and scallions to frying pan, and cook until tender, about 2 minutes. Mix cornstarch with water. Add juice, rind, sugar, stock, turmeric, salt and pepper, and cornstarch mixture to pan and cook, stirring constantly, until sauce boils and thickens. Pour over fish and serve.

FISH IN OYSTER MUSHROOM SAUCE

SERVES 4

2 tablespoons butter

1 lb (500 g) white-fleshed or oily fish fillets, skinned

2 cups (7 oz/220 g) sliced oyster mushrooms

1/3 cup (1/2 oz/15 g) chopped scallions (spring onions/shallots)

2 tablespoons all-purpose (plain) flour

1 cup (8 fl oz/250 ml) fish stock (see page 260)

2 tablespoons dry vermouth

2 tablespoons light whipping cream

salt and freshly ground pepper

Melt butter in frying pan over medium heat. Add fish and cook 2 to 3 minutes per side or until fish is opaque and beginning to flake when tested. Remove and keep warm.

Add mushrooms and scallions to pan and cook over medium heat until tender, 2 to 3 minutes. Stir in flour and cook 1 minute. Stir in stock, vermouth, and cream and cook until sauce thickens and boils. Season with salt and pepper, pour over fish, and serve.

FISH WITH FENNEL AND PARMESAN SAUCE

SERVES 4

1 tablespoon butter

1 fennel bulb, sliced

1 lb (500 g) white-fleshed or oily fish fillets, skinned

1/3 cup (3 fl oz/90 ml) light whipping cream

1/4 cup (2 fl oz/60 ml) fish stock (see page 260) or dry white wine

salt and freshly ground pepper

2 tablespoons grated parmesan cheese

1 tablespoon chopped fennel top or fresh dill

Melt butter in frying pan over medium heat. Add fennel and cook until tender, about 5 minutes. Remove and keep warm.

Add fish to frying pan and cook over medium heat 2 to 3 minutes per side or until fish is opaque and beginning to flake when tested. Remove and keep warm.

Add cream, stock, and salt and pepper to frying pan and bring to boil. Simmer 1 minute or until sauce thickens. Add fennel, parmesan, fennel top, and fish. Heat through and serve.

FISH IN PASSIONFRUIT AND PISTACHIO SAUCE

SERVES 4

3 tablespoons butter

1 lb (500 g) white-fleshed fish fillets, skinned

1 tablespoon all-purpose (plain) flour

1 cup (8 fl oz/250 ml) fish stock (see page 260)

1/2 cup (4 fl oz/125 ml) passionfruit pulp

2 tablespoons chopped pistachios

freshly ground pepper

Melt butter in frying pan over medium heat. Add fish and cook 2 to 3 minutes per side or until fish is opaque and beginning to flake when tested. Remove and keep warm.

Add flour to pan juices and cook 1 minute. Gradually add stock and pulp, and cook stirring constantly, until sauce boils and thickens. Add nuts, season with pepper, and pour over fish. Serve immediately.

Fish in Passionfruit and Pistachio Sauce

FISH WITH PISTACHIO BEARNAISE

SERVES 4

½ cup (4 fl oz/125 ml) dry white wine

⅓ cup (3 fl oz/90 ml) white wine vinegar

3 scallions (spring onions/shallots), halved

3 egg yolks

7 oz (220 g) hot melted butter

½ cup (2 oz/60 g) chopped pistachios

2 tablespoons chopped chives

1 tablespoon chopped fresh parsley

2 teaspoons chopped fresh thyme

2 tablespoons butter

1 lb (500 g) white-fleshed fish fillets, skinned

salt and freshly ground pepper

Combine wine, vinegar, and scallions in saucepan and bring to boil over high heat. Boil until reduced to ¼ cup (2 fl oz/60 ml). Strain.

Combine reduction and yolks in food processor or blender and blend well. With motor running, gradually add melted butter, blending until all is incorporated. Add nuts, chives, parsley, and thyme and process just until combined. Keep warm over hot water.

Melt 2 tablespoons butter in frying pan over medium heat. Add fillets and season with salt and pepper. Cook 2 to 3 minutes per side or until fish is opaque and beginning to flake when tested.

To serve, place fillets on plates and spoon sauce over.

FISH IN PEPPERED CORNMEAL WITH CUCUMBER SALAD

SERVES 4

1 cup (7 oz/220 g) cornmeal

2 teaspoons crushed pepper

1 lb (500 g) white-fleshed or oily fish fillets, skinned

2 cucumbers, seeded and finely chopped

⅓ cup (½ oz/15 g) finely chopped scallions (spring onions/shallots)

½ cup (4 fl oz/125 ml) olive oil

2 tablespoons lemon juice

2 teaspoons seeded mustard

salt and freshly ground pepper

Combine cornmeal and pepper in bowl and mix well. Coat fillets in mixture, pressing firmly.

Place cucumbers and scallions in bowl. Combine half the oil, juice, mustard, and salt and pepper. Pour over vegetables, and mix well. Chill if desired.

Heat remaining oil in frying pan over medium heat. Add fillets and cook 2 to 3 minutes per side or until fish is golden and is beginning to flake when tested. Place on plates and serve with cucumber salad.

FISH WITH BARBECUED MEDITERRANEAN VEGETABLES

SERVES 4

The vegetables take a little time to prepare but are really worth it! I remember my mother serving them when I was a child, with barbecued octopus, and it was truly delicious. She used to add lots of freshly chopped parsley (straight from the garden) and lemon juice. The capsicums may be quartered and seeded prior to cooking, however I find that they do not remain as moist as when prepared in the manner below.

2 red bell peppers (capsicums)

1 eggplant (aubergine), sliced

2 tablespoons olive oil

1/3 cup (3 fl oz/80 ml) extra virgin olive oil

2 cloves garlic, chopped

salt and freshly ground pepper

1 lb (500 g) white-fleshed fish fillets, skinned

Preheat barbecue, grill, or broiler to medium heat.

Cook whole peppers until skin blisters and blackens, about 15 to 20 minutes. Cool, then peel off skin, remove seeds, and cut flesh into strips. Place in bowl.

Cook eggplant 2 to 3 minutes per side, brushing well with oil. Cool slightly and cut into strips. Add to peppers with extra virgin oil, garlic, and salt and pepper. Mix well.

Cook fillets 2 to 3 minutes per side or until fish is opaque and beginning to flake when tested. Serve with room-temperature vegetables.

Following pages: Barbecued Fish with Artichokes and Black Olives (page 160), Barbecued Fish with Bean and Onion Salad (page 161), Barbecued Fish with Peperonata (page 160)

Barbecued Fish with Artichokes and Black Olives

SERVES 4

1/4 cup (2 fl oz/60 ml) extra virgin olive oil

1 tablespoon balsamic vinegar

2 teaspoons chopped fresh oregano or 1 teaspoon dried

1 clove garlic, chopped

salt and freshly ground pepper

13 oz (400 g) can artichoke hearts, drained and halved

1 purple (Spanish) onion, sliced

1/2 cup (4 oz/125 g) black olives

4 white fleshed or oily fish steaks (cutlets), about 8 oz (250 g) each

2 tablespoons olive oil

Combine oil, vinegar, oregano, garlic, and salt and pepper in bowl. Add artichokes, onion and olives and mix well.

Preheat barbecue, grill, or broiler and brush with oil to prevent fish from sticking. Add fish and brush with oil. Season with salt and pepper. Cook 3 to 4 minutes per side or until fish is opaque and beginning to flake when tested.

To serve, place fish on plate and top with artichokes and olives.

Barbecued Fish with Peperonata

SERVES 4

Peperonata needs long, slow cooking to allow the flavors to develop fully. It can be made several days in advance and refrigerated. Can also be served with panfried fish, or shrimp (prawns).

1/3 cup (3 fl oz/90 ml) olive oil

1 onion, sliced

3 cloves garlic, chopped

1 green bell pepper (capsicum), seeded and sliced

1 red bell pepper (capsicum), seeded and sliced

1 yellow bell pepper (capsicum), seeded and sliced

salt and freshly ground pepper

2 tablespoons olive oil, for cooking fish

1 lb (500 g) white-fleshed or oily fish fillets, skinned

Place oil, onion, and garlic in frying pan over medium heat and garlic and cook until tender, about 5 minutes. Add peppers and season with salt and pepper. Cover and cook over low heat 30 to 40 minutes or until tender.

Preheat barbecue, grill, or broiler and brush with oil to prevent fish from sticking. Brush fish with oil and season with salt and pepper. Cook 2 to 3 minutes per side or until fish is opaque and beginning to flake when tested. Serve with warm peppers.

BARBECUED FISH WITH BEAN AND ONION SALAD

SERVES 4

Dried beans need a lot of preparation, so if you don't have the time, a can of beans, rinsed well, makes a good substitute.

1/2 cup (3 oz/90 g) dried red kidney beans or one 10 oz (300 g) can

1 onion, thinly sliced

1 tablespoon chopped capers

1 teaspoon chopped fresh oregano or 1/2 teaspoon dried

1/3 cup (3 fl oz/80 ml) extra virgin olive oil

1 tablespoon water

salt and freshly ground pepper

2 tablespoons olive oil, for cooking fish

1 lb (500 g) white-fleshed or oily fish fillets, skinned

If using dried beans, soak in plenty of water overnight. Drain. Place in large saucepan with plenty of fresh water and bring to boil. Simmer until beans are tender, 1 to 1 1/2 hours. Drain and cool.

Combine cooked or canned beans with onion, capers, oregano, oil, and water and season with salt and pepper. Mix well.

Preheat barbecue, grill, or broiler and brush with oil to prevent fish from sticking. Brush fillets with oil. Season with salt and pepper. Cook 2 to 3 minutes per side or until fish is opaque and beginning to flake when tested. Serve with the bean salad.

BARBECUED FISH WITH ROASTED EGGPLANT SAUCE

SERVES 4

2 large eggplants (aubergines)

2 tablespoons olive oil

1 head garlic

1/3 cup (3 fl oz/90 ml) extra virgin olive oil

2 tablespoons lemon juice

salt and freshly ground pepper

2 tablespoons olive oil, for cooking fish

1 lb (500 g) white-fleshed or oily fish fillets, skinned

Preheat oven to 425°F (220°C/Gas 7). Brush eggplant with oil and place on baking sheet with whole head of garlic. Bake 30 minutes or until eggplant and garlic are soft to touch and eggplant skin is darkened and blistered. Cool.

Peel eggplant. Chop flesh and place in food processor or blender. Cut top off garlic and squeeze flesh over eggplant. Process until smooth. Pour in oil, lemon juice, and salt and pepper and blend well.

Preheat barbecue, grill, or broiler and brush well with oil to prevent fish from sticking. Brush fillets with oil. Season with salt and pepper. Cook 2 to 3 minutes per side or until fish is opaque and beginning to flake when tested. Serve with eggplant sauce.

BARBECUED SHRIMP WITH TOMATOES AND PECORINO POLENTA

SERVES 4

Polenta is the Italian name for cornmeal. It has many uses, including breads and pancakes, puddings and porridge. In this case it is simmered first with water or stock, then poured into a pan, cooled, sliced, and broiled (grilled) until crisp and golden.

1 cup (6 oz/180 g) polenta

1 teaspoon salt

1 cup (8 fl oz/250 ml) cold water

2 cups (16 fl oz/500 ml) boiling water or fish stock (see page 260)

1/4 cup (1 oz/30 g) grated pecorino cheese

olive oil, for cooking

1 1/2 lb (750 g) uncooked jumbo shrimp (large prawns), peeled and deveined

small bunch arugula (rocket), trimmed and washed

4 plum (egg) tomatoes, quartered

1/3 cup (3 fl oz/90 ml) extra virgin olive oil

2 tablespoons balsamic vinegar

3 tablespoons chopped fresh basil

3 cloves garlic, chopped

freshly ground pepper

Combine polenta, salt, and cold water in saucepan and mix well. Pour in boiling water or stock and bring to boil. Cook over medium heat 10 minutes, stirring constantly. Cover and continue to cook, over very low heat 15 minutes. Stir in pecorino. Pour into oiled 8 in. x 8 in. (20 cm x 20 cm) square cake tin and let cool.

Using sharp knife, cut polenta into 3 in. (7 cm) squares. Brush with oil and broil (grill) until golden and toasted.

Preheat barbecue, grill, or broiler and brush with oil to prevent sticking. Brush shrimp with oil and cook 1 to 2 minutes per side or until tender.

To serve, place polenta squares on plates. Top with some arugula, then shrimp and tomato. Combine extra virgin olive oil, vinegar, basil, and garlic and drizzle over. Grind pepper over and serve.

Barbecued Shrimp with Tomatoes and Pecorino Polenta

BARBECUED TUNA WITH GARLIC, ANCHOVY, AND CAPER MAYONNAISE

SERVES 4

1 egg yolk

2 tablespoons lemon juice

1 clove garlic, chopped

4 anchovy fillets

4 capers

$^1/_2$ cup (4 fl oz/125 ml) olive oil

2 tablespoons chopped fresh parsley

2 tablespoons olive oil, for cooking

4 tuna steaks, about 8 oz (250 g) each

salt and freshly ground pepper

Combine yolk, lemon juice, garlic, anchovy fillets, and capers in food processor or blender and puree until smooth. With motor running, gradually add $^1/_2$ cup oil, blending until all oil is incorporated. Stir in parsley.

Preheat barbecue, grill, or broiler and brush with oil to prevent fish from sticking. Brush tuna with oil and season with salt and pepper. Cook 3 to 4 minutes per side, brushing further with oil during cooking, until fish is opaque and beginning to flake when tested. Serve fish immediately with the mayonnaise.

BARBECUED TUNA WITH MARINATED VEGETABLES

SERVES 4

4 tuna steaks, about 8 oz (250 g) each

1/4 cup (2 fl oz/60 ml) olive oil

3 cloves garlic, chopped

salt and freshly ground pepper

1 cup (2 oz/60 g) watercress

5 oz (150 g) asparagus, blanched

4 oz (125 g) green beans, blanched

8 new potatoes, cooked

1/3 cup (3 fl oz/80 ml) extra virgin olive oil

2 tablespoons balsamic vinegar

1 tablespoon chopped fresh parsley

2 teaspoons creamed horseradish

1 teaspoon dijon mustard

2 tablespoons olive oil, for cooking

Place tuna in glass bowl. Combine 1/4 cup oil, 2 cloves garlic, and salt and pepper and pour over tuna. Marinate 30 minutes in refrigerator, or longer if possible.

Combine watercress, asparagus, beans, and potatoes in bowl. Combine extra virgin olive oil, vinegar, 1 clove garlic, parsley, horseradish, mustard, and salt and pepper, pour over vegetables, and toss well. Marinate 10 minutes.

Preheat barbecue, grill, or broiler and brush with oil to prevent sticking. Drain tuna, and cook 3 to 4 minutes per side or until fish is opaque and beginning to flake when tested, basting frequently with oil.

To serve, place tuna on plates and surround with vegetables.

BARBECUED FISH WITH GARLIC DRESSING

SERVES 4

1/4 cup (2 fl oz/60 ml) olive oil

1 tablespoon red wine vinegar

2 cloves garlic, chopped

1 teaspoon dijon mustard

1 tablespoon chopped fresh parsley

1 tablespoon olive oil, for cooking

4 white fleshed or oily fish steaks (cutlets), about 8 oz (250 g) each

salt and freshly ground pepper

Combine 1/4 cup oil, vinegar, garlic, mustard, and parsley in small saucepan, and stir over medium heat 1 to 2 minutes to infuse garlic flavor into oil.

Preheat barbecue, grill, or broiler and brush with oil to prevent fish from sticking. Brush fish with oil and season with salt and pepper. Cook 3 to 4 minutes per side or until fish is opaque and beginning to flake when tested. Place on plates and spoon dressing over. Serve at once.

Following pages: Baked Citrus Fish (page 168), Baked Fish with Crunchy Topping (page 168), Baked Snapper with Vegetables (page 169)

BAKED FISH WITH CRUNCHY TOPPING

SERVES 4

This can be prepared several hours in advance, covered, and refrigerated until ready for baking. Serve with baked potatoes and salad.

1 lb (500 g) white-fleshed or oily fish fillets, skinned

salt and freshly ground pepper

3 tablespoons melted butter

1 1/2 cups (3 oz/90 g) fresh breadcrumbs (see glossary)

1/4 cup (1 oz/30 g) grated parmesan cheese

2 cloves garlic, chopped

3 tablespoons chopped fresh parsley

2 teaspoons chopped fresh oregano or 1/2 teaspoon dried

Preheat oven to 350°F (180°C/Gas 4). Place fillets in greased baking dish and season with salt and pepper.

Combine butter, breadcrumbs, parmesan, garlic, parsley, and oregano in bowl and mix well. Top fillets evenly with breadcrumb mixture. Cover dish with foil and bake 15 minutes or until topping is golden and fish is opaque and beginning to flake when tested. Remove foil and bake 10 minutes more to allow top to brown.

BAKED CITRUS FISH

SERVES 4

3 lb (1.5 kg) whole fish, scaled and cleaned

3 orange slices

3 lemon slices

small bunch parsley

1/2 cup (4 fl oz/125 ml) orange juice

1/4 cup (2 fl oz/60 ml) lemon juice

2 tablespoons melted butter

salt and freshly ground pepper

Preheat oven to 350°F (180°C/Gas 4). Using sharp knife, make 2 to 3 diagonal slits on both sides of fish. Fill fish cavity with orange, lemon and parsley. Place fish in greased baking dish.

Combine juices and butter and pour over fish. Season to taste with salt and pepper, and bake until fish is opaque and beginning to flake when tested, about 30 minutes. Serve immediately.

BAKED SNAPPER WITH VEGETABLES

2 tablespoons butter

13 oz (400 g) mixed julienned vegetables (carrots, celery, fennel, asparagus)

4 small whole fish, about 8 oz (250 g) each, scaled and cleaned

salt and freshly ground pepper

1 tablespoon madeira or sherry

3/4 cup (6 fl oz/180 ml) fish stock (see page 260)

1/4 cup (2 fl oz/60 ml) light whipping cream

1 teaspoon cornstarch (cornflour) mixed with 1 tablespoon water, if needed for thickening

Preheat oven to 350 F°(180°C/Gas 4).

Melt butter in frying pan over medium heat. Add vegetables and cook just until tender crisp.

Spread vegetables in greased baking dish. Using a sharp knife, make 2 to 3 diagonal slits on each side of fish. Place on top of vegetables and season well with salt and pepper. Combine madeira, stock, and cream and pour over fish. Cover dish with foil and bake until fish is opaque and beginning to flake when tested, 20 to 25 minutes.

To serve, place fish on four plates. Remove vegetables with slotted spoon and divide equally among fish. Pour pan juices over or, if they require thickening, pour pan juices into small saucepan and place over high heat. Add cornstarch mixture and bring to boil, stirring constantly until sauce thickens. Pour sauce over vegetables and serve.

BAKED FISH IN TAHINI

This Lebanese dish is luscious. The sesame paste over the top lends a lot of flavor and results in a very moist fish. Tahini is semi-liquid, but when the other ingredients are added, it becomes a thick paste. Serve this with a green salad.

1 cup (8 fl oz/250 ml) tahini

1/2 cup (4 fl oz/125 ml) lemon juice

3 cloves garlic, chopped

2 red chilies, seeded and chopped

3 tablespoons chopped cilantro (fresh coriander leaves)

3 tablespoons chopped fresh parsley

2 teaspoons ground cumin

2 teaspoons ground coriander

1/2 teaspoon salt

3 lb (1.5 kg) whole fish, scaled, cleaned and scored

Preheat oven to 350°F (180°C/Gas 4).

In large bowl combine tahini, juice, garlic, chilies, cilantro, parsley, cumin, coriander, and salt and mix well. Spread paste all over fish. Place on greased baking sheet and bake until fish is opaque and beginning to flake when tested, about 30 minutes. Serve immediately.

ROASTED MARINATED FISH AND VEGETABLES

SERVES 4

This is a wonderfully flavorful and attractive dish. The variety of vegetables gives it lots of color and texture.

1/3 cup (3 fl oz/80 ml) olive oil

2 cloves garlic, chopped

2 teaspoons fennel seeds

2 teaspoons chopped fresh oregano

2 leeks, halved lengthwise

4 zucchini (courgette)

4 small yellow squash

2 golden nugget squash, halved and seeds removed

1 lb (500 g) white-fleshed or oily fish fillets, skinned

4 small whole tomatoes

Preheat oven to 425°F (220°C/Gas 7).

Combine oil, garlic, fennel seeds, and oregano in small bowl and mix well.

Arrange leeks, zucchini, and squash on rimmed baking dish and brush with oil mixture.

Place fish in glass bowl and pour remaining oil mixture over; let stand.

Bake vegetables 15 minutes. Drain fish. Add fish and tomatoes to vegetables and bake about 15 minutes until fish is opaque and beginning to flake when tested. Serve hot.

BAKED WHOLE FISH WITH LEMON, ROSEMARY, AND HONEY

SERVES 4

1/4 cup (2 fl oz/60 ml) lemon juice

1/4 cup (2 fl oz/60 ml) honey

1 tablespoon chopped fresh rosemary or 2 teaspoons dried

grated rind of 1 lemon

3 lb (1.5 kg) whole fish, scaled and cleaned

Preheat oven to 350°F (180°C/Gas 4).

Combine juice, honey, rosemary, and rind in small saucepan and stir. Bring to boil over medium heat and simmer 1 minute.

Using a sharp knife, make 2 to 3 diagonal cuts on each side of fish. Brush well with lemon mixture. Bake until fish is opaque and beginning to flake when tested, about 30 minutes, basting frequently with lemon mixture. Serve immediately.

Roasted Marinated Fish and Vegetables

LIME BAKED FISH

SERVES 4

4 lb (2 kg) whole fish, scaled
and cleaned

grated rind 1 lime

1/2 cup (4 fl oz/125 ml) lime juice

2 cloves garlic, chopped

2 teaspoons fresh thyme

3 tablespoons melted butter

salt and freshly ground pepper

Using a sharp knife, make 2 to 3 diagonal cuts on either side of fish. Place in large glass dish. Combine rind and juice, garlic, and thyme and pour over fish. Marinate 1 hour, or longer if time allows.

Preheat oven to 350°F (180°C/Gas 4). Drain fish and pat dry with paper towel. Brush all over with butter and season with salt and pepper. Place in greased baking dish and bake until fish is opaque and beginning to flake when tested, about 40 minutes. Serve hot.

BAKED FISH GREEK STYLE

SERVES 4

This can be cooked successfully on the barbecue. After marinating fish, wrap in greased foil and barbecue for 30 to 40 minutes, turning every 15 minutes or so.

3 lb (1.5 kg) whole fish,
scaled and cleaned

1/3 cup (3 fl oz/80 ml) olive oil

2 cloves garlic, chopped

2 teaspoons chopped fresh
oregano or 1 teaspoon dried

1 onion, grated

juice of 1 lemon

4 bay leaves, crushed

1/4 teaspoon cracked pepper

Using a sharp knife, make 2 to 3 diagonal slits on each side of fish. Place fish in glass dish. Combine oil, garlic, oregano, onion, juice, bay leaves, and pepper and rub over fish. Marinate in refridgerator 1 hour, or longer if time allows.

Preheat oven to 350°F (180°C/Gas 4). Drain fish, reserving marinade. Place fish in greased baking dish, cover, and bake until fish is opaque and beginning to flake when tested, about 30 minutes, basting often with reserved marinade.

Serve immediately.

STEAMED ASIAN FISH

SERVES 4

This preparation method results in very moist, tender fish. Fillets and steaks or cutlets are successfully cooked this way, using the same marinade. Wrap them in foil packages and refrigerate until ready to cook. Try barbecuing the packages for about 10 minutes.

3 lb (1.5 kg) whole fish, scaled and cleaned

2 tablespoons sherry

2 tablespoons soy sauce

1 tablespoon honey

1 tablespoon oyster sauce

2 teaspoons sesame oil

1/4 teaspoon five spice powder

2 scallions (spring onions/ shallots), chopped

2 cloves garlic, chopped

Using sharp knife, make 2 to 3 deep diagonal cuts on both sides of fish. Lay fish on large sheet of foil, bringing up sides to hold in marinade.

Preheat oven to 350°F (180°C/Gas 4). Combine sherry, soy sauce, honey, oyster sauce, oil, five spice, scallions and garlic in small bowl and mix well. Pour over fish. Fold foil over fish to form large parcel. Place on baking sheet and leave to marinate for a least 30 minutes. Bake until fish is opaque and beginning to flake when tested, about 30 minutes. Serve hot.

STEAMED FISH IN PEPPERED TOMATO SAUCE

SERVES 4

This sauce is tangy, peppery, and very tasty. It can also be used to simmer fish or shellfish on top of the stove; just cover and simmer until fish is tender.

1 tablespoon vegetable oil

2 onions, chopped

2 cloves garlic, chopped

14 oz (440 g) can peeled tomatoes, chopped

1/4 cup (2 fl oz/60 ml) white vinegar

1/4 cup (2 fl oz/60 ml) soy sauce

1 tablespoon sugar

2 teaspoons cracked pepper

2 bay leaves

3 lb (1.5 kg) whole fish, scaled and cleaned

Heat oil in saucepan over medium heat. Add onions and garlic and cook until tender about 4 minutes. Add tomatoes, vinegar, soy sauce, sugar, pepper, and bay leaves, cover, and simmer 15 to 20 minutes. Cool slightly, then puree in food processor or blender.

Preheat oven to 375°F (190°C/Gas 5). Using a sharp knife, make 2 to 3 deep diagonal cuts on either side of the fish. Place in baking dish. Pour tomato sauce over and cover. Bake until fish is opaque and beginning to flake when tested, about 30 minutes. Serve immediately.

STEAMED FISH PARCELS IN BUTTER MUSTARD SAUCE

SERVES 4

This simple recipe produces beautifully moist, tender fish. The parcels can be prepared several hours in advance and refrigerated, or frozen for up to 4 months. They can also be barbecued for about 10 minutes, if preferred.

4 white-fleshed or oily fish fillets, about 8 oz (250 g) each, skinned

3 tablespoons butter, softened

2 tablespoons lemon juice

1 tablespoon dijon mustard

3 tablespoons chopped mixed fresh herbs (parsley, thyme, chives)

salt and freshly ground pepper

Preheat oven to 350°F (180°C/Gas 4).

Place each fillet on small sheet of greased foil. Combine butter, lemon juice, mustard, herbs, and salt and pepper in small bowl and mix well. Divide among fillets. Wrap up fish parcels, double-folding edges for a tight seal. Arrange parcels on baking sheet. Bake 15 to 20 minutes or until fish is opaque and beginning to flake when tested. Serve hot.

STEAMED SALMON PACKAGES

SERVES 4

This easy recipe can be prepared several hours ahead and refrigerated until ready for cooking. The packages are also great on the barbecue — just place over hot coals and cook 8 to 10 minutes.

4 salmon steaks, about 8 oz (250 g) each

salt and freshly ground pepper

3 tablespoons mixed fresh herbs (parsley, chives, tarragon)

4 tablespoons dry white wine

4 tablespoons melted butter

Preheat oven to 350°F (180°C/Gas 4).

Place each salmon steak on piece of foil or baking paper and fold edges upwards to hold liquid. Season with salt and pepper. Sprinkle with herbs, then pour 1 tablespoon each wine and butter over each steak. Wrap fish in foil, double-folding edges for a tight seal. Arrange on baking sheet. Bake 10 to 15 minutes or until fish is tender and beginning to flake when tested. Serve hot.

Steamed Salmon Packages

STEAMED SNAPPER IN CAPER, OLIVE, AND PINE NUT SAUCE

SERVES 4

This unusual sauce is extremely tasty. It can be used to simmer any variety of seafood, including mollusks, fish steaks or cutlets, or shrimp (prawns).

1/4 cup (2 fl oz/60 ml) olive oil

1 onion, chopped

1 clove garlic, chopped

14 oz (440 g) can peeled tomatoes, chopped

2 tablespoons tomato paste

2 teaspoons paprika

1/3 cup (3 oz/90 g) black olives

1/3 cup (1 1/2 oz/45 g) pine nuts

2 tablespoons capers

4 small whole snapper, 10 oz (300 g) each, scaled and cleaned

Heat oil in large frying pan over medium heat. Add onion and cook 4 minutes or until tender. Add garlic and sauté until fragrant, about 1 minute. Pour in tomatoes, tomato paste, and paprika, cover, and simmer 15 minutes.

Add olives, nuts, capers, and fish, cover, and simmer 20 minutes or until fish is opaque and beginning to flake when tested. Serve hot.

OVEN-STEAMED FISH

SERVE 4

Wasabi, a Japanese horseradish, is extremely hot and should be added sparingly according to taste.

3 lb (1.5 kg) whole fish, scaled and cleaned

2 cups (4 oz/125 g) sliced mushrooms

2 tablespoons soy sauce

1 tablespoon mirin or sherry

2 teaspoons sesame oil

1 tablespoon lemon juice

1/2 teaspoon wasabi or to taste

1/3 cup (1/2 oz/15 g) chopped scallions (spring onions/shallots)

1 clove garlic, chopped

1 teaspoon chopped fresh ginger

Preheat oven to 350°F (180°C/Gas 4).

Using a sharp knife, make 2 to 3 deep diagonal cuts in either side of fish. Place in greased baking dish or on large sheet of greased foil. Top with mushrooms.

Combine soy sauce, mirin, sesame oil, juice, wasabi, scallions, garlic, and ginger and pour over fish. Cover dish or fold foil to form large parcel. Bake until fish is opaque and beginning to flake when tested, about 30 minutes. Serve hot.

POACHED SALMON WITH LEMON AND DILL MAYONNAISE

SERVES 4

For more advice on poaching, see page 18.

1 egg yolk
1 teaspoon grated lemon rind
2 tablespoons lemon juice
1 cup (8 fl oz/250 ml) olive oil
2 tablespoons chopped fresh dill
salt and freshly ground pepper
4 salmon steaks, about 8 oz
(250 g) each

Combine egg yolk, rind, and juice in food processor or blender and mix well. With motor running, gradually add oil, processing until all is incorporated and mayonnaise is thick and creamy. Stir in dill and season to taste with salt and pepper. Chill.

Arrange salmon in large frying pan and pour in enough water to cover. Bring to boil, then simmer 10 to 15 minutes or until fish is tender and beginning to flake when tested. Drain well on paper towels. Serve with dill mayonnaise.

POACHED SALMON IN ORANGE, HONEY, AND WINE

SERVES 4

This recipe results in beautifully moist and tender fish. Try it with whole fish and other fish steaks cutlets too. For more advice on poaching, see page 18.

grated rind of 1 orange
1/2 cup (4 fl oz/125 ml)
orange juice
1/4 cup (2 fl oz/60 ml) honey
1/4 cup (2 fl oz/60 ml)
dry white wine
4 salmon steaks, 8 oz
(250 g) each

Combine rind, juice, honey, and wine in large frying pan over medium heat and bring to boil, stirring constantly. Add fish and cook over low heat until fish is tender and beginning to flake when tested, about 10 to 15 minutes. Remove fish with slotted spoon, drain on paper towels, keep warm.

Bring poaching liquid to boil over high heat and cook until slightly reduced and thickened. Spoon a small amount over fish and serve.

CHILLED POACHED SALMON

SERVES 6

For more advice on poaching, see page 18. Serve with Russian mayonnaise, tartare sauce, or garlic and herb mayonnaise (see pages 262 to 266).

4 lb (2 kg) whole salmon, scaled

1 onion, quartered

4 lemon slices

1 cup (8 fl oz/250 ml) dry white wine

Place fish in fish kettle or saucepan large enough to hold it. Add onion, lemon slices, wine, and water to cover. Bring to boil, then immediately turn down heat, cover, and simmer gently about 20 to 25 minutes. Cool in poaching liquid.

Drain fish well on paper towels. Using a sharp knife, remove skin on both sides by making a shallow cut close to head, taking hold of skin and pulling away gently. Chill.

To serve, segment fish with a sharp knife and lift away flesh with two spoons.

POACHED FISH WITH DRIED FRUITS

SERVES 4

For more advice on poaching, see page 18.

1 tablespoon oil

1 onion, chopped

2 teaspoons ground coriander

1 teaspoon ground allspice

1 1/2 cups (12 fl oz/375 ml) fish stock (see page 260)

1/2 cup (4 fl oz/125 ml) dry white wine

1/2 cup (3 oz/90 g) chopped dried apricots

1/2 cup (3 oz/90 g) chopped prunes

1 tablespoon seeded mustard

4 white-fleshed fish steaks (cutlets), about 8 oz (250 g) each

steamed rice, to serve

Heat oil in frying pan over medium heat. Add onion and cook until tender, about 5 minutes. Stir in coriander and allspice and cook 1 minute. Stir in stock, wine, apricots, prunes, and mustard and bring to boil. Cover and simmer, 5 minutes or until slightly thickened.

Add fish, cover, and simmer about 15 minutes or until fish is opaque and beginning to flake when tested. Serve with rice and spoon sauce over.

Poached Fish with Dried Fruits

178

POACHED FISH WITH EGG AND LEMON SAUCE

SERVES 4

A light, frothy sauce of Greek origin. It is quite tangy, which makes it perfect for any poached or steamed fish or shellfish. For more advice on poaching, see page 18.

1/2 cup (4 fl oz/125 ml) hot lemon juice

grated rind of 1 lemon

1/2 cup (4 fl oz/125 ml) hot fish stock (see page 260)

1/4 cup (2 fl oz/60 ml) light whipping cream

2 eggs

freshly ground pepper

4 white-fleshed fish steaks (cutlets), about 8 oz (250 g) each

Combine juice, rind, stock, and cream. Place eggs over simmering water in double boiler and beat with hand mixer until thick and creamy. Gradually add lemon mixture, beating until all liquid is incorporated. Season to taste with pepper. Keep warm over double boiler.

Place fish in frying pan and add enough water to cover. Bring to boil over high heat. Reduce heat and simmer until fish is cooked through, about 15 minutes. Drain well and serve with sauce.

180

BARBECUED FISH WITH LIME MARMALADE GLAZE

SERVES 4

4 small whole fish, about 8 oz (250 g) each, scaled and cleaned

3 tablespoons lime marmalade

3 tablespoons lime juice

2 tablespoons melted butter

Preheat barbecue, grill, or broiler. Oil lightly to prevent fish from sticking.

Mix marmalade, juice, and butter.

Using a sharp knife, make 2 to 3 diagonal cuts on each side of fish. Cook fish 4 to 5 minutes per side or until it is opaque and beginning to flake when tested, basting very frequently with lime mixture. Serve immediately.

BARBECUED KEBABS

SERVES 4

If using bamboo skewers, soak them in water for 30 minutes beforehand to keep them from burning. Kebabs can be prepared several hours in advance and refrigerated. They can also be frozen, uncooked, for up to 4 months.

1 lb (500 g) white-fleshed or oily fish fillets, skinned and ground (minced)

1 onion, grated

1/2 teaspoon ground coriander

1/2 teaspoon ground cumin

1/2 teaspoon garam masala

1/4 teaspoon chili powder

2 tablespoons mango chutney

2 tablespoons plain yogurt

3 tablespoons chopped cilantro (fresh coriander leaves)

Combine fish, onion, coriander, cumin, garam masala, and chili powder and mix well. Divide into 16 parts and roll each into a sausage shape, using wet hands. Thread onto skewers, allowing 2 per skewer.

Mix chutney and yogurt.

Preheat barbecue, grill or broiler and brush well with oil to prevent kebabs from sticking. Cook kebabs 2 to 3 minutes per side, brushing with chutney mixture. Serve sprinkled with cilantro.

Stir-Fried Fish with Snow Peas

SERVES 4

The fish can be marinated several hours in advance, covered, and refrigerated until ready for cooking. The longer the fish marinates, the better the flavor, so marinating overnight is preferred.

1 lb (500 g) white-fleshed or oily fish fillets, skinned and chopped

1/4 cup (2 fl oz/60 ml) soy sauce

1 tablespoon sherry

1 clove garlic, chopped

1 teaspoon chopped fresh ginger

1 tablespoon vegetable oil

7 oz (220 g) snow peas (mange-tout)

1 teaspoon cornstarch (cornflour)

1/2 cup (4 fl oz/125 ml) fish stock (see page 260)

steamed rice, to serve

Place fish in bowl with soy sauce, sherry, garlic, and ginger. Mix well and marinate 30 minutes, or longer if time allows.

Heat oil in frying pan or wok over high heat. Add snow peas and stir-fry until tender crisp, about 1 to 2 minutes. Remove.

Mix cornstarch and 1 tablespoon stock in cup. Drain fish, reserving marinade. Add fish to hot pan and stir-fry until tender, about 1 to 2 minutes. Pour in reserved marinade, cornstarch mixture, remaining stock and snow peas and stir until sauce boils and thickens. Serve immediately with steamed rice.

Stir-Fried Shrimp with Broccoli

SERVES 4

1 1/2 lb (750 g) uncooked jumbo shrimp (large prawns), peeled and deveined

1 red chili, seeded and chopped

1 clove garlic, chopped

1 tablespoon oyster sauce

1 tablespoon soy sauce

1 tablespoon peanut oil

10 oz (300 g) broccoli florets

2 teaspoons cornstarch (cornflour)

1/2 cup (4 fl oz/125 ml) fish stock (see page 260)

cooked rice or noodles, to serve

Place shrimp in large bowl. Add chili, garlic, and sauces and mix well. Marinate 30 minutes, or longer if time allows.

Heat oil in large frying pan or wok over high heat. Add broccoli and stir-fry 2 to 3 minutes. Remove.

Mix cornstarch with 1 tablespoon stock in cup. Drain shrimp, reserving marinade. Add shrimp to hot pan and stir-fry 1 minute, or just until they turn opaque. Add broccoli, reserved marinade, cornstarch mixture, and remaining stock, and cook, stirring constantly, until sauce boils and thickens. Serve immediately with rice or noodles.

Stir-Fried Shrimp with Broccoli

FISH WITH MAPLE SYRUP AND MUSTARD MARINADE

SERVES 4

2 tablespoons maple syrup

1 tablespoon seeded mustard

1 tablespoon soy sauce

1 lb (500 g) white-fleshed or oily fish fillets, skinned

Combine maple syrup, mustard, and soy sauce in bowl and mix well. Add fillets and marinate, covered, 30 minutes, or longer if time allows in refrigerator.

Drain well, reserving marinade. Panfry, broil, grill, or barbecue fish 2 to 3 minutes per side or until fish is opaque and beginning to flake when tested, basting frequently with marinade. Serve immediately.

TROPICAL MARINATED FISH

SERVES 4

1/4 cup (2 fl oz/60 ml) olive oil

1 cup (8 fl oz/250 ml) orange juice

1/2 cup (4 fl oz/125 ml) pineapple juice

1 teaspoon chopped fresh ginger

2 tablespoons chopped fresh mint

1 lb (500 g) white-fleshed or oily fish fillets, skinned

1 tablespoon olive oil, for frying

1 tablespoon cornstarch (cornflour)

2 tablespoon water

1 mango, sliced, or 13 oz (400 g) can mango slices, drained

Combine oil, juices, ginger, and mint in large bowl. Add fillets and marinate 30 minutes. Drain, reserving marinade. Pat fish dry with paper towels.

Heat 1 tablespoon oil in frying pan over medium heat. Add fish and cook 2 to 3 minutes per side or until fish is opaque and beginning to flake when tested. Remove and keep warm.

Mix cornstarch and water in cup. Add to pan with reserved marinade and bring to boil. Cook until sauce boils and thickens. Add mango and warm through. To serve, place fish on plates and spoon sauce over.

WHOLE FISH WITH MINTED YOGURT

SERVES 4

This marinade is suited to fish fillets and steaks or cutlets as well as whole fish. After marinating, the fish ,can be barbecued, broiled, grilled, or fried.

2 onions, grated

1 teaspoon chopped fresh ginger

2 cloves garlic, chopped

2 teaspoons ground coriander

2 teaspoons ground cumin

7 oz (220 g) plain yogurt

1/2 teaspoon salt

1/2 cup (2/3 oz/20 g) chopped fresh mint

4 small whole fish, 8 oz (250 g) each, scaled and cleaned

Combine onions, ginger, garlic, coriander, cumin, yogurt, salt, and mint in large glass bowl and mix well.

Using a sharp knife, make 2 to 3 deep diagonal cuts in each side of fish. Add to bowl and marinate 30 minutes, or longer if time permits.

Preheat oven to 350°F (180°C/Gas 4). Drain excess marinade from fish. Place fish in greased baking dish and bake about 20 minutes or until fish is opaque and beginning to flake when tested. Serve immediately.

WHOLE FISH WITH FENNEL SEED AND GARLIC

SERVES 4

1/4 cup (2 fl oz/60 ml) olive oil

2 tablespoons butter

grated rind of 1 orange

2 tablespoons orange juice

2 cloves garlic, chopped

2 teaspoons fennel seeds

salt and freshly ground pepper

4 whole fish, about 8 oz (250 g) each, scaled and cleaned

Combine oil, butter, orange rind and juice, garlic, fennel seeds, and salt and pepper in small saucepan and bring to boil, then reduce heat and simmer 1 minute. Cool slightly.

Preheat broiler (grill) and brush with oil to prevent fish from sticking. Using a sharp knife, make 2 to 3 deep diagonal cuts in each side of fish. Brush well with basting mixture and cook 4 to 5 minutes per side or until fish is opaque and beginning to flake when tested, basting frequently. Serve immediately.

APRICOT-STUFFED FISH WITH HONEY GINGER SAUCE

SERVES 4

4 small whole fish, about 8 oz (250 g) each, scaled and cleaned

1 tablespoon butter

1 onion, chopped

1 cup (6 oz/180 g) cooked rice

1/2 cup (3 oz/90 g) chopped dried apricots

1/4 cup (1 1/2 oz/45 g) chopped walnuts

2 tablespoons chopped fresh parsley

salt and freshly ground pepper

1 tablespoon cornstarch (cornflour)

3/4 cup (6 fl oz/180 ml) fish stock (see page 260)

1 tablespoon ginger wine or sherry

1 tablespoon olive oil

2 teaspoons chopped fresh ginger

1/2 teaspoon ground ginger

2 tablespoons honey

Preheat oven to 350°F (180°C/Gas 4). Using sharp knife, make 2 to 3 diagonal slits on each side of the fish.

Melt butter in small saucepan over medium heat. Add onion and sauté 3 to 4 minutes or until tender. Place in bowl with rice, apricots, walnuts, parsley, and salt and pepper and mix well.

Fill cavity of each fish with rice mixture, packing firmly. Arrange fish in greased baking dish and bake until fish is opaque and is beginning to flake when tested, about 20 minutes.

Combine cornstarch, stock, and wine in cup and mix well. Heat oil in frying pan. Add fresh ginger and cook 1 minute. Stir in ground ginger, honey, cornstarch mixture and bring to boil. Cook, stirring, until sauce thickens. Serve with baked fish.

Apricot-Stuffed Fish with Honey Ginger Sauce

LEMON AND HERB MARINATED FISH

SERVES 4

This marinade can be used for all types of fish and shellfish — fillets, steaks or cutlets, and shrimp (prawns), for example.

1 tablespoon fresh thyme

2 tablespoons chopped
fresh rosemary

grated rind of 1 lemon

1/4 cup (2 fl oz/60 ml) lemon juice

1/4 cup (2 fl oz/60 ml) olive oil

2 cloves garlic, chopped

3 lb (1.5 kg) whole fish such as
trout, scaled and cleaned

Combine herbs, rind, juice, oil, and garlic in food processor or blender and process until smooth.

With sharp knife, make 2 to 3 diagonal cuts on either side of fish. Place in glass bowl, pour in marinade and rub all over fish. Marinate in refrigerator 1 hour, or longer if time permits. Drain.

Preheat oven to 350°F (180°C/Gas 4). Place fish in greased baking dish and cover with foil. Bake until fish is opaque and beginning to flake when tested, about 30 minutes. Serve hot.

TROUT WITH COUSCOUS AND PECAN STUFFING

SERVES 4

An unusual stuffing suitable for almost any type of small whole fish makes this dish extremely tasty. Serve with lots of lemon wedges and steamed vegetables.

1/2 cup (3 oz/90 g) instant
couscous

3/4 cup (6 fl oz/180 ml)
boiling water

1 tablespoon vegetable oil

1 onion, chopped

1 clove garlic, chopped

1/2 cup (2 oz/60 g) grated carrot

1/2 cup (2 oz/60 g) chopped pecans

salt and freshly ground pepper

4 whole fish such as trout, about
8 oz (250 g) each, cleaned

3 tablespoons melted butter

Place couscous in bowl and add water. Cover and let stand until all water is absorbed, about 5 minutes. (Quantities and time may vary depending on brand.)

Heat oil in frying pan over medium heat. Add onion and garlic and cook until tender, about 5 minutes. Add to couscous with carrot, nuts, and salt and pepper and mix well.

Preheat oven to 350°F (180°C/Gas 4). Pack stuffing into trout cavities, packing firmly. Arrange trout in greased baking dish and brush with butter. Bake until fish is opaque and beginning to flake when tested, about 20 minutes. Serve immediately.

CITRUS AND HERBED YOGURT BREAM

SERVES 4

4 oz (125 g) plain yogurt
1 tablespoon chopped fresh dill
1 tablespoon chopped fresh mint
1 tablespoon chopped fresh basil
grated rind of 1 lemon
grated rind of 1 orange
1/4 cup (2 fl oz/60 ml) lemon juice
2 tablespoons orange juice
salt and freshly ground pepper
3 lb (1.5 kg) whole fish such as bream, scaled and cleaned

Combine yogurt, dill, mint, basil, rinds, juices and salt and pepper in food processor or blender and process until smooth.

Using a sharp knife, make 2 to 3 diagonal cuts on each side of fish. Place fish in glass dish. Pour yogurt mixture over and marinate 30 minutes, or longer if time permits.

Preheat oven to 350°F (180°C/Gas 4). Place fish in greased baking dish and bake until fish is opaque and beginning to flake when tested, about 30 minutes. Serve immediately.

TROUT WITH ALMOND, ORANGE, AND CELERY STUFFING

SERVES 4

2 tablespoons butter
1 onion, chopped
1/3 cup (1 1/2 oz/45 g) chopped celery
1/3 cup (1 1/2 oz/45 g) flaked almonds
grated rind of 1 orange
1 1/2 cups (3 oz/90 g) fresh breadcrumbs (see glossary)
1/2 cup (2 fl oz/125 ml) orange juice
freshly ground pepper
4 small whole fish such as trout, about 8 oz (250 g) each, cleaned
2 tablespoons melted butter

Preheat oven to 350°F (180°C/Gas 4).

Melt butter in frying pan over medium heat. Add onion and celery and cook until tender, about 5 minutes. Stir in almonds and cook until crisp and golden, about 1 minute.

Transfer onion mixture to large bowl. Add rind, breadcrumbs, 1/4 cup juice, and pepper and mix well. Stuff trout with mixture, packing firmly. Arrange in greased baking dish. Combine butter and remaining juice and brush over trout. Season with pepper. Cover dish with foil and bake until fish is opaque and beginning to flake when tested, about 20 minutes. Serve immediately.

Following pages: Trout with Almond, Orange, and Celery Stuffing (page 189), Trout with Couscous and Pecan Stuffing (page 188), Trout with Orange, Maple Syrup, and Macadamia Nuts (page 192)

Trout Baked with Red Wine and Vegetables

SERVES 4

Try any small whole fish like red mullet or else experiment with fish steaks, reducing cooking time to about 20 minutes.

2 tablespoons olive oil

1 onion, chopped

1/2 cup (2 oz/60 g) chopped fennel

1/2 cup (2 oz/60 g) chopped carrot

1/2 cup (2 oz/60 g) chopped red bell pepper (capsicum)

4 whole trout, about 8 oz (250 g) each, cleaned

1/2 cup (4 fl oz/125 ml) red wine

about 1/2 cup (4 fl oz/125 ml) fish stock (see page 260)

1 tablespoon all-purpose (plain) flour

1 tablespoon butter, softened

salt and freshly ground pepper

Heat oil in frying pan over medium heat. Add onion, fennel, carrot, and pepper and cook until tender, about 5 minutes.

Preheat oven to 350°F (180°C/Gas 4). Spread vegetables on greased baking dish. Arrange trout on top. Combine wine and stock and pour over. Cover with foil and bake until fish is opaque and beginning to flake when tested, about 20 minutes.

Remove fish and keep warm. Place baking dish over medium heat on stove and bring pan juices to boil. Blend flour and butter to paste and add to pan. Cook, stirring, until sauce thickens. Add more stock if sauce becomes too thick.

To serve, place fish on plates and spoon vegetable sauce over.

Trout With Orange, Maple Syrup, and Macadamia Nuts

SERVES 4

This sauce goes well with any type of small whole fish.

3 tablespoons butter

4 whole trout, about 8 oz (250 g) each, cleaned

1/3 cup (11/2 oz/45 g) chopped macadamia nuts

2 tablespoons chopped scallions (spring onions, shallots)

grated rind of 1 orange

1/4 cup (2 fl oz/60 ml) orange juice

2 tablespoons maple syrup

Melt 2 tablespoons butter in frying pan over medium heat. Add trout and fry 4 to 5 minutes per side or until fish is opaque and beginning to flake when tested. Remove and keep warm.

Melt remaining butter in same frying pan over medium heat. Add nuts and cook 1 to 2 minutes or until golden. Add scallions, rind, juice, and syrup. Bring to boil. Simmer until sauce thickens slightly. Pour over trout and serve.

PANFRIED TROUT WITH HOT VINAIGRETTE

SERVES 4

4 small whole fish such as trout, 8 oz (250 g) each

seasoned flour (see glossary)

1/4 cup (2 fl oz/60 ml) olive oil

3 cloves garlic, chopped

2 tablespoons balsamic vinegar

2 tablespoons water

2 teaspoons chopped fresh oregano or 1 teaspoon dried

Wash trout well and pat dry with paper towel. Place flour in plastic bag. Add trout and shake until fish is well coated. Remove from bag and shake off excess.

Heat oil in frying pan over high heat. Add trout and cook 4 to 5 minutes per side or until fish is opaque and beginning to flake when tested. Remove and keep warm.

Add garlic to pan juices and cook over medium heat until fragrant, about 1 minute. Add vinegar, water, and oregano and bring to boil. Remove from heat, pour over trout, and serve.

TUNA STEAKS WITH TOMATO SALAD

Tuna is wonderful to barbecue or grill. But it is important, not to overcook it, or it will dry out. Brushing it with oil during cooking will help keep it moist. It is quite acceptable to serve tuna pink in the middle. The salad is better if prepared ahead to allow flavors to develop.

3 plum (egg) tomatoes, quartered

1 teaspoon chopped fresh oregano or 1/4 teaspoon dried

1/4 cup (2 fl oz/60 ml) extra virgin olive oil

1 clove garlic, chopped

salt and freshly ground pepper

4 tuna steaks, about 8 oz (250 g) each

2 tablespoons olive oil, for cooking

Combine tomatoes, oregano, oil, garlic, and salt and pepper in bowl and mix well.

Preheat barbecue, grill, or broiler and brush with oil to prevent sticking. Brush tuna with oil and season with salt and pepper. Cook fish 2 to 3 minutes per side or until tender and beginning to flake when tested.

To serve, place on plates and top with tomato salad.

TUNA STEAKS WITH EGG AND LEMON DRESSING

SERVES 4

This is a light, creamy dressing similar to mayonnaise but with a thinner consistency. It can be made in advance and stored in the refrigerator for up to 3 days. It makes a great dressing for many seafood salads.

1/3 cup (3 fl oz/90 ml) olive oil

1/4 cup (2 fl oz/60 ml) lemon juice

1 egg yolk

2 tablespoons grated parmesan cheese

2 tablespoons chopped fresh parsley

4 tuna steaks, about 8 oz (250 g) each

2 tablespoons olive oil, for cooking

salt and freshly ground pepper

Combine oil, juice, yolk, parmesan, and parsley in food processor or blender and process until thick and creamy.

Preheat barbecue, grill, or broiler and brush with oil to prevent sticking. Brush tuna with oil and season with salt and pepper. Cook fish 2 to 3 minutes per side or until tender and beginning to flake when tested.

To serve, place tuna on plate and spoon dressing over.

Tuna Steaks with Tomato Salad

FISH WITH CHERMOULLA

SERVES 6

Chermoulla is a north African marinade. The longer the fish marinates, the better — so marinate overnight if possible. The traditional method for this recipe uses whole fish, filling the cavity with the marinade mixture and then baking. This version is a little quicker yet loses none of the flavor. Serve with rice or couscous.

1/3 cup (1/2 oz/15 g) chopped cilantro (fresh coriander leaves)

1/3 cup (1/2 oz/15 g) chopped fresh parsley

2 cloves garlic, chopped

2 red chilies, seeded and chopped

2 teaspoons ground cumin

2 teaspoons paprika

1/2 cup (4 fl oz/125 ml) olive oil

1/3 cup (3 fl oz/90 ml) lime juice

6 white-fleshed or oily fish steaks, about 8 oz (250g) each

Combine cilantro, parsley, garlic, chilies, cumin, paprika, oil, and juice in food processor or blender and puree until smooth. Pour into glass dish, add fish and mix well. Marinate several hours in refrigerator, overnight if time allows.

Remove fish from marinade. Panfry, broil, grill, or barbecue, 3 to4 minutes per side or until fish is opaque and beginning to flake when tested.

BLACKENED FISH

SERVES 4

For success with this Cajun recipe it is important to have a really hot frying pan, so when the fish is added it begins to sizzle immediately. This will result in a crisp, very dark coating.

1 tablespoon all-purpose (plain) flour

1 teaspoon onion powder

1/2 teaspoon powdered thyme

1/2 teaspoon powdered oregano

1/2 teaspoon salt

1/4 teaspoon chili powder

1/4 teaspoon freshly ground white pepper

1/4 teaspoon freshly ground black pepper

1/4 teaspoon paprika

1 lb (500 g) white-fleshed or oily fish fillets, skinned

4 tablespoons melted butter

1 tablespoon oil, for frying

Combine flour and spices and mix well. Brush fillets with butter, then rub spice mixture all over fillets.

Heat oil in iron frying pan over high heat until very hot. Add fillets and cook 2 to 3 minutes per side or until fish is opaque and beginning to flake when tested. Serve immediately.

PESCE AL PARMIGIANO

SERVES 4

This rich dish should be off-set by a crisp green salad and served with lots of crusty bread to mop up the sauce. It can be prepared several hours in advance and refrigerated until baking time.

6 tablespoons olive oil

1 onion, chopped

1 clove garlic, chopped

14 oz (440 g) can peeled tomatoes, chopped

1/4 cup (2 fl oz/60 ml) red wine

3 tablespoons chopped fresh basil

salt and freshly ground pepper

1 lb (500 g) white-fleshed or oily fish fillets, skinned

seasoned flour (see glossary)

1 egg, beaten

1 cup (4 oz/125 g) dry breadcrumbs

2 cups (8 oz/250 g) shredded mozzarella cheese

1/4 cup (1 oz/30 g) grated parmesan cheese

Heat 2 tablespoons oil in large saucepan over medium heat. Add onion and garlic and cook until tender, about 2 minutes. Add tomatoes, wine, basil, and salt and pepper and bring to boil. Cover and simmer 15 minutes. Cool.

Coat fish with flour and shake off excess. Dip into egg and then breadcrumbs, pressing coating on firmly. Heat remaining oil in frying pan over medium heat, Add fish and cook 2 to 3 minutes per side or until golden. Drain well on paper towels.

Preheat oven to 350°F (180°C/Gas 4). Place fish in greased baking dish. Sprinkle mozzarella over. Pour on tomato sauce and sprinkle with parmesan. Bake 15 minutes or until cheese is golden.

DORY ROLLS

1 cup (7 oz/220 g) ricotta cheese

1/3 cup (2 oz/60 g) chopped prosciutto

1/4 cup (1 oz/30 g) grated parmesan cheese

1 teaspoon chopped fresh marjoram

1/4 teaspoon cracked pepper

4 thin fish fillets, such as Dory, about 4 oz (125 g) each

3 tablespoons melted butter

freshly ground pepper

Combine ricotta, prosciutto, parmesan, marjoram, and pepper in bowl and mix well.

Preheat oven to 350°F (180°C/Gas 4). Place fillets skin side up on work surface and divide cheese mixture evenly among fish. Roll up firmly, using toothpicks if necessary to secure. Arrange rolls seam side down in greased baking dish. Brush with butter and sprinkle with pepper. Cover dish with foil and bake for 15 to 20 minutes or until fish is opaque and beginning to flake when tested. Serve immediately.

DORY WITH SPINACH SAUCE

Almost any other type of fish fillet, white-fleshed or oily, may be substituted. Serve with boiled buttered potatoes and steamed vegetables.

2 tablespoons butter

1 lb (500 g) Dory fillets

3 cups (5 oz/155 g) chopped fresh spinach

1/3 cup (3 fl oz/80 ml) dry white wine

1 tablespoon dijon mustard

1/2 cup (4 fl oz/125 ml) light whipping cream

salt and freshly ground pepper

Melt butter in frying pan over medium heat. Add fillets and cook 2 to 3 minutes per side or until fish is opaque and beginning to flake when tested. Remove and keep warm.

Add spinach to pan juices and cook over medium heat until tender, about 2 to 3 minutes. Add wine, mustard, cream, and salt and pepper and cook until sauce thickens and boils, about 3 to 4 minutes.

Place the fish on plates and pour the sauce over. Serve immediately.

Dory Rolls

DORY KIEV

SERVES 4

This recipe can be made well in advance and refrigerated until ready to cook. It also freezes successfully; once the rolls have been prepared, cover well with plastic wrap, place in a freezer bag, and freeze up to 4 months. Defrost, then fry as below.

1/2 cup (4 oz/125 g) butter, softened

2 cloves garlic, chopped

1/3 cup (1/2 oz/15 g) chopped mixed fresh herbs (chives, parsley, tarragon)

salt and freshly ground pepper

4 thin fish fillets, such as Dory, about 5 oz (150 g) each

seasoned flour (see glossary)

1 egg

2 tablespoons milk

1 cup (4 oz/125 g) dry breadcrumbs

1/2 cup (11/2 oz/45 g) ground almonds

1/3 cup (3 fl oz/90 ml) olive oil

Combine butter, garlic, herbs, and salt and pepper in small bowl and mix well.

Place fish on work surface skin side up. Divide butter mixture into 4 parts and place one part in the middle of each fillet. Roll fillets to enclose butter, using toothpicks if necessary to secure. Chill rolls until butter is firm, about 15 minutes.

Dip rolls into flour, shaking off excess. Beat egg with milk in shallow dish. Combine breadcrumbs and nuts in another dish. Dip fish rolls into egg mixture, then into crumb mixture, pressing crumbs on firmly. Chill 15 minutes.

Heat oil in frying pan over medium heat. Add rolls and cook until crisp and golden on all sides, about 10 minutes. Serve immediately.

DORY AND SCALLOPS IN LEMON AND BASIL BEARNAISE

SERVES 4

2 tablespoons lemon juice

grated rind of 1 lemon

1/4 teaspoon salt

2 egg yolks

1/3 cup (1/2 oz/15 g) chopped fresh basil

1/2 cup (4 oz/125 g) hot melted butter

3 tablespoons butter, for cooking

1 lb (500 g) fish fillets, such as Dory

freshly ground pepper

8 oz (250 g) scallops, deveined if necessary

7 oz (220 g) asparagus, steamed lightly and kept warm

Combine lemon juice, rind, salt, yolks, and basil in food processor or blender and puree until smooth. With motor running, gradually add melted butter, blending until all is incorporated. Keep sauce warm over hot water.

Melt 3 tablespoons butter in frying pan over medium heat. Add fillets, season with pepper, and cook 2 to 3 minutes per side or until fish is opaque and beginning to flake when tested. Remove and keep warm.

Add scallops and asparagus to frying pan, season with pepper, and cook just until scallops are opaque and asparagus is warm, about 1 to 2 minutes.

To serve, divide fish among four plates, top with scallops and asparagus and spoon sauce over.

DORY WITH HONEY AND ALMONDS

SERVES 4

This simple dish is equally suited to small whole fish, particularly trout.

2 tablespoons butter
1 lb (500 g) Dory fillets
1/3 cup (1 oz/30 g) flaked almonds
2 tablespoons honey
2 tablespoons white wine

Melt butter in frying pan over medium heat. Add fillets and fry 2 to 3 minutes per side or until fish is opaque and beginning to flake when tested. Remove and keep warm.

Add almonds to pan and stir over medium heat until golden. Pour in honey and wine and cook until sauce is slightly thickened. Pour over fish and serve.

PANFRIED DORY WITH SLIVERED ALMONDS AND SNOW PEAS

SERVES 4

6 tablespoons butter

1 lb (500 g) white-fleshed or oily fish fillets, such as Dory

1/3 cup (1 1/2 oz/45 g) slivered almonds

1/3 cup (1/2 oz/15 g) chopped scallions (spring onions/shallots)

7 oz (220 g) snow peas (mange-tout), steamed until tender crisp

2 tablespoons dry white wine

salt and freshly ground pepper

Melt 2 tablespoons butter in frying pan over medium heat. Add fish and cook 2 to 3 minutes per side or until fish is opaque and beginning to flake when tested. Remove and keep warm.

Add almonds to pan juices and cook over medium heat until golden, about 1 to 2 minutes. Stir in remaining butter, scallions, snow peas, wine, and salt and pepper. Stir until sauce boils and thickens slightly.

To serve, place fillets on plates and pour sauce over.

Panfried Dory with Slivered Almonds and Snow Peas

HUNGARIAN CREAM FISH

SERVES 4

2 tablespoons butter

1 onion, finely chopped

1 red bell pepper (capsicum), finely chopped

2 teaspoons paprika

$1/2$ cup (4 fl oz/125 ml) sour cream

1 lb (500 g) white-fleshed or oily fish fillets, skinned

salt and freshly ground pepper

rice or noodles, to serve

Melt 1 tablespoon butter in frying pan over medium heat. Add onion and bell pepper and sauté until tender, about 5 minutes. Add paprika and sour cream and stir to heat through.

Melt remaining 1 tablespoon butter in another frying pan over medium heat. Add fillets and season to taste with salt and pepper. Fry 2 to 3 minutes per side, or until fish is opaque and beginning to flake when tested.

To serve, place fish on plates with rice or noodles and pour sauce over.

INDIAN CUTTLEFISH CASSEROLE

SERVES 4

Other types of seafood that can be used as substitutes include uncooked shrimp (prawns), about $1^1/2$ lb (750g), and octopus, about 2 lb (1kg), after it has simmered for 30 minutes.

2 tablespoons vegetable oil

1 onion, sliced

2 cloves garlic, chopped

2 red chilies, seeded and chopped

2 teaspoons ground cumin

1 teaspoon ground coriander

1 teaspoon ground fenugreek seed

$1/2$ teaspoon chili powder

1 cup (8 fl oz/250 ml) fish stock (see page 260)

2 lb (1 kg) cuttlefish, cleaned and honeycombed (see page 34)

cooked rice or noodles, to serve

Heat oil in saucepan over medium heat. Add onion and cook until tender, about 4 minutes. Add garlic, chilies, cumin, coriander, fenugreek, and chili powder and cook 1 minute. Stir in stock and bring to boil.

Add cuttlefish and simmer uncovered until tender, about 5 minutes. Serve with rice or noodles.

THAI CRISPY FISH WITH HOT SOUR CHILI SAUCE

SERVES 4

Thanks to the quick cooking process, deep-fried fish is very moist. The oil must be hot enough to make the fish sizzle immediately; this will seal the surface of the fish and trap in moisture.

1 tablespoon vegetable oil

3 red chilies, seeded and chopped

2 cloves garlic, chopped

2 tablespoons chopped cilantro (fresh coriander leaves)

2 tablespoons oyster sauce

1 tablespoon fish sauce

1 tablespoon sweet chili sauce

2 tablespoons lime juice

1/2 cup (4 fl oz/125 ml) Thai fish stock (see page 260) or water

2 tablespoons chopped fresh basil

4 small whole fish, about 8 oz (250 g) each, scaled and cleaned

coarse salt

oil for deep frying

steamed jasmine rice, to serve

Heat oil in saucepan over medium heat. Add chilies, garlic, and cilantro and cook until fragrant, about 1 minute. Pour in sauces, juice, and stock and bring to boil, stirring constantly. Cook until sauce thickens slightly, about 4 minutes. Stir in basil.

With a sharp knife, make 2 to 3 deep diagonal cuts on each side of the fish. Rub generously with salt.

Heat oil in large saucepan over medium heat until hot. Immerse fish and cook until golden and crisp, about 10 minutes. Drain on paper towels.

Serve fish with sauce and rice.

Following pages: Indian Cuttlefish Casserole (page 204), Thai Crispy Fish with Hot Sour Chili Sauce (page 205), and Thai Fish Curry (page 208)

THAI FISH CURRY

SERVES 4

The same curry works well with shrimp (prawns), or honeycombed squid (calamari).

1 teaspoon vegetable oil

2 tablespoons green curry paste

1½ cups (12 fl oz/375 ml) thin coconut cream

1 tablespoon fish sauce

1 tablespoon sugar

3 tablespoons chopped fresh basil leaves

2 tablespoons chopped cilantro (fresh coriander leaves)

1 cup (4 oz/125 g) chopped zucchini (courgette)

1½ lb (750 g) white-fleshed or oily fish fillets, skinned and cut into cubes

steamed rice, to serve

Heat oil in large saucepan over medium heat. Add curry paste and cook until oil separates from paste, about 1 to 2 minutes. Add coconut cream, fish sauce, sugar, basil, cilantro, and zucchini and bring to boil. Reduce heat and simmer 10 minutes or until zucchini is tender.

Add fish and bring to boil. Simmer 5 minutes or until fish is tender and flakes easily. Serve with rice.

CUTTLEFISH, BASIL, AND PEANUT CURRY

SERVES 4

This can be made using shrimp (prawns), squid (calamari), or chopped fish fillets if desired.

1 tablespoon oil

1 tablespoon red curry paste

1½ cups (12 fl oz/375 ml) thin coconut cream

¼ cup (2 oz/60 g) crunchy peanut butter

⅓ cup (½ oz/15 g) chopped fresh basil

2 lb (1 kg) cuttlefish, cleaned and cut into pieces

steamed rice, to serve

Heat oil in saucepan over medium heat. Add curry paste and cook 1 minute. Add coconut cream, peanut butter, and basil and bring to boil, then simmer 5 minutes. Add cuttlefish and cook until tender, about 2 to 3 minutes. Serve with rice.

CLASSIC FISH CURRY

SERVES 4

2 tablespoons vegetable oil

1 onion, chopped

2 cloves garlic, chopped

1 red chili, seeded and chopped

1 tablespoon chopped lemongrass

1 teaspoon ground cumin

1 teaspoon garam masala

1 teaspoon turmeric

1/2 teaspoon ground cardamom

1 cup (8 fl oz/250 ml) thin coconut cream

1 cup (8 fl oz/250 ml) fish stock (see page 260)

1 teaspoon salt

1 cup (4 oz/125 g) peas

4 white-fleshed or oily fish steaks (cutlets), about 6 oz (180 g) each

2 tablespoons chopped cilantro (fresh coriander leaves)

steamed rice, to serve

Heat oil in saucepan over medium heat. Add onion and cook until tender, about 4 minutes. Add garlic, chili, lemongrass, cumin, garam masala, turmeric and cardamom and cook 1 minute. Add coconut cream, stock, and salt and bring to boil. Reduce heat and simmer 10 minutes.

Add fish and peas, cover, and simmer 10 to 15 minutes or until fish flakes when tested. Stir in cilantro and serve with rice.

SHRIMP KORMA

SERVES 4

1 onion, chopped

2 teaspoons chopped fresh ginger

2 red chilies, seeded and chopped

2 cloves garlic, chopped

1/3 cup (2 oz/60 g) chopped cashews

2 teaspoons ground coriander

2 teaspoons ground cumin

1 teaspoon garam masala

1/4 teaspoon cinnamon

1/4 teaspoon ground cardamom

1/2 cup (4 fl oz/125 ml) water

2 tablespoons olive oil

7 oz (220 g) plain yogurt

salt

1 1/2 lbs (750 g) uncooked shrimp (prawns), peeled and deveined

3 tablespoons chopped cilantro (fresh coriander leaves)

steamed rice, to serve

Combine onion, ginger, chilies, garlic, and cashews in food processor or blender and grind finely. Add coriander, cumin, garam masala, cinnamon, cardamom, and water and blend.

Heat oil in large saucepan over medium heat. Add processed mixture and cook until fragrant, about 1 to 2 minutes. Add yogurt and salt to taste and bring to boil. Simmer 5 minutes, stirring occasionally. Add shrimp and cook until tender, 3 to 5 minutes. Stir in cilantro and serve with rice.

Shrimp Korma

INDIAN FISHBALLS IN TOMATO AND CREAM

SERVES 4

These fishballs are truly outstanding. They can be prepared up to four months in advance and frozen, ready to plunge into the simmering sauce. Serve with fluffy, steamed rice. Make smaller fishballs to serve with predinner drinks — the sauce acts as a dip.

Sauce:

2 tablespoons butter

1 onion, chopped

1 clove garlic, chopped

1 red chili, seeded and chopped

1 teaspoon garam masala

1 teaspoon ground cumin

14 oz (440 g) can peeled tomatoes, chopped

1/2 cup (4 fl oz/125 ml) water

1/2 cup (4 fl oz/125 ml) light whipping cream

2 tablespoons chopped cilantro (fresh coriander leaves)

1/2 teaspoon salt

Fishballs:

1 lb (500 g) white-fleshed or oily fish fillets, skinned and chopped

1 onion, grated

1 clove garlic, chopped

1/4 teaspoon chili powder

1 teaspoon garam masala

1/2 teaspoon ground ginger

1/2 teaspoon salt

For sauce: Melt butter in saucepan over medium heat. Add onion and cook until tender, about 4 minutes. Add garlic, chili, garam masala, and cumin and cook 1 minute. Pour in tomatoes and water, cover, and simmer 15 minutes, stirring occasionally. Add cream, cilantro, and salt.

For fishballs: Place fish in food processor or blender and puree. Add onion, garlic, chili powder, garam masala, ginger, and salt and blend well. Using wet hands, shape tablespoonsful of mixture into balls. Chill 10 minutes.

Bring sauce to boil. Add fishballs, cover, and simmer 10 minutes, stirring occasionally.

LOBSTER MEDALLIONS WITH CHERVIL AND ASPARAGUS

SERVES 4

6 tablespoons butter

2 lb (1 kg) uncooked lobster tails

1 clove garlic, chopped

7 oz (220 g) asparagus, steamed until tender crisp

grated rind of 1 lime

1 tablespoon lime juice

2 tablespoons chopped fresh chervil

2 tablespoons chopped scallions (spring onions/shallots)

salt and freshly ground pepper

Extract meat from lobster tails and cut into medallions (see page 24).

Melt 2 tablespoons butter in frying pan over medium heat. Add lobster and cook until tender, about 1 to 2 minutes. Remove and keep warm.

Melt remaining butter in same pan over medium heat. Add garlic, asparagus, rind, and juice, chervil, scallions and salt and pepper, and bring to boil. Simmer just until asparagus is heated through.

To serve, divide lobster medallions among four plates and spoon sauce over.

LOBSTER TAILS WITH LIME BUTTER

SERVES 4

4 uncooked lobster tails, about 8 oz (250 g) each

1/3 cup (2 oz/60 g) butter

1/4 cup (2 fl oz/60 ml) lime juice

2 tablespoons lime marmalade

3 tablespoons chopped chives

Extract meat from lobster tails and cut into medallions (see page 24).

Melt 2 tablespoons butter in frying pan over medium heat. Add lobster and cook until tender, about 1 to 2 minutes. Remove and keep warm.

Add remaining butter, juice, marmalade, and chives to pan and bring to boil, stirring constantly. Remove from heat and pour over lobster. Serve immediately.

LOBSTER THERMIDOR

SERVES 4

This impressive dish can be assembled several hours ahead and refrigerated until ready for baking.

2 cooked lobsters, about 2 lb (1 kg) each (see page 25)

2 tablespoons butter

3 tablespoons chopped scallions (spring onions/shallots)

2 tablespoons all-purpose (plain) flour

1¼ cups (10 fl oz/300 ml) milk

¾ cup (3 oz/90 g) grated gruyère cheese

½ teaspoon salt

1 teaspoon dijon mustard

Cut lobsters in half along length of body and extract meat, reserving shells (see page 22 to 25). Cut into bite-size pieces and place in large bowl.

Melt butter in saucepan over medium heat. Add scallions, cook 1 minute. Add flour and cook 1 minute. Remove from heat.

Gradually whisk in milk, return to heat, and cook, stirring constantly, until sauce thickens and boils.

Remove from heat and add ½ cup gruyère, salt, and mustard; stir until cheese melts. Add to lobster and mix well. Return mixture to lobster shells.

Preheat oven to 350°F (180°C/Gas 4). Place lobster shells on baking sheet and sprinkle with remaining gruyère. Bake 15 to 20 minutes or until heated through and golden.

Lobster Thermidor

LOBSTER WITH ORANGE AND PISTACHIO BUTTER

SERVES 4

4 lobster tails,
about 8 oz (250 g) each

1/2 cup (4 oz/125 g) butter

salt and freshly ground pepper

grated rind of 1 orange

1/4 cup (2 fl oz/60 ml) orange juice

2 tablespoons orange marmalade

2 tablespoons chopped pistachios,
toasted

Extract meat from lobster tails and cut into medallions (see page 24).

Melt 1 tablespoon butter in frying pan over medium heat. Add lobster, season to taste with salt and pepper, and cook until tender, 1 to 2 minutes.

Add remaining butter, rind, juice, marmalade, and nuts and stir to coat lobster with sauce. Serve immediately.

CRAB IN YOGURT

SERVES 4

1 tablespoon vegetable oil

2 teaspoons chopped fresh ginger

2 cloves garlic, chopped

1 red chili, seeded and chopped

1 teaspoon turmeric

1 teaspoon curry powder

1/3 cup (1/2 oz/15 g) chopped scallions (spring onions/shallots)

1/2 cup (4 oz/125 g) plain yogurt

1 cup (8 fl oz/250 ml) fish stock (see page 260)

2 lb (1 kg) uncooked crab, segmented (see page 26)

steamed rice, to serve

Heat oil in frying pan over medium heat. Add ginger, garlic, chili, turmeric, curry powder, and scallions and cook until fragrant, about 1 minute. Stir in yogurt and stock and bring to boil. Add crab, cover, and cook 15 to 20 minutes or until crab is cooked through. Test by cracking open a segment. Serve with rice.

CHILI CRAB

This sauce is very hot and spicy. If you prefer a milder sauce, simply reduce the number of chilies and the amount of chili sauce. Serve with rice or noodles.

2 tablespoons peanut oil

2 teaspoons sesame oil

1/3 cup (1/2 oz/15 g) chopped scallions (spring onions, shallots)

3 cloves garlic, chopped

2 teaspoons chopped fresh ginger

2 red chilies, chopped

2 tablespoons soy sauce

2 tablespoons oyster sauce

2 tablespoons sweet chili sauce

1 tablespoon chili sauce

1/2 cup (4 fl oz/125 ml) fish stock (see page 260)

2 lb (1 kg) uncooked crabs, segmented (see page 26)

Heat oils in frying pan or wok over medium heat. Add scallions, garlic, ginger, and chilies and sauté until fragrant, about 1 minute. Pour in sauces and stock, bring to boil, cover, and simmer 5 minutes. Add crabs, cover, and simmer 10 to 15 minutes or until crabs are cooked through. Test by cracking open a segment.

CRAB FRITTATA

Served hot or at room temperature, this makes a superb light meal when served with a salad or serve it sliced as part of a buffet or as finger-food at a party.

4 tablespoons butter

1 zucchini (courgette), sliced

1 red bell pepper (capsicum), sliced

1/2 cup (2 oz/60 g) chopped leek

1 cup (6 oz/180 g) crabmeat, cooked or canned

6 eggs, beaten

salt and freshly ground pepper

1/2 cup (2 oz/60 g) grated cheddar cheese

3 tablespoons chopped fresh parsley

Melt 2 tablespoons butter in frying pan over medium heat. Add zucchini, pepper, and leek and cook until tender, about 5 minutes. Cool. Place in large bowl with crabmeat, eggs, and salt and pepper to taste.

Preheat broiler (grill). Melt remaining 2 tablespoons butter in frying pan with heat-proof handle over medium heat. Pour in egg mixture and cook until bottom sets, about 6 to 8 minutes. Sprinkle with cheese and parsley. Broil (grill) until top sets and is golden brown.

SPICY TOMATO OCTOPUS

SERVES 4

2 tablespoons butter

1 onion, chopped

2 cloves garlic, chopped

2 teaspoons ground cumin

2 teaspoons ground coriander

1 teaspoon turmeric

1/4 teaspoon chili powder

14 oz (440 g) can peeled tomatoes, chopped

salt and freshly ground pepper

2 lb (1 kg) octopus, cleaned and segmented

1/2 cup (4 fl oz/125 ml) light whipping cream

steamed rice, to serve

Heat butter in saucepan over medium heat. Add onion and cook until tender, about 5 minutes. Stir in garlic, cumin, coriander, turmeric, and chili powder and cook 1 minute. Pour in tomatoes, cover, and simmer 15 minutes, stirring occasionally. Season with salt and pepper. Add octopus and simmer until tender, about 40 to 50 minutes. Stir in cream and heat through. Serve with rice.

Spicy Tomato Octopus

OCTOPUS AND POTATO CASSEROLE

SERVES 4

This simple, hearty dish, was taught to me by my parents. Octopus varies greatly in size. The longer octopus simmers, the more tender it will be. If you purchase large octopus, it can take up to 1 hour to become tender, so when preparing this recipe, adjust the cooking time if necessary.

1/4 cup (2 fl oz/60 ml) olive oil

1 onion, chopped

2 cloves garlic, chopped

1 red chili, seeded and chopped

2 lb (1 kg) baby octopus, cleaned and cut into small pieces

1 lb (500 g) boiling potatoes, peeled and chopped

1/2 cup (4 fl oz/125 ml) fish stock (see page 260)

1/2 cup (4 fl oz/125 ml) dry white wine

salt and freshly ground dry pepper

3 tablespoons chopped fresh parsley

Heat oil in large saucepan over medium heat. Add onion and cook until tender, about 4 minutes. Add garlic, chili, octopus, and potatoes and cook, stirring constantly, until octopus and potatoes are just beginning to cook, 5 to 6 minutes.

Add stock, wine, and salt and pepper and bring to boil. Cover and simmer until octopus is tender, about 30 to 40 minutes. Stir in parsley and serve.

POTATO AND FISH CAKES

SERVES 6

These can be made several days in advance, covered, and refrigerated until ready for cooking. They also freeze well for up to four months.

1 lb (500 g) white-fleshed or oily fish fillets, skinned and ground (minced)

8 oz (250 g) baking potatoes, cooked and mashed

salt and freshly ground pepper

2 tablespoons chopped fresh parsley

2 tablespoons chopped scallions (spring onions/shallots)

2 tablespoons mayonnaise

2 tablespoons chopped gherkin

1½ cups (6 oz/185 g) dry breadcrumbs

oil for shallow frying

Combine fish, potatoes, salt and pepper, parsley, scallions, mayonnaise, and gherkin in large bowl and mix well. Using wet hands, shape into 12 patties.

Coat patties with breadcrumbs, pressing firmly. Chill 30 minutes.

Heat ¼ inch (¾ cm) depth of oil in frying pan over medium heat. Add patties and cook 2 to 3 minutes per side. Drain on paper towels and serve hot or cold.

SEAFOOD PIZZAS

SERVES 4

Pizza dough can be made in advance, covered with plastic wrap, and kept in the refrigerator for up to 6 hours prior to baking.

1/2 oz (15 g) compressed yeast or 2 teaspoons active dry yeast

1 teaspoon sugar

1 cup (8 fl oz/250 ml) warm water

2 cups (8 oz/250 g) all-purpose (plain) flour

1 teaspoon salt

14 oz (440 g) can peeled tomatoes, chopped

1 onion, chopped

1 clove garlic, chopped

1/4 cup (2 fl oz/60 ml) olive oil

salt and freshly ground pepper

8 oz (250 g) mussels, scrubbed, debearded, and steamed open

8 oz (250 g) uncooked shrimp (prawns), peeled and deveined

8 oz (250 g) squid (calamari), cleaned and chopped

3 oz (90 g) scallops, deveined if necessary

1/2 cup (2 oz/60 g) shredded mozzarella cheese

2 tablespoons chopped fresh basil

2 teaspoons chopped fresh oregano

Combine yeast, sugar, and 1/4 cup (2 fl oz/60 ml) warm water in small bowl and mix well. Cover with cloth and let stand in warm place for 10 minutes or until frothy, creamy, and nearly tripled in volume.

Place flour and salt in a large bowl and make a well in middle. Pour in yeast mixture and remaining water. Mix well, adding more warm water if necessary to make a firm dough. Turn out onto well-floured surface and knead 10 minutes, or until dough is smooth and elastic and springs back when indented with finger. Place dough in oiled bowl, brush with oil, cover loosely with plastic wrap and cloth, and let stand in a warm place 30 to 40 minutes or until doubled in bulk.

Combine tomatoes, onion, garlic, oil, and salt and pepper in saucepan. Simmer and bring to boil 10 to 15 minutes or until slightly thickened. Cool.

Preheat oven to 450°F (230°C/Gas 8). Punch down dough. Turn out onto lightly floured surface and knead 1 to 2 minutes or until smooth and elastic. Divide in half. Roll out each half on lightly floured surface into 10 in. (25 cm) round. Transfer to well-oiled baking sheets. Spread tomato mixture over dough, top with seafood, and sprinkle with cheese and herbs. Bake 10 to 15 minutes or until golden and bubbly and bottom of pizza is crisp and browned. Serve immediately.

Seafood Pizzas

SEAFOOD PAELLA

SERVES 4 TO 6

This paella may be a little time consuming, but it's really worth the effort. Add more stock if necessary throughout cooking.

1/4 cup (2 fl oz/60 ml) olive oil

2 tablespoons butter

2 cloves garlic, chopped

1 onion, chopped

1 red bell pepper (capsicum), seeded and chopped

2 tomatoes, peeled, seeded, and chopped

1 1/2 cups (9 oz/270 g) short-grain rice

3 1/2 cups (28 fl oz/875 ml) fish stock (see page 260)

1 teaspoon salt

1/4 teaspoon saffron threads, crumbled

1/4 teaspoon pepper

1 lb (500 g) uncooked crabs, segmented (see page 26)

1 lb (500 g) mussels, scrubbed and debearded

1 lb (500 g) uncooked shrimp (prawns), peeled and deveined

7 oz (220 g) scallops, deveined if necessary

3 tablespoons chopped fresh parsley

2 teaspoons chopped fresh oregano

1 teaspoon fresh thyme

Heat oil and butter in large frying pan over medium heat. Add garlic, onion, and pepper and cook until tender, about 5 minutes. Stir in tomatoes and cook 5 minutes.

Add rice and stir to coat well. Stir in stock, salt, saffron, and pepper, cover, and bring to boil. Simmer 5 minutes, stirring occasionally. Add crabs and cook covered 10 minutes. Add mussels and shrimp, stir well, and cook covered 5 minutes. Add scallops, parsley, oregano, and thyme and cook covered until tender, about 1 to 2 minutes. Serve immediately.

SEAFOOD GUMBO

SERVES 4 TO 6

Gumbo, a soup-stew from Louisiana, takes its name from an African word for okra. Okra is a glutinous, pod-shaped vegetable that gives gumbo its characteristic gelatinous texture.

2 tablespoons olive oil

2 tablespoons butter

1 onion, chopped

1 clove garlic, chopped

1 red bell pepper (capsicum), seeded and chopped

1 tablespoon all-purpose (plain) flour

2 cups (16 fl oz/500 ml) fish stock (see page 260)

14 oz (440 g) can peeled tomatoes, chopped

1 tablespoon tomato paste

salt and freshly ground pepper

10 oz (300 g) okra, trimmed

8 oz (250 g) octopus, cleaned and cut into small pieces

10 oz (300 g) white-fleshed or oily fish fillets, skinned and cut into small pieces

1 lb (500 g) uncooked shrimp (prawns), peeled and deveined

8 oz (250 g) mussels, scrubbed and debearded

2 tablespoons chopped fresh parsley

2 teaspoons fresh thyme or 1 teaspoon dried

steamed rice, for serving

Heat oil and butter in large saucepan over medium heat. Add onion, garlic, and pepper and cook until tender, about 5 minutes. Add flour and stir 1 minute. Add stock, tomatoes, tomato paste, and salt and pepper, cover, and simmer until thickened slightly, about 10 to 15 minutes.

Add okra and octopus, cover, and cook 30 minutes or until octopus is tender. Add fillets and shrimp and cook 3 to 5 minutes. Stir in mussels, parsley, and thyme and cook just until mussels open; discard any that do not open. Serve over rice.

Following pages: Indonesian Seafood Rice (page 228), Seafood Paella (page 224), Seafood Gumbo (page 225)

INDONESIAN SEAFOOD RICE

SERVES 4

Fried onion flakes are crisp, golden pieces of onion that are used for added flavor and texture. They are available in delicatessens and supermarkets. Shrimp paste, also known as blachan, is a strongly flavored puree of shrimp (prawns). It is quite salty, so use it sparingly as a flavoring agent in Asian recipes.

2 tablespoons vegetable oil

2 eggs, beaten

1 onion, chopped

1 clove garlic, chopped

1 red chili, seeded and chopped

1 teaspoon shrimp paste

8 oz (250 g) uncooked shrimp (prawns), peeled and deveined

8 oz (250 g) scallops, deveined if necessary

13 oz (400 g) squid (calamari), cleaned and cut into strips

3 cups (1 lb/500 g) cooked rice

1/3 cup (1/2 oz/15 g) chopped scallions (spring onions/shallots)

2 tablespoons soy sauce

1 tablespoon chili sauce

3 tablespoons chopped scallions (spring onions/shallots), for serving

3 tablespoons fried onion flakes, for serving

Heat 1 tablespoon oil in frying pan or wok over medium heat. Pour in eggs to make thin omelette and cook until set on bottom. Turn and cook other side until set. Cut into long strips and set aside.

Heat remaining oil in same pan. Add onion and cook until tender and golden, about 5 minutes. Add garlic, chili, and shrimp paste and cook until fragrant, about 1 minute.

Add shrimp, scallops, and squid and cook just until seafood is no longer translucent. Stir in rice, scallions, and sauces and mix just until rice is heated through.

To serve, divide rice among four plates and sprinkle with omelette, extra scallions, and onion flakes.

SPANISH HOT POT

SERVES 4

The tomato sauce in this recipe is particularly tasty. It can also be used to simmer fillets, fish steaks or cutlets, or shellfish such as shrimp (prawns) or squid (calamari). Serve with plenty of crusty bread to soak it up.

1 cup (5 oz/150 g) chopped tomato

1/3 cup (1/2 oz/15 g) chopped fresh parsley

3 cloves garlic, chopped

1 red chili, seeded and chopped

2 tablespoons olive oil

1/4 cup (2 fl oz/60 ml) water

1 1/2 lb (750 g) sardines, cleaned

Combine tomato, parsley, garlic, and chili in food processor or blender and process until smooth.

Heat oil in frying pan over medium heat. Add tomato puree and cook until sauce boils and thickens slightly, about 4 minutes. Stir in water. Add sardines and bring to a boil. Reduce heat, cover, and simmer just until fish is beginning to flake when tested, about 5 minutes.

CUTTLEFISH AND ESCAROLE RISOTTO

SERVES 4

Squid (calamari) may be substituted for the cuttlefish in this recipe, and spinach or arugula (rocket) make ideal substitutes for the escarole.

2 tablespoons butter

2 tablespoons olive oil

1 onion, chopped

2 cloves garlic, chopped

1 1/2 lb (750 g) cuttlefish, cleaned and chopped

2 cups (8 oz/250 g) chopped escarole (curly endive)

1 1/2 cups (10 oz/300 g) short-grain rice

1/2 cup (4 fl oz/125 ml) dry white wine

salt and freshly ground pepper

3 cups (24 fl oz/750 ml) hot fish stock (see page 260)

Heat butter and oil in saucepan over medium heat. Add onion and cook until tender, about 5 minutes. Add garlic, cuttlefish, and escarole and cook until cuttlefish is white, about 5 minutes. Add rice and stir 1 minute to coat with oil. Add wine and stir over medium heat until absorbed. Season with salt and pepper. Add stock, 1/2 cup at a time, stirring frequently and allowing each addition of stock to be absorbed before adding the next. Rice should be tender, moist, and creamy; add extra stock if necessary. Serve immediately.

INDIVIDUAL SEAFOOD PIES

SERVES 4

8 oz (250 g) white-fleshed fish fillets, skinned and cut into small pieces

10 oz (300 g) uncooked shrimp (prawns), peeled and deveined

1/2 cup (4 fl oz/125 ml) fish stock (see page 260)

1/2 cup (4 fl oz/125 ml) dry white wine

8 oz (250 g) scallops, deveined if necessary

2 tablespoons butter

2 tablespoons all-purpose (plain) flour

1/2 cup (4 fl oz/125 ml) milk

1/2 teaspoon dry mustard

salt and freshly ground pepper

12 freshly shucked oysters or 1 small jar oysters, drained

1/3 cup (1/2 oz/15 g) finely chopped scallions (spring onions/shallots)

2 tablespoons chopped fresh parsley

1 tablespoon chopped fresh tarragon

1 egg yolk, beaten

2 sheets commercial puff pastry

Combine fish, shrimp, stock, and wine in frying pan and bring to boil over medium heat. Simmer 3 to 5 minutes or until seafood is just tender. Remove with slotted spoon. Add scallops and cook 1 minute. Remove. Reserve 1 cup (8 fl oz/250 ml) cooking liquid.

Melt butter in saucepan over medium heat. Add flour and cook 1 minute, stirring constantly. Remove from heat and gradually whisk in reserved cooking liquid, milk, dry mustard, and salt and pepper. Return to heat and cook, stirring constantly, until sauce boils and thickens.

Preheat oven to 375°F (190°C/Gas 5). Pour sauce into large bowl. Add cooked seafood, oysters, scallions, parsley, and tarragon and mix well. Divide mixture among four 1 cup (8 fl oz/250 ml) soufflé dishes or molds, filling almost full. Brush rims of dishes with some of the egg yolk and place pastry on top, trimming to fit with sharp knife. Brush pastry with egg yolk. Place dishes on baking sheet and bake until golden 15 to 20 minutes. Serve hot.

Individual Seafood Pies

MIXED VEGETABLE AND FISH PARCELS

SERVES 4

Cooking fish in a protective package of foil or waxed (greaseproof) paper produces moist and tender results. The ingredients steam in the heat of the oven, which allows strong flavors to develop. The packages can be made several hours ahead and refrigerated until ready for cooking. They are also very successful on the barbecue; cook for about 15 minutes without turning.

4 white-fleshed or oily fish fillets, about 5 oz (150 g) each, skinned

salt and freshly ground pepper

8 oz (250 g) mixed julienned vegetables, blanched

5 oz (150 g) scallops, deveined if necessary

3 oz (90 g) butter, softened

1 clove garlic, chopped

3 tablespoons chopped chives

Place each fillet on a separate sheet of greased foil. Season well with salt and pepper. Top with vegetables, then scallops.

Combine butter, garlic, and chives in bowl and mix well. Divide among packages, spooning over scallops. Lift edges of foil and double-fold to form a tight seal.

Preheat oven to 350°F (180°C/Gas 4). Arrange packages on baking sheet and bake 15 to 20 minutes or until fish is opaque and beginning to flake when tested. Serve immediately.

SALADE NIÇOISE

2 tablespoons butter

4 tuna steaks, 3 oz (90 g) each

2 plum (egg) tomatoes, quartered

6 oz (180 g) green beans, steamed until tender

8 anchovy fillets

1/3 cup (1 1/2 oz/45 g) black olives

1 head radicchio, torn

1/3 cup (3 fl oz/90 ml) olive oil

1/4 cup (2 fl oz/60 ml) tarragon vinegar

2 teaspoons dijon mustard

salt and freshly ground pepper

2 hard-cooked (boiled) eggs, quartered

Melt butter in frying pan over high heat. Add tuna and cook 2 to 3 minutes per side, turning only once. Place on serving plates.

Combine tomatoes, beans, anchovy fillets, olives, and radicchio in large bowl.

Mix oil, vinegar, mustard and salt and pepper. Pour over salad and toss well. Pile salad and egg beside tuna.

WARM FISH SALAD

12 new potatoes, cooked until tender

7 oz (220 g) snow peas (mange-tout), blanched

1 small lettuce (any type), washed and torn

2 plum (egg) tomatoes, quartered

3 tablespoons chopped chives

1 tablespoon olive oil, for cooking

1 lb (500 g) white-fleshed fish fillets, skinned and cut into strips

salt and freshly ground pepper

1/3 cup (3 fl oz/90 ml) extra virgin olive oil

2 tablespoons lemon juice

1 teaspoon seeded mustard

2 teaspoons fresh thyme

Combine potatoes, snow peas, lettuce, tomatoes, and chives in large bowl.

Heat 1 tablespoon oil in frying pan over medium heat. Add fish, season with salt and pepper, and cook about 2 minutes per side or until fish is opaque and beginning to flake when tested. Cool slightly and add to salad.

Combine extra virgin olive oil, juice, mustard, thyme, and salt and pepper and mix well. Pour over salad and toss to combine. Pile onto individual plates and serve.

SOUPS

Bouillabaisse (page 236)

BOUILLABAISSE

SERVES 4

The most famous of all fish soups, bouillabaisse originated in France, although most European countries have their own versions. Use a variety of seafood for best flavor, choosing types that are in season to get the best quality and price. If small whole fish are unavailable, try either steaks (cutlets) or fish fillets cut into big chunks.

1/4 cup (2 fl oz/60 ml) olive oil

1 onion, chopped

1 clove garlic, chopped

1/3 cup (1 1/2 oz/45 g) chopped fennel

4 cups (32 fl oz/1 l) fish stock (see page 260)

14 oz (440 g) can peeled tomatoes, chopped

1/4 teaspoon turmeric

1/4 teaspoon salt

1/4 teaspoon pepper

4 small whole fish (such as garfish or red mullet), cleaned and scaled

1 lb (500 g) white-fleshed fish fillets, cut into pieces

1 lb (500 g) uncooked shrimp (prawns), peeled and deveined

1 lb (500 g) mussels, scrubbed and debearded

1/3 cup (1/2 oz/15 g) chopped fresh parsley

4 slices French bread, toasted

green aïoli (see page 262)

chopped fresh parsley, to serve

Heat oil in large saucepan over medium heat. Add onion, garlic, and fennel and cook until tender, about 3 to 4 minutes. Add stock, tomatoes, turmeric, salt, and pepper, bring to boil, and simmer 15 minutes.

Add whole fish and simmer 5 minutes. Add fish pieces and shrimp and simmer 2 minutes. Add mussels and parsley and cook 2 to 3 minutes or just until mussels open; discard any that do not open.

To serve, place French bread in soup bowls. Top with seafood and broth and spoon 1 tablespoon of aïoli on top. Sprinkle with extra parsley.

KAKAVIA

SERVES 4

A tasty fish and vegetable stock makes this classic Greek soup irresistible. You can use any type of mollusk, including mussels, clams, and cockles.

2 lb (1 kg) fish bones, washed

1 onion, chopped

1 lemon, sliced

small bunch parsley

6 cups (48 fl oz/1.5 l) water

1/4 cup (2 fl oz/60 ml) olive oil

1/2 cup (2 oz/60 g) chopped celery

1 onion, chopped

2 cloves garlic, chopped

1/2 cup (2 oz/60 g) chopped fennel

1/2 cup (2 oz/60 g) chopped carrot

2 cups (7 oz/220 g) peeled and chopped tomato

1/4 cup (2 fl oz/60 ml) dry white wine

1 lb (500 g) white-fleshed fish fillets, chopped

1 lb (500 g) mollusks soaked for 30 minutes in cold water

2 tablespoons chopped fresh parsley

Combine bones, onion, lemon, parsley, and water in large saucepan and bring to boil over high heat. Simmer uncovered 20 minutes, skimming as necessary. Strain; reserving stock and discarding remainder.

Heat oil in large saucepan over medium heat. Add celery, onion, garlic, fennel, and carrot and cook until tender, about 5 minutes. Add tomato, wine, and reserved stock, bring to boil, and simmer 30 minutes. Strain vegetables, reserving stock.

Puree vegetables in food processor. Return stock and puree to saucepan and bring to boil. Add fish and mollusks and simmer 2 to 3 minutes or until shells open; discard any that do not open. Stir in parsley and serve.

FISHERMAN'S SOUP

This well-flavored soup is a favorite East European dish.

1/4 cup (2 fl oz/60 ml) olive oil

1/2 cup (2 oz/60 g) chopped celery

1/2 cup (2 oz/60 g) chopped carrot

1 onion, finely chopped

3 cloves garlic, chopped

1/3 cup (1/2 oz/15 g) chopped fresh
parsley

2 bay leaves

1 cup (4 oz/125 g) peeled,
seeded, and chopped tomatoes

1/2 cup (4 fl oz/125 ml) dry
white wine

4 cups (32 fl oz/1 l) fish stock
(see page 260)

1/3 cup (2 oz/60 g) short-grain rice

1 lb (500 g) white-fleshed or
oily fish fillets, cubed

1 lb (500 g) mussels, scrubbed
and debearded

Heat oil in large saucepan over medium heat. Add celery, carrot, and onion and cook until tender, about 5 minutes. Add garlic, parsley, bay leaves, tomatoes, wine, and stock and simmer 15 minutes.

Add rice and simmer 8 minutes, stirring occasionally. Add fish and mussels and simmer 4 minutes or until rice is tender and mussels have opened; discard any that do not open. Serve immediately.

THAI FISH AND NOODLE SOUP

A Thai-style soup that is hot and spicy with a light lemony tang. A meal in itself.

2 tablespoons vegetable oil

1 onion, chopped

2 cloves garlic, chopped

2 tablespoons chopped
lemongrass

1 tablespoon green curry paste

3 cups (24 fl oz/750 ml) fish stock
(see page 260)

1 cup (8 oz/250 ml) thin
coconut cream

1 lb (500 g) white-fleshed fish
fillets, cubed

3 tablespoons chopped fresh
mint leaves

4 oz (125 g) soft Asian noodles

Heat oil in large saucepan over medium heat. Add onion and cook until tender, about 3 to 4 minutes. Stir in garlic, lemongrass, and curry paste and sauté until fragrant, about 1 minute. Pour in fish stock and coconut cream and simmer 15 minutes.

Add fish, mint, and noodles and cook 5 minutes or until fish is tender. Serve piping hot.

Fisherman's Soup

FISHBALL AND NOODLE SOUP

SERVES 4 TO 6

This big, hearty soup makes a great starter to an Asian menu.

8 oz (250 g) white-fleshed or oily fish fillets, skinned and ground (minced)

2 teaspoons red curry paste

1 tablespoons chopped cilantro (fresh coriander leaves)

1/4 teaspoon salt

1 tablespoon vegetable oil

1 tablespoon chopped lemongrass

1 red chili, seeded and chopped

1 clove garlic, chopped

4 cups (32 fl oz/1 l) Thai fish stock (see page 260)

2 tablespoons fish sauce

1 tablespoon lemon juice

1 cup (4 oz/125 g) sliced oyster mushrooms

3 oz (90 g) soft Asian noodles

1/2 cup (2 oz/60 g) mung bean sprouts

2 tablespoons chopped fresh mint

Combine fish, curry paste, cilantro, and salt in bowl and mix well. Shape teaspoonsful of mixture, into small balls with wet hands. Set aside.

Heat oil in large saucepan over medium heat. Add lemongrass, chili, and garlic and cook until fragrant, about 1 minute. Pour in stock, fish sauce, and juice and bring to boil. Add mushrooms, noodles, and sprouts simmer 2 minutes. Add fishballs and mint and simmer 2 to 3 minutes or until fishballs are tender. Serve piping hot.

Curry Soup with Mixed Mollusks

A mild curry soup that is easy and fast to make. Serve with crusty bread for a complete meal. For the best flavor, use a variety of mollusks, such as mussels, clams, and cockles.

2 tablespoons butter

1 onion, chopped

1 clove garlic, chopped

1 red chili, seeded and chopped

2 tablespoons all-purpose (plain) flour

2 teaspoons green curry paste

2 tablespoons tomato paste

4 cups (32 fl oz/1 l) fish stock (see page 260)

2 tomatoes, peeled, seeded, and chopped

1¹/₂ lbs (750 g) mixed mollusks

2 tablespoons chopped fresh basil

salt and freshly ground pepper

Melt butter in large saucepan over medium heat. Add onion and cook until tender, about 4 minutes. Add garlic and chili and cook until fragrant, about 1 minute. Stir in flour, curry paste, and tomato paste and cook 1 minute. Gradually stir in fish stock and tomatoes and bring to boil, stirring constantly. Simmer 15 minutes.

Add mollusks and simmer about 3 minutes just until they open, discard any that do not open; stir in basil and salt and pepper to taste. Serve hot.

Indian Fish Soup

1 tablespoon oil

1 onion, finely chopped

1 clove garlic, chopped

1 teaspoon chopped fresh ginger

1 teaspoon ground cumin

1 teaspoon ground coriander

4 cups (32 fl oz/1 l) fish stock (see page 260)

salt and freshly ground pepper

¹/₂ cup (3 oz/90 g) long-grain rice

1 lb (500 g) white-fleshed fish fillets, cubed

2 tablespoons chopped cilantro (fresh coriander leaves)

Heat oil in large saucepan over medium heat. Add onion and cook until tender, about 3 to 4 minutes. Stir in garlic, ginger, cumin, and coriander and cook until fragrant, about 1 minute. Pour in stock, season with salt and pepper, and bring to boil.

Add rice and simmer 12 minutes or until rice is tender.

Add fish and cilantro and simmer 2 to 3 minutes, until fish is tender and beginning to flake when tested. Serve at once.

Following pages: Fishball and Noodle Soup (page 240), Seafood Laksa (page 244), Curry Soup with Mixed Mollusks (page 241)

SEAFOOD LAKSA

SERVES 4 TO 6

This recipe for the famous Malaysian soup allows for quick, easy preparation. Use any seafood you like.

1 tablespoon oil

1 onion, chopped

2 cloves garlic, chopped

2 teaspoons ground cumin

1 teaspoon ground coriander

1/2 teaspoon turmeric

6 cups (48 fl oz/1.5 l) Thai fish stock (see page 260)

1 cup (8 fl oz/250 ml) thin coconut cream

7 oz (220 g) soft Asian noodles

1 lb (500 g) uncooked shrimp (prawns), peeled and deveined

1 lb (500 g) squid (calamari), cleaned and cut into rings

8 oz (250 g) white-fleshed fish fillets, skinned and cubed

3 tablespoons chopped cilantro (fresh coriander leaves)

3 tablespoons chopped fresh mint

Heat oil in large saucepan over medium heat. Add onion and cook until tender, about 4 minutes. Add garlic, cumin, coriander, and turmeric and sauté until fragrant, about 1 minute. Pour in stock and coconut cream and bring to boil. Add noodles, shrimp, squid, and fish and simmer 4 to 5 minutes, or until tender. Stir in cilantro and mint and season to taste with salt and pepper. Serve hot.

SPICY FISH AND LENTIL SOUP

SERVES 4

1 tablespoon olive oil

1 onion, chopped

3 cloves garlic, chopped

2 teaspoons ground coriander

2 teaspoons ground cumin

1/4 teaspoon chili powder

1 teaspoon turmeric

7 oz (220 g) brown lentils

3 cups (24 fl oz/750 ml) fish stock (see page 260)

1 lb (500 g) white-fleshed or oily fish fillets, skinned and chopped

1 cup (8 fl oz/250 ml) thin coconut cream

2 tablespoons chopped cilantro (fresh coriander leaves)

Heat oil in large saucepan over medium heat. Add onion and cook until tender, about 4 minutes. Add garlic, coriander, cumin, chili powder, and turmeric and sauté until fragrant, about 1 minute. Add lentils and stock and simmer 45 minutes or until lentils are tender.

Stir in fish and coconut cream and bring to boil. Simmer 2 to 3 minutes or until fish is tender and beginning to flake when tested. Stir in cilantro and serve.

FISH AND SWEET CORN SOUP

A light Chinese soup that is easy to make. Serve as a starter to any meal. Egg strands are long, thin strips of egg which have been created by constant stirring of soup as beaten egg is poured in. It is stirred just long enough for strands to solidify, about 1 to 2 minutes.

4 cups (32 fl oz/1 l) fish stock (see page 260)

13 oz (400 g) can creamed corn

2 tablespoons sherry

2 tablespoons soy sauce

1 teaspoon sesame oil

1/2 teaspoon salt

1 tablespoon cornstarch (cornflour)

1 tablespoon water

8 oz (250 g) white-fleshed fish fillets, skinned and ground (minced)

1/3 cup (1/2 oz/15 g) finely chopped scallions (spring onions/shallots)

1 egg, beaten

Combine stock, corn, sherry, soy sauce, oil, and salt in a large saucepan over high heat and bring to boil.

Mix cornstarch and water in cup. Add to saucepan with fish and stir vigorously to break up fish. Simmer until fish is cooked through, about 4 minutes.

Return to boil, add scallions and egg, and stir well with wooden spoon to create egg strands. Serve piping hot.

FISH, POTATO, AND SORREL SOUP

2 tablespoons butter

2 onions, sliced

1 lb (500 g) boiling potatoes, peeled and finely chopped

2 carrots, peeled and chopped

6 cups (48 fl oz/1.5 l) fish stock (see page 260)

1/2 teaspoon salt

1 1/2 lb (750 g) white-fleshed fish fillets, skinned and chopped

4 oz (125 g) chopped sorrel

freshly ground pepper

2 teaspoons chopped fresh tarragon

Melt butter in large saucepan over medium heat and cook onions until tender about 4 minutes. Add potatoes and carrots, and cook 5 minutes. Add stock and salt and bring to boil. Reduce heat, cover, and simmer 15 minutes or until vegetables are tender.

Add fish and simmer 2 to 3 minutes until fish is just beginning to flake when tested. Add sorrel, pepper, and tarragon and cook just until sorrel is tender, no longer than 1 to 2 minutes. Serve immediately.

LEMONY FISH SOUP

SERVES 4

This tangy soup has the wonderful taste of fennel, with a hint of tomato. Should fennel be unavailable, celery makes a good substitute.

4 cups (32 fl oz/1 l) fish stock
(see page 260)

1/4 cup (2 fl oz/60 ml) lemon juice

3 cups (12 oz/375 g) finely
chopped fennel

3 tablespoons tomato paste

1 lb (500 g) white-fleshed fish
fillets, cubed

1/4 teaspoon salt

1/4 teaspoon freshly ground
pepper

3 tablespoons chopped
fresh dill

Combine stock, juice, fennel, and tomato paste in medium saucepan and bring to boil over high heat. Simmer 10 minutes or until fennel is tender.

Add fish, salt, and pepper and simmer 2 minutes. Stir in dill and serve.

FENNEL AND OYSTER SOUP

SERVES 4

A delicate soup with a touch of creaminess and the subtle taste of fennel.

2 tablespoons butter

1 onion, chopped

2 cups (4 oz/125 g) chopped
fennel

1 teaspoon fennel seeds

3 cups (24 fl oz/750 ml) fish stock
(see page 260)

2 dozen oysters on the half shell
or 1 small jar oysters, drained

1/2 cup (4 fl oz/125 ml) light
whipping cream

salt and freshly ground pepper

Melt butter in saucepan over medium heat. Add onion, fennel, and fennel seeds and cook until vegetables are tender, about 5 minutes. Pour in fish stock and simmer 15 minutes.

Puree mixture in food processor or blender. Return puree to saucepan with cream. Season with salt and pepper. Bring just to boil, add oysters (without shells) and warm through. Serve hot.

Fennel and Oyster Soup

246

HEARTY FISH, BEAN, AND VEGETABLE SOUP

SERVES 4 TO 6

A meal-in-one soup, similar to Italian minestrone, that makes an ideal winter warmer.

1 onion, quartered

2 lb (1 kg) fish bones, washed

small bunch parsley

4 cups (32 fl oz/1 l) water

1 tablespoon olive oil

1/2 cup (2 oz/60 g) chopped carrot

1/2 cup (2 oz/60 g) chopped celery

1/2 cup (2 oz/60 g) chopped leek

1/2 cup (2 oz/60 g) chopped potato

1/2 cup (2 oz/60 g) peas

1 cup (4 oz/125 g) peeled and chopped tomatoes

10-oz (300 g) can red kidney beans, undrained

1 lb (500 g) white-fleshed fish fillets, cubed

salt and freshly ground pepper

Combine onion, fish bones, parsley, and water in large saucepan and bring to boil over high heat. Reduce heat and simmer uncovered 20 minutes, skimming when necessary. Strain and reserve liquid.

Heat oil in large saucepan over medium heat. Add carrot, celery, leek, potato, and peas and cook 5 minutes. Add tomatoes and reserved stock, bring to boil, and simmer 20 minutes, or until vegetables are tender.

Add beans, fish, and salt and pepper. Return to a boil and simmer 5 minutes. Serve hot.

MOLLUSK AND RICE SOUP

SERVES 4

A deliciously light soup that works with clams, cockles or mussels.

1 1/2 lb (750 g) mollusks

2 tablespoons butter

3 cloves garlic, chopped

1/2 cup (4 fl oz/125 ml) dry white wine

1 tablespoon olive oil

1 onion, chopped

1 cup (4 oz/125 ml) sliced button mushrooms

1 tablespoon tomato paste

4 cups (32 fl oz/1 l) fish stock (see page 260)

1/2 cup (3 oz/90 g) short-grain rice

1/4 teaspoon salt

1/4 teaspoon freshly ground pepper

3 tablespoons chopped fresh parsley

Soak mollusks in large container or sink of cold water for 30 minutes to remove sand.

Melt butter in large saucepan over medium heat. Add garlic and cook until fragrant, about 1 minute. Add mollusks and wine, cover, and bring to boil. Cook until mollusks open; discard any that do not. Remove mollusks from shells and chop if necessary. Reserve 1/2 cup (4 fl oz/125 ml) cooking liquid.

Heat oil in large saucepan over medium heat. Add onion and cook until tender, about 4 minutes. Add mushrooms and tomato paste and cook 1 minute. Pour in fish stock and reserved cooking liquid and bring to boil. Add rice and cook 12 minutes or until tender. Add salt, pepper, parsley, and mollusks. Heat through, and serve.

SHRIMP AND ONION SOUP

SERVES 6

This is a variation on the classic French onion soup. The soup can be prepared in advance up to the point of adding the stock. Just before serving, reheat to boiling and add shrimp.

4 tablespoons butter

1 lb (500 g) brown onions, sliced

4 cups (32 fl oz/1 l) fish stock (see page 260)

salt and freshly ground pepper

1 lb (500 g) uncooked shrimp (prawns), peeled and deveined

4 oz (125 g) grated emmenthal cheese

6 slices French bread, toasted and buttered

Melt butter in large saucepan over medium heat. Add onion and cook slowly over low heat until tender and golden, about 15 minutes.

Add stock and bring to boil. Simmer 15 minutes. Season with salt and pepper. Add shrimp, and cook just until shrimp are no longer translucent, about 3 to 4 minutes.

Broil (grill) cheese onto bread; place bread in soup bowls and pour soup over. Serve immediately.

SHRIMP, TOMATO, AND CHILI SOUP

SERVES 4

1 tablespoon olive oil

1 onion, sliced

2 cloves garlic, chopped

1 lb (500 g) uncooked shrimp (prawns), peeled (reserve shells) and deveined

3 cups (24 fl oz/750 ml) water

1/2 cup (4 fl oz/125 ml) dry white wine

2 tablespoons tomato paste

1 cup (4 oz/125 g) peeled and chopped tomatoes

1 chili, seeded and chopped

1/4 teaspoon salt

3 tablespoons chopped fresh basil

Heat oil in large saucepan over medium heat. Add onion, garlic, and reserved shrimp shells and sauté until onion is tender, about 4 minutes. Add water and wine and simmer 15 minutes. Strain; reserve liquid and discard onion and shells.

Return stock to saucepan. Add tomato paste, tomatoes, and chili and bring to boil over high heat. Reduce heat and simmer 10 minutes.

Add shrimp, salt, and basil and simmer 3 to 4 minutes or until shrimp no longer translucent. Serve immediately.

Shrimp and Onion Soup

TOM YAM GOONG

SERVES 4

This most famous of Thai soups is hot, spicy, and very easy to make. Adjust seasonings to your taste.

4 cups (32 fl oz/ 1 l) Thai fish stock (see page 260)

1 tablespoon chopped lemongrass

6 kaffir lime leaves

1/3 cup (3 fl oz/90 ml) lime juice

2 tablespoons fish sauce

2 red chilies, seeded and chopped

2 tablespoons sweet chili sauce

3 tablespoons chopped cilantro (fresh coriander leaves)

1 lb (500 g) uncooked shrimp (prawns), peeled and deveined

2 tablespoons chopped scallions (spring onions/shallots)

Combine stock, lemongrass, leaves, juice, fish sauce, chilies, chili sauce, and cilantro in large saucepan and bring to boil over medium heat. Simmer 15 to 20 minutes.

Add shrimp and bring to boil, then turn down heat and cook 3 to 5 minutes or until no longer translucent. Stir in scallions and serve.

LONG SOUP WITH SEAFOOD AND SHREDDED LETTUCE

SERVES 4

A super-fast dish that makes a great all-in-one meal, especially good on cold days! It is called 'long soup' because of the long noodles used as opposed to 'short soup' which uses short noodles. Straw mushrooms are small elongated mushrooms, that are readily available in cans — if fresh ones are difficult to find.

2 teaspoons sesame oil

1 clove garlic, chopped

1 teaspoon chopped fresh ginger

4 cups (32 fl oz/1 l) fish stock (see page 260)

2 tablespoons soy sauce

2 tablespoons sherry

8 oz (250 g) uncooked shrimp (prawns), peeled and deveined

8 oz (250 g) white-fleshed fish fillets, cubed

3 oz (90 g) scallops, deveined

1 cup (3 oz/90 g) shredded iceberg lettuce

1 cup (4 oz/125 g) straw mushrooms

3 oz (90 g) soft Asian noodles

1/3 cup (1/2 oz/15 g) chopped scallions (spring onions/shallots)

Heat oil in large saucepan over medium heat. Add the garlic and ginger and cook until fragrant, about 1 minute. Pour in stock, soy sauce, and sherry and bring to boil. Stir in shrimp, fillets, scallops, lettuce, mushrooms, noodles, and scallions and simmer 5 minutes or until seafood is tender. Serve piping hot.

MUSSEL, TOMATO, AND CHERVIL SOUP

SERVES 4

This delicate soup is a lovely starter for an elegant dinner party. Other mollusks, including clams or cockles, may be substituted for the mussels with equally appealing results.

2 lb (1 kg) mussels, scrubbed and debearded

1 cup (8 fl oz/250 ml) water

2 tablespoons butter

3 tablespoons chopped scallions (spring onions/shallots)

1/4 cup (1 oz/30 g) all-purpose (plain) flour

3 cups (24 fl oz/750 ml) fish stock (see page 260)

1/4 teaspoon turmeric

1/4 cup (2 fl oz/60 ml) cream

1 tablespoon chopped chives

1/4 teaspoon salt

1/3 cup (1 1/2 oz/45 g) peeled, seeded and chopped tomato

1 tablespoon chopped fresh chervil

Place mussels in large saucepan with water, cover, and bring to boil. Simmer about 2 to 3 minutes, just until mussels open; discard any that do not open. Remove mussels from shells and chop into small pieces. Reserve 1 cup (8 fl oz/250 ml) cooking liquid.

Melt butter in medium saucepan over medium heat. Add scallions and cook 1 minute. Add flour and cook 1 minute. Remove from heat and gradually add fish stock, turmeric, and reserved cooking liquid. Return to heat and bring to boil, stirring constantly. Add cream, mussels, chives, salt, tomato, and chervil and simmer until heated through. Serve hot.

LOBSTER BISQUE

SERVES 4

A delicate soup with a beautifully creamy consistency. You can also use rock lobster, scampi, crayfish, or shrimp (prawns).

2 lb (1 kg) uncooked lobster

1 stalk celery, chopped

1 carrot, peeled and chopped

1 onion, chopped

1 bay leaf

small bunch parsley

10 cups (80 fl oz/2.5 l) water

3 tablespoons butter

1/4 cup (1 oz/30 g) all-purpose (plain) flour

1 cup (8 fl oz/250 ml) milk

2 tablespoons sherry

2 teaspoons chopped fresh chervil

2 teaspoons chopped chives

2 teaspoons chopped fresh tarragon

salt and white pepper

Wash lobster well. Separate head from body (tail) by inserting sharp knife into first membrane layer holding the two together (see pages 22 to 25).

Combine head, celery, carrot, onion, bay leaf, parsley, and water in large saucepan and bring to a boil. Simmer 15 minutes, skimming as necessary. Add lobster tail to stock and simmer 10 to 15 minutes, again skimming as necessary. Strain; reserve 8 cups (64 fl oz/2 l) stock and tail.

Using scissors, extract meat from reserved tail by cutting through shell and carefully peeling away meat (see page 24). Place lobster meat in food processor or blender with 1/4 cup (2 fl oz/60 ml) reserved stock and puree until smooth.

Melt butter in large saucepan over medium heat. Add flour and cook 1 minute. Remove from heat and gradually add reserved stock and milk. Return to heat and bring to boil, stirring constantly. Reduce heat and simmer until thick and creamy.

Add pureed lobster, sherry, chervil, chives, tarragon, and salt and pepper. Serve hot.

CLAM CHOWDER

SERVES 4

Substitute crabmeat or cubed fish fillets for a different version of this chowder.

2 lb (1 kg) clams, soaked for 30 minutes to remove sand

3 tablespoons butter

2 bacon strips (rashers), finely chopped

1 onion, finely chopped

1/2 cup (2 oz/60 g) finely chopped celery

1/4 cup (1 oz/30 g) all-purpose (plain) flour

2 cups (16 fl oz/500 ml) milk

1 cup (8 fl oz/250 ml) fish stock (see page 260)

1 1/2 cups (6 oz/180 g) finely diced boiling potato

3 tablespoons chopped fresh parsley

salt and freshly ground pepper

Place clams in large saucepan with 1 cup (8 fl oz/250 ml) water. Cover, bring to boil, and cook about 2 to 3 minutes, just until clams open; discard any that do not open. Cool. Reserve 1 cup (4 fl oz/250 ml) liquid.

Melt butter in large saucepan over medium heat. Add bacon, onion, and celery and cook until tender, about 5 minutes. Add flour and cook 1 minute. Remove from heat and gradually stir in milk, stock, and reserved liquid. Return to heat and bring to boil, stirring constantly until thickened. Add potato, cover, and simmer 15 minutes or until tender.

Remove clams from shells; discard shells. Add clams to soup with parsley. Season with salt and pepper and heat through. Serve piping hot.

SCALLOP AND LEEK SOUP

SERVES 4

Serve this soup in small portions; it's deliciously rich and creamy. Oysters would make a good substitute for scallops.

2 tablespoons butter

1 cup (4 oz/125 g) sliced leeks

2 cloves garlic, chopped

1/2 cup (4 fl oz/125 ml) milk

1 egg yolk, beaten

2 cups (16 fl oz/500 ml) fish stock (see page 260)

8 oz (250 g) scallops, deveined

2 tablespoons chopped fresh dill

salt and freshly ground pepper

Melt butter in medium saucepan over medium heat. Add leeks and garlic and cook until tender, about 3 minutes.

Whisk together milk and yolk. Pour milk mixture into saucepan with stock, bring to boil, and stir until thickened. Add scallops, dill, and salt and pepper and simmer 1 to 2 minutes until scallops are tender. Serve hot.

SCALLOP AND POTATO SOUP

SERVES 4

A light, clear soup that is full of flavor. Substitute oysters or mussels for scallops if you wish.

2 tablespoons olive oil

1 cup (4 oz/125 g) thinly sliced leeks

1 cup (4 oz/125 g) finely chopped potato

1/2 cup (2 oz/60 g) finely chopped celery

1/2 cup (2 oz/60 g) finely chopped carrot

1 cup (8 oz/250 ml) tomato puree

4 cups (32 fl oz/1 l) fish stock (see page 260)

1 lb (500 g) scallops, deveined

3 tablespoons finely chopped chives

salt and freshly ground pepper

Heat oil in large saucepan over medium heat. Add leeks, potato, celery, and carrot and cook until tender, about 10 minutes.

Add tomato and stock and bring to boil. Simmer 15 minutes.

Add scallops, chives, and salt and pepper, and simmer 1 to 2 minutes until scallops are tender. Serve hot.

SAUCES

Herbed Butter Sauce (Page 269)

FISH STOCK

MAKES 4 CUPS (32 FL OZ/1 L)

Fish stock is quick and easy to make. The bones must be washed well to remove any blood and intestines. Do not simmer longer than 20 minutes or the stock will be bitter. Skim often to remove scum, otherwise you will end up with a cloudy stock. Once stock is made, it can be refrigerated for 1 week or frozen up to 4 months. Remember if freezing to allow room in the container for frozen stock to expand.

2 lb (1 kg) fish bones, washed
1 onion, chopped
1 cup (8 oz/250 ml) dry white wine
3 lemon slices
4 cups (32 fl oz/1 l) water
small bunch parsley
1/2 teaspoon peppercorns

Combine bones, onion, wine, lemon, water, parsley, and peppercorns in large pot and bring to boil over high heat, skimming as necessary. Reduce heat and simmer uncovered 20 minutes, skimming occasionally. Strain. Cool before refrigerating or freezing.

THAI FISH STOCK

MAKES ABOUT 6 CUPS (48 FL OZ/1.5 L)

The same rules apply as for a traditional fish stock — see the notes above. This fish stock can be used in soups, sauces, or for poaching. Store in refrigerator, covered, for up to 5 days or else keep in freezer for up to 4 months.

1 lb (500 g) fish bones, washed
8 cups (64 fl oz/2 l) water
2 cilantro (fresh coriander) roots
6 kaffir lime leaves
1 in. (2.5 cm) piece fresh ginger
2 cloves garlic, bruised (see glossary)
1 onion, quartered

Combine bones, water, cilantro roots, lime leaves, ginger, garlic, and onion in large saucepan and bring to boil over high heat. Simmer uncovered 20 minutes, skimming occasionally. Strain. Cool before refrigerating or freezing.

260

SAVORY BUTTERS

MAKES 4 OZ (125 G)

Savory butters not only add flavor but also act as a sauce as they melt over just-cooked seafood. Spoon a small amount over panfried, broiled, grilled, or barbecued shellfish or fish. May be made up to 1 week in advance and stored in an airtight container in the refrigerator, or in the freezer for up to 4 months. Combine all ingredients in food processor or blender and process until smooth. Chill.

ANCHOVY BUTTER

1/2 cup (4 oz/125 g) butter, softened
6 anchovy fillets

LEMON BUTTER

1/2 cup (4 oz/125 g) butter, softened
1 teaspoon grated lemon rind
2 tablespoons lemon juice

GARLIC, TOMATO, AND BASIL BUTTER

1/2 cup (4 oz/125 g) butter, softened
1 clove garlic, chopped
1/3 cup (1/2 oz/15 g) finely chopped fresh basil
2 tablespoons tomato paste

HERB BUTTER

1/2 cup (4 oz/125 g) butter, softened
3 tablespoons finely chopped fresh parsley
1 tablespoon chopped fresh tarragon
1 tablespoon chopped fresh basil

GREEN AIOLI

MAKES ABOUT 1 CUP (8 FL OZ/250 ML)

Aïoli traditionally accompanies fish soups such as bouillabaisse (see page 236) but is equally delicious served with hot or cold seafood. Make up to 1 week ahead and store in airtight container in refrigerator.

2 egg yolks
2 tablespoons lemon juice
salt and freshly ground pepper
3 cloves garlic, chopped
2 tablespoons chopped
    fresh parsley
2 tablespoons chopped chives
1 tablespoon chopped fresh
    tarragon
1 cup (8 fl oz/250 ml) olive oil

Combine yolks, lemon juice, salt and pepper, garlic, parsley, chives, and tarragon in food processor or blender and mix until smooth. With motor running, gradually pour in oil until all is incorporated. Serve at room temperature, if possible.

GARLIC AND HERB MAYONNAISE

MAKES ABOUT 1 CUP (8 FL OZ/250 ML)

Serve with hot or cold poached fish, fish that has been barbecued, grilled, or broiled, and cold shellfish. Store tightly covered for up to one week in refrigerator.

2 egg yolks
1/4 teaspoon salt
freshly ground pepper
2 tablespoons lemon juice
1 cup (8 fl oz/250 ml) olive oil
1 clove garlic, chopped
1 tablespoon chopped fresh dill
1 tablespoon chopped chives
1 tablespoon chopped fresh
    parsley

Combine yolks, salt, pepper to taste, and lemon juice in food processor or blender and blend well. With motor running, gradually pour in oil until all is incorporated and mixture is thick and creamy. Mix in garlic and herbs.

Serve chilled or at room temperature.

Grilled Fish with Garlic and Herb Mayonnaise

RED PEPPER MAYONNAISE

MAKES 1½ CUPS (12 FL OZ/375 ML)

This terrific mayonnaise goes particularly well with deep-fried battered seafood, as well as barbecued seafood. It keeps well in an airtight container in the refrigerator for up to 3 days. May be served chilled or at room temperature. Before broiling (grilling), the pepper may be quartered and seeded first, but I find this produces a drier result than cooking whole.

1 red bell pepper (capsicum)
1 egg yolk
2 tablespoons lemon juice
1 cup (8 fl oz/250 ml) olive oil

Place whole pepper under preheated broiler (grill) and cook, turning, until skin blackens and blisters, about 15 minutes. Let cool, then peel away skin and remove seeds.

Place pepper in food processor or blender with yolk and juice and process until smooth. With motor running, gradually pour in oil and blend until all is incorporated. Serve at room temperature if possible.

RUSSIAN MAYONNAISE

MAKES ABOUT 1½ CUPS (12 FL OZ/375 ML)

This is a truly delicious variation of mayonnaise. It is really good served chilled with a whole poached fish such as salmon (see page 178), or with a chilled seafood platter.

2 egg yolks
2 tablespoons lemon juice
1 teaspoon prepared mustard
salt and freshly ground pepper
1 cup (8 fl oz/250 ml) olive oil
3 tablespoons chopped gherkins
3 tablespoons red caviar
2 tablespoons ketchup (tomato sauce)
1 scallion (spring onion/ shallot), chopped
1 teaspoon creamed horseradish

Combine yolks, juice, mustard, and salt and pepper in food processor or blender and process until well combined. With motor running, gradually pour in oil until all is incorporated.

Fold in gherkins, caviar, ketchup, scallion, and creamed horseradish. Serve chilled or at room temperature.

SKORTHALIA

MAKES 2 CUPS (16 FL OZ/500 ML)

This is a Greek garlic sauce (although more like a thick dip) that goes very well with fried or barbecued fish and shellfish. The type of potato used will determine the final result — the floury type is best as the waxy variety do not mash as well. If the sauce is too thick, simply add more olive oil and lemon juice to taste. May be stored for 1 to 2 days in an airtight container in refrigerator, but warm to room temperature before serving.

1 cup (10 oz/300 g) mashed potato, cooled

4 cloves garlic, crushed

1/2 cup (4 fl oz/125 ml) olive oil

1/2 cup (2 oz/60 g) ground almonds

1/4 cup (2 fl oz/60 ml) lemon juice

2 tablespoons chopped fresh parsley

salt and freshly ground pepper

Combine potato, garlic, oil, almonds, lemon juice, parsley, and salt and pepper to taste in large bowl and mix well. Serve at room temperature.

SEAFOOD DIPPING SAUCE

MAKES ABOUT 1 1/4 CUPS (10 FL OZ/300 ML)

This tangy sauce goes very well with chilled shellfish or seafood salads. It can be made up to 4 days in advance and stored in an airtight container in the refrigerator.

1/2 cup (4 fl oz/125 ml) whole-egg mayonnaise

1/2 cup (4 fl oz/125 ml) sour cream

1/4 cup (2 fl oz/60 ml) ketchup (tomato sauce)

2 teaspoons dijon mustard

1 tablespoon worcestershire sauce

Combine mayonnaise, sour cream, ketchup, mustard, and worcestershire in large bowl and mix well. Chill before serving.

SEAFOOD SAUCE

MAKES ABOUT 3/4 CUP (6 FL OZ/180 ML)

This light and creamy sauce can be made 2 days in advance and refrigerated in an airtight container. Serve with chilled shellfish.

1/2 cup (4 fl oz/125 ml) whipping cream, lightly whipped

2 tablespoons ketchup (tomato sauce)

2 tablespoons whole-egg mayonnaise

1 tablespoon lemon juice

dash hot pepper sauce, such as tabasco

salt and freshly ground pepper

Combine cream, ketchup, mayonnaise, juice, sauce, and salt and pepper to taste in medium bowl and mix well. Chill before serving.

TARTARE SAUCE

MAKES 1 1/4 CUPS (10 FL OZ/300 ML)

This mayonnaise-based sauce is flavored with gherkins and capers. It is traditionally served with deep-fried seafood such as calamari rings (see page 142). Stores well for up to 5 days in an airtight container in refrigerator. Serve chilled.

1 egg yolk

1 teaspoon dijon mustard

2 tablespoons lemon juice

1 cup (8 fl oz/250 ml) olive oil

2 tablespoons chopped gherkins

2 tablespoons chopped capers

1 tablespoon chopped chives

Combine yolk, mustard, and juice in food processor or blender and process until smooth. With motor running, gradually pour in oil until all is incorporated.

Add gherkins, capers, and chives and stir just until combined.

Tartare Sauce

CURRIED AVOCADO SAUCE

MAKES ABOUT 1 CUP (8 FL OZ/250 ML)

A thick, creamy mixture that can be used a dipping sauce for cold shellfish or spooned over barbecued, broiled, or grilled fish. Sauce can be made up to 1 hour in advance — any longer and it will go brown.

1 avocado, mashed
1/2 cup (4 fl oz/125 ml) mayonnaise
2 tablespoons lemon juice
1 teaspoon curry powder

Combine avocado, mayonnaise, juice, and curry powder in glass bowl and mix well. Chill before serving.

GARLIC AVOCADO SAUCE

MAKES ABOUT 1 CUP (8 FL OZ/250 ML)

This thick, creamy sauce is perfect with a chilled seafood platter or as an accompaniment to freshly shucked oysters. It can be made up to 1 hour in advance, covered, and refrigerated until ready to serve.

1 avocado, peeled and chopped
2 tablespoons mayonnaise
2 tablespoons lemon juice
1 tablespoon ketchup (tomato sauce)
2 cloves garlic, chopped
salt and freshly ground pepper

Combine avocado, mayonnaise, juice, ketchup, garlic, and salt and pepper to taste in food processor, blender, or glass bowl and mix until smooth. Chill until ready to use.

HERBED BUTTER SAUCE

MAKES ABOUT 1 CUP (8 FL OZ/250 ML)

This beautiful sauce is quick to make using a food processor or blender. Serve warm with poached or panfried seafood. Keep sauce warm over a double boiler if necessary for up to 15 minutes. Simmer water only, as boiling will cause sauce to curdle.

1/3 cup (3 fl oz/90 ml) fish stock (see page 260)

1/3 cup (3 fl oz/80 ml) lemon juice

3 tablespoons chopped scallions (spring onions/shallots)

2 egg yolks

1/2 cup (4 oz/125 g) unsalted butter, melted until bubbly

2 tablespoons chopped fresh chervil

2 tablespoons chopped chives

Combine stock, juice, and scallions in saucepan and bring to boil over high heat. Boil until liquid is reduced to 1/3 cup (3 fl oz/90 ml). Strain, discarding scallions.

Place egg yolks and reduction in food processor or blender and mix well. With motor running, gradually pour in hot butter until all is incorporated. Add chervil and chives and mix briefly. Serve warm.

BEURRE BLANC

MAKES ABOUT 3/4 CUP (6 FL OZ/180 ML)

This warm white butter sauce makes a suitable accompaniment to poached, steamed, or panfried fish. For variations, try adding 1 teaspoon grated orange rind, 2 tablespoons chopped nuts, or 1 tablespoon chopped fresh herbs.

The sauce can be kept warm for about 30 minutes in a double boiler over barely simmering water. Beurre blanc cannot be re-emulsified if it separates, so be sure it is made over low heat and in a non-aluminum pan to prevent sauce discoloration.

3 scallions (spring onions/ shallots), halved

1/4 cup (2 fl oz/60 ml) white wine vinegar

1/4 cup (2 fl oz/60 ml) dry white wine

1/2 cup (4 oz/125 g) butter, diced

salt and white pepper

Combine scallions, vinegar, and wine using a wooden spoon in non-aluminum saucepan over high heat and bring to boil. Boil until reduced to 2 tablespoons. Strain, discarding scallions.

Return reduction to saucepan and place over low heat. Whisk in butter piece by piece until all is incorporated. Season with salt and pepper. Serve sauce warm.

COURT BOUILLON

MAKES 4 CUPS (32 FL OZ/1 L)

Court bouillon is an aromatic liquid used for poaching fish and shellfish. It imparts a slightly lemony flavor with a hint of herbs. Bouquet garni is a small bunch of herbs tied together, usually consisting of parsley, thyme, and bay leaves. It is also readily available in dried form, resembling tea bags. The sauce will keep in the refrigerator for up to 1 week, or may be frozen for up to 4 months.

4 cups (32 fl oz/1 l) water
1 cup (8 fl oz/250 ml) dry white wine
2 carrots, peeled and chopped
1 onion, chopped
1 cup (2 oz/60 g) chopped celery
1 bouquet garni
1 lemon, sliced

Combine water, wine, carrots, onion, celery, bouquet garni, and lemon in large saucepan and bring to boil over high heat. Reduce heat and simmer 40 minutes. Strain before using.

RED PEPPER VINAIGRETTE

MAKES ABOUT 1 CUP (8 FL OZ/250 ML)

This vinaigrette goes well with chilled seafood and seafood salads. Try spooning some over barbecued fish or octopus for an unusual sauce. It keeps well for about 3 days in an airtight container in the refrigerator.

1 red bell pepper (capsicum)
1/4 cup (2 fl oz/60 ml) balsamic vinegar
1 clove garlic, chopped
1/2 cup (4 fl oz/125 ml) olive oil
salt and freshly ground pepper

Preheat broiler (grill). Cook whole pepper, turning until skin blackens and blisters, about 15 minutes. Let cool, then peel away skin and remove seeds. Alternatively, quarter and seed pepper first; cook for 5 to 10 minutes and peel.

Place pepper in food processor or blender with vinegar, garlic, oil, and salt and pepper to taste and blend until smooth.

Red Pepper Vinaigrette

270

MORNAY SAUCE

MAKES ABOUT 1 CUP (8 FL OZ/250 ML)

This is a rich, creamy sauce well suited to poached fish and shellfish. It can be enriched with the addition of cream, egg yolks, or wine. You can make this sauce 1 week in advance and refrigerate it; reheat in the microwave or over gentle heat, mixing it with a little milk or cream if necessary. To prevent a skin from forming during refrigeration, simply place a piece of plastic wrap directly on the surface.

1 tablespoon butter

1 tablespoon all-purpose (plain) flour

1 cup (8 fl oz/250 ml) milk

1/3 cup (1 1/2 oz/45 g) grated cheddar cheese

1 teaspoon dijon mustard

salt and white pepper

Melt butter in saucepan over medium heat. Add flour and cook 1 minute, stirring constantly. Remove from heat and gradually add milk. Return to medium heat and bring to boil, stirring constantly until sauce thickens and boils. Remove from heat and add cheese, mustard, and salt and pepper to taste, stirring until cheese melts. Serve hot.

BEARNAISE SAUCE

MAKES ABOUT 1 CUP (8 FL OZ/250 ML)

Make sure the butter is really hot before adding it to the eggs; this will ensure a good emulsion. Should the sauce break and curdle, just incorporate 1 to 2 tablespoons of ice water. This should bring it back together. Sauce can be kept warm over hot water for about 15 minutes. Do not boil the water as the sauce will curdle. Place plastic film directly over sauce to prevent a skin forming. It is important to use a non-aluminum pan otherwise the sauce will discolor.

1/4 cup (2 fl oz/60 ml) tarragon vinegar

1/4 cup (2 fl oz/60 ml) dry white wine

2 scallions (spring onions/ shallots), chopped

1 tablespoon chopped fresh tarragon

3 egg yolks

1/2 cup (4 oz/125 g) melted butter

Combine vinegar, wine, scallions, and tarragon using a wooden spoon in non-aluminum saucepan over high heat and bring to boil. Boil until reduced to 2 tablespoons. Strain.

Place eggs and reduction in food processor or blender and process until well combined. With motor running, gradually add hot butter, mixing until all is incorporated. Serve hot.

HOLLANDAISE SAUCE

MAKES 1 CUP (8 FL OZ/250 ML)

A classic, hollandaise is a delicate emulsified sauce flavored with lemon juice. You can vary it by adding 2 tablespoons chopped nuts, 2 teaspoons prepared mustard, or 2 tablespoons chopped fresh herbs. Should the sauce curdle, just blend in 1 to 2 tablespoons ice water.

3 egg yolks
1/4 cup (2 fl oz/60 ml) lemon juice
1/2 cup (4 oz/125 g) butter, melted
salt and white pepper

Combine yolks and juice in food processor or blender and mix well. With motor running, gradually pour in hot butter until all is incorporated. Season to taste with salt and pepper. Serve immediately.

CAPER HOLLANDAISE

MAKES 1 1/2 CUPS (12 FL OZ/375 ML)

Try this hollandaise with panfried seafood, including shrimp (prawns), lobster, fillets, and fish steaks or cutlets. Serve warm as the sauce will solidify if it is allowed to cool.

3 egg yolks
2 tablespoons lemon juice
salt and freshly ground pepper
1/2 cup (4 oz/125 g) butter, melted
2 tablespoons chopped capers
2 tablespoons chopped
fresh parsley

Combine yolks, lemon juice, and salt and pepper to taste in food processor or blender and process to combine. With motor running, gradually add hot butter, mixing until all is incorporated. Add capers and parsley and blend briefly. Serve warm.

WATERCRESS SAUCE

MAKES ¾ CUP (6 FL OZ/180 ML)

This delicious sauce is good with either hot or cold seafood. It can be kept in the refrigerator for up to 3 days. If watercress is hard to find, try parsley or basil.

1 cup (1½ oz/45 g) watercress leaves
6 anchovy fillets
2 tablespoons capers
1 clove garlic, chopped
1 tablespoon lemon juice
½ cup (4 fl oz/125 ml) olive oil
salt and freshly ground pepper

Combine watercress, anchovy fillets, capers, garlic, and juice in food processor or blender and process until smooth. With motor running, gradually pour in oil until all is incorporated. Season to taste with salt and pepper. Serve chilled.

TURKISH ALMOND SAUCE

MAKES ABOUT 1 CUP (8 FL OZ/250 ML)

This unusual thick sauce has a slightly coarse consistency. It makes a good accompaniment to broiled, grilled or barbecued fish or shellfish.

½ cup (2 oz/60 g) finely ground almonds
2 cloves garlic, chopped
½ cup (4 fl oz/125 ml) olive oil
⅓ cup (3 fl oz/90 ml) lemon juice
2 tablespoons chopped fresh parsley
salt and freshly ground black pepper

Combine almonds, garlic, oil, juice, parsley, and salt and pepper to taste in food processor or blender and process until well combined. Serve chilled.

Watercress Sauce

MUSTARD SAUCE

MAKES 1 CUP (8 FL OZ/250 ML)

This sauce is simple to make yet very tasty. Serve it with poached, broiled, or grilled fillets, fish steaks or cutlets. Try to make it just before serving, but it may be kept warm in a double boiler if necessary.

1/2 cup (4 fl oz/125 ml) fish stock (see page 260)

1/2 cup (4 fl oz/125 ml) cream

2 tablespoons sherry

2 egg yolks, beaten

salt and freshly ground pepper

1 tablespoon prepared mustard

1 tablespoon chopped scallions (spring onions/shallots)

Combine stock, cream, sherry, yolks, salt and pepper, mustard, and scallions in saucepan and bring to boil over medium heat. Reduce heat and simmer, stirring constantly, until sauce thickens. Serve immediately.

ROUILLE

MAKES 1 CUP (8 FL OZ/250 ML)

This rich garlicky sauce is traditionally served with fish soups such as bouillabaisse (see page 236), although it is equally good with fried, battered, or barbecued seafood.

1 red bell pepper (capsicum), seeded and chopped

3 cloves garlic, chopped

2 red chilies, seeded and chopped

1 egg yolk

2 slices (2 oz/60 g) bread, crusts trimmed, soaked in water and squeezed dry

1/2 cup (4 oz/125 ml) olive oil

1 teaspoon chopped fresh thyme

1/4 teaspoon salt

Combine pepper, garlic, and chilies in food processor or blender and process until smooth. Add yolk and bread and blend well. With motor running, gradually pour in oil until all is incorporated and sauce is thick and creamy. Mix in thyme and salt. Serve at room temperature.

VELOUTÉ SAUCE

MAKES ABOUT 1¹/₂ CUPS (12 FL OZ/375 ML)

This velvety rich sauce can be enriched even further by the addition of wine and cream: at the end of cooking simply add 2 tablespoons of light whipping cream. To flavor with wine, replace ¹/₂ cup of the fish stock with ¹/₂ cup dry white wine. Do not make more than 3 days in advance and store, covered, in the refrigerator. Thin with a little extra stock if necessary. This sauce is good with poached or steamed fish and shellfish.

2 tablespoons butter

2 tablespoons all-purpose (plain) flour

2 cups (16 fl oz/500 ml) fish stock (see page 260)

salt and freshly ground pepper

Melt butter in saucepan over medium heat. Add flour and cook 2 minutes, stirring constantly. Remove from heat and gradually whisk in stock. Season with salt and pepper. Return to medium heat and cook, stirring constantly, until the sauce boils and thickens, about 5 minutes. Reduce heat and simmer gently until sauce has reduced and thickened, about 20 minutes. Serve hot.

LEMON AND DILL SAUCE

MAKES 1 CUP (8 FL OZ/250 ML)

This sauce can be made 3 days in advance and stored in an airtight container in the refrigerator. Serve it with chilled shellfish, such as oysters or shrimp (prawns).

¹/₂ cup (4 fl oz/125 ml) good quality mayonnaise

¹/₂ cup (4 fl oz/125 ml) sour cream

1 tablespoon chopped fresh dill

grated rind of 1 lemon

1 tablespoon lemon juice

salt and freshly ground pepper

Combine mayonnaise, sour cream, dill, rind, juice, and salt and pepper to taste in glass bowl and mix well. Chill before serving.

BASIC RECIPES

Beer Batter (page 280)

BASIC BATTER

MAKES ENOUGH FOR 1 LB (500 G) SEAFOOD.

Batters can be successfully made in a food processor or blender. Place all ingredients in the container and process just until smooth. Do not overprocess or you will end up with a tough coating. Use this batter with white-fleshed or oily fish fillets, shrimp (prawns), cuttlefish, or squid (calamari).

1 egg, beaten
1 cup (8 fl oz/250 ml) milk
salt and freshly ground pepper
1 cup (4 oz/125 g) all-purpose
(plain) flour

Blend egg, milk, and salt and pepper in measuring cup. Place flour in bowl. Make a well in middle and gradually pour in milk mixture. Mix well to form a smooth batter.

Dip seafood into batter, allowing excess to drip away. Plunge into hot oil to deep fry (see Introduction). Cook until golden. Drain on kitchen paper towels before serving.

BEER BATTER

MAKES ENOUGH FOR 1 LB (500 G) SEAFOOD.

This batter is beautifully crisp and has a wonderful taste — it's one of my favorites! It can be used with white-fleshed or oily fish fillets, shrimp (prawns), cuttlefish, or squid (calamari).

1 cup (4 oz/125 g) all-purpose
(plain) flour
1 teaspoon salt
1 egg, beaten
1 cup (8 fl oz/250 ml) beer

Sift flour and salt into bowl. Make a well in middle and gradually mix in egg and beer (beer will froth up; keep mixing to allow bubbles to subside). Mix well to form smooth batter.

Dip seafood into batter, allowing excess to drip away. Plunge into hot oil to deep fry (see Introduction). Cook until golden. Drain on paper towels before serving.

LEMON AND WINE BATTER

MAKES ENOUGH FOR 1 LB (500 G) SEAFOOD

This thin and crispy batter has a tangy flavor with a hint of wine. Use for fish fillets, shrimp (prawns), scallops, or squid (calamari).

1 cup (4 oz/125 g) all-purpose (plain) flour

1 teaspoon salt

1/2 cup (4 fl oz/125 ml) lemon juice

1/2 cup (4 fl oz/125 ml) dry white wine

2 egg whites, beaten to soft peaks

Sift flour and salt into bowl and make a well in middle. Combine juice and wine and gradually pour in. Mix well to form smooth batter. Lightly fold in egg whites. Use batter immediately.

Dip seafood into batter, allowing excess to drip away. Plunge into hot oil to deep fry (see Introduction). Cook until golden. Drain on paper towels before serving.

TEMPURA BATTER

MAKES ENOUGH FOR 1 LB (500 G) SEAFOOD

Tempura is a light, crisp Japanese batter, used to coat seafood and vegetables. Try a variety of fish pieces, shrimp (prawns), squid, and a few small vegetables. Special tempura flour is available but plain flour works well if you take care. The ice water makes for added crispness as it meets with the hot oil.

3/4 cup (3 oz/90 g) all-purpose (plain) flour

1 cup (8 fl oz/250 ml) ice water

1 egg yolk, beaten

Place flour in bowl and make a well in middle. Combine water and yolk and gradually pour in. Mix until just combined; do not overmix or batter will be heavy.

Dip seafood lightly into batter. Plunge into hot oil to deep fry (see Introduction). Cook until golden. Drain on paper towels before serving.

Following pages: Fish with Lemon and Sesame Coating (page 284), Fish with Parmesan and Almond Coating (page 285), Fish with Spiced Cashew Coating (page 285)

FISH WITH LEMON AND SESAME COATING

1/2 cup (2 oz/60 g) all-purpose (plain) flour

1/2 cup (2 oz/60 g) sesame seeds

1/4 teaspoon lemon pepper

2 teaspoons grated lemon rind

1 lb (500 g) white-fleshed or oily fish fillets, skinned

1/3 cup (3 fl oz/90 ml) olive oil

1 tablespoon sesame oil

Combine flour, seeds, pepper, and rind in bowl and mix well. Press fillets into coating and shake off excess.

Heat oils in frying pan over medium heat. Add fillets and cook 2 to 3 minutes per side or until crust is crispy and golden and fish is opaque and beginning to flake when tested. Serve hot.

FISH WITH OATMEAL AND HAZELNUT COATING

1/2 cup (2 oz/60 g) quick-cooking rolled oats

1/2 cup (2 oz/60 g) ground hazelnuts

2 teaspoons grated lemon rind

1 lb (500 g) white-fleshed or oily fish fillets, skinned

1 egg, beaten

oil for shallow frying

Mix oats, hazelnuts, and rind in shallow bowl. Dip fillets into egg and then into oat mixture. Shake off excess coating.

Heat enough oil to cover base of frying pan over medium heat. Add fillets and cook 2 to 3 minutes per side or until crust is crisp and golden and fish is opaque and begins to flake when tested. Serve hot.

FISH WITH PARMESAN AND ALMOND COATING

SERVES 4

1 cup (4 oz/125 g) dry breadcrumbs

1/2 cup (2 oz/60 g) almond meal

1/4 cup (1 oz/30 g) grated parmesan cheese

2 tablespoons chopped mixed fresh herbs (parsley, tarragon, chives)

1 lb (500 g) white-fleshed or oily fish fillets, skinned

Combine breadcrumbs, almond meal, parmesan, and herbs and mix well. Place fillets in coating and press well to help coating adhere.

Heat oil in frying pan over medium heat. Add fish and cook 2 to 3 minutes per side or until crust is crisp and golden and fish is opaque and beginning to flake when tested. Serve hot.

FISH WITH SPICED CASHEW COATING

SERVES 4

1/2 cup (2 oz/60 g) all-purpose (plain) flour

1/4 cup (1 oz/30 g) ground cashews

2 teaspoons ground cardamom

1 teaspoon nutmeg

1/4 teaspoon garlic powder

1/4 teaspoon chili powder

1 lb (500 g) white-fleshed or oily fish fillets, skinned

3 tablespoons butter

Combine flour, cashews, cardamom, nutmeg, garlic powder, and chili powder and mix well. Add fillets and coat with mixture, shaking off excess.

Melt butter in frying pan over medium heat. Add fillets and cook 2 to 3 minutes per side or until crust is crisp and golden and fish is opaque and beginning to flake when tested. Serve hot.

FISH WITH CORNMEAL COATING

SERVES 4

Cornmeal, also known as polenta, makes a great coating, as the result is golden and crispy.

1 lb (500 g) white-fleshed or oily fish fillets, skinned

seasoned flour (see glossary)

1 egg, beaten

1 cup (3 oz/90 g) cornmeal (polenta)

oil for shallow frying

Coat fillets in flour, shaking off excess. Dip fillets into egg and drain away excess. Dip into cornmeal, pressing firmly with fingertips to help coating adhere.

Heat enough oil to cover the base of frying pan over medium heat. Add fillets and cook 2 to 3 minutes per side or until crust is golden and fish is opaque and beginning to flake when tested. Serve hot.

FISH WITH CURRIED COCONUT COATING

SERVES 4

1/2 cup (2 oz/60 g) dry breadcrumbs

1/2 cup (1 oz/30 g) unsweetened shredded coconut

1/2 cup (2 oz/60 g) almond meal

2 teaspoons curry powder

1 lb (500 g) white-fleshed or oily fish fillets, skinned

3 tablespoons butter

Combine breadcrumbs, coconut, almond meal, and curry powder in bowl and mix well. Add fillets, pressing well to help coating adhere. Shake off excess coating.

Melt butter in frying pan over medium heat. Add fillets and cook 2 to 3 minutes per side or until crust is crispy and golden and fish is opaque and beginning to flake when tested. Serve hot.

Fish with Curried Coconut Coating

CRUMBED FISH

SERVES 4

To avoid mess, try placing fish and flour in a plastic bag and shaking to coat the fish. Crumbed fish can be made well in advance and stored in the refrigerator for 2 days or frozen for up to 4 months. For variety, herbs, ground nuts, grated lemon rind, or unsweetened shredded coconut can be added to the breadcrumbs. Serve the fish with lemon wedges.

1 lb (500 g) white-fleshed or oily fish fillets, skinned

seasoned flour (see glossary)

1 egg, beaten

dry breadcrumbs

oil for shallow frying

Dust fillets in flour, shaking off excess. Dip into egg, then breadcrumbs, pressing firmly. Chill 30 minutes.

Heat enough oil to cover the base of frying pan over medium heat. Add fillets and cook 2 to 3 minutes per side or until fish is opaque and beginning to flake when tested. Serve hot.

SPICY FRIED FISH

SERVES 4

1/2 cup (2 oz/60 g) all-purpose (plain) flour

1 tablespoon ground coriander

1 teaspoons ground cumin

1/2 teaspoon salt

1/2 teaspoon chili powder

1 lb (500 g) white-fleshed or oily fish fillets, skinned

1/4 cup (2 fl oz/60 ml) olive oil

Combine flour, coriander, cumin, salt, and chili powder and mix well. Add fillets and coat evenly, shaking off excess. Heat oil in frying pan over medium heat. Add fish and cook 2 to 3 minutes per side or until fish is opaque and beginning to flake when tested. Serve hot.

ASIAN MARINADE

MAKES ABOUT 1 CUP (8 FL OZ/250 ML)

Use with oily or white-fleshed fish fillets and steaks (cutlets), shrimp (prawns), cuttlefish, and squid (calamari). This recipe makes enough for 1 lb (500 g) seafood.

1/2 cup (4 fl oz/125 ml) hoisin sauce

1/4 cup (2 fl oz/60 ml) ketchup (tomato sauce)

1/4 cup (2 fl oz/60 ml) lemon juice

2 tablespoons honey

2 tablespoons soy sauce

3 tablespoons chopped scallions (spring onions/shallots)

1/4 teaspoon cracked pepper

Combine hoisin sauce, ketchup, juice, honey, soy sauce, scallions, and pepper and mix well. Add seafood and allow to marinate 30 minutes, or longer if time allows.

Drain well, reserving marinade. Broil, grill, barbecue, or panfry the seafood (see Introduction), basting with marinade during cooking.

JAPANESE MARINADE

MAKES ABOUT 3/4 CUP (6 FL OZ/180 ML

Use white-fleshed or oily fish fillets, shrimp (prawns), octopus, or squid (calamari). This recipe makes enough for 1 lb (500 g) seafood.

1/3 cup (3 fl oz/80 ml) soy sauce

1/4 cup (2 fl oz/60 ml) mirin or sake

2 tablespoons sesame oil

1 tablespoon brown sugar

3 tablespoons chopped scallions (spring onions/shallots)

1 clove garlic, chopped

Combine soy sauce, mirin, oil, sugar, scallions, and garlic and mix well. Add seafood and marinate 30 minutes, or longer if time allows.

Drain well, reserving marinade. Barbecue, broil, grill, or panfry (see Introduction), basting well with marinade during cooking.

TANDOORI MARINADE

MAKES $1/2$ CUP (4 FL OZ/125 ML); ENOUGH FOR 1 LB (500 G) SEAFOOD.

Suitable for 1 lb (500 g) whole fish, fish fillets, steaks (cutlets), and shrimp (prawns). The authentic Indian method involves marinating ingredients overnight and than baking a traditional clay oven called a tandoor, resulting in an exotic blend of spicy flavours. This version is the best alternative I've found.

$1/2$ cup (4 fl oz/125 ml) plain yogurt

3 cloves garlic, chopped

2 teaspoons ground ginger

$1/2$ teaspoon chili powder

$1/2$ teaspoon ground coriander

$1/2$ teaspoon ground cumin

$1/2$ teaspoon garam masala

$1/2$ teaspoon paprika

$1/2$ teaspoon turmeric

Combine yogurt, garlic, ginger, chili powder, coriander, cumin, garam masala, paprika, and turmeric in glass bowl and mix well. Add seafood and marinate 30 minutes, or longer if time allows.

Drain, reserving marinade. Barbecue, broil, grill, or bake (see Introduction), basting with marinade throughout cooking.

If baking fish, preheat oven to 425°F (220°C/Gas 7). Place fish in a single layer in baking dish, bake for 10 to 15 minutes or until opaque and beginning to flake when tested.

THAI-STYLE MARINADE

MAKES ABOUT $1/2$ CUP (4 FL OZ/125 ML)

Use white-fleshed or oily fish fillets, shrimp (prawns), cuttlefish, octopus, or squid (calamari). This recipe makes enough for 1 lb (500 g) seafood.

2 cloves garlic, chopped

2 tablespoons fish sauce

$1/3$ cup ($1/2$ oz/15 g) chopped cilantro (fresh coriander leaves)

2 tablespoons chopped lemongrass

2 tablespoons chopped fresh mint

$1/3$ cup (3 fl oz/90 ml) lime juice

2 tablespoons sweet chili sauce

Combine garlic, fish sauce, cilantro, lemongrass, mint, lime juice, and chili sauce in glass bowl and mix well. Add seafood and marinate 30 minutes, or overnight if time allows.

Drain well and barbecue, broil, grill, or panfry (see Introduction), basting with reserved marinade.

Tandoori Marinade

SOUR CREAM MARINADE

MAKES 3/4 CUP (6 FL OZ/180 ML)

This deliciously tangy marinade can be used for all fish or shellfish. This recipe makes enough for 1 lb (500 g) seafood.

1/2 cup (4 fl oz/125 ml) sour cream
1/4 cup (2 fl oz/60 ml) lemon juice
1 teaspoon ground cumin
1 teaspoon ground coriander
1/4 teaspoon cinnamon
1 clove garlic, chopped

Combine sour cream, juice, cumin, coriander, cinnamon, and garlic in glass bowl and mix well. Add seafood and marinate 30 minutes, or overnight if time allows.

Drain excess marinade. Barbecue, broil, grill, or panfry (see Introduction).

SPICY YOGURT MARINADE

MAKES 2/3 CUP (5 FL OZ/150 ML)

Try this with 1lb (500 g) white-fleshed fish fillets, shrimp (prawns), squid (calamari), and octopus.

2/3 cup (5 fl oz/150 ml) plain yogurt
2 cloves garlic, chopped
2 teaspoons chopped fresh ginger
2 teaspoons garam masala
1 teaspoon ground cumin
1 teaspoon ground coriander
1 red chili, seeded and chopped

Combine yogurt, garlic, ginger, garam masala, cumin, coriander, and chili in glass bowl and mix well. Add seafood and marinate 30 minutes, or longer if time allows.

Drain and barbecue, broil, or grill (see Introduction), basting with reserved marinade.

LEMON ROSEMARY MARINADE

MAKES ABOUT 1/2 CUP (4 FL OZ/125 ML)

This marinade is particularly good with whole fish. Make sure the fish is scored, as this will allow the flavors to penetrate and will help the fish cook evenly. You can also use the marinade on fish fillets or steaks (cutlets). This recipe makes enough for 1 lb (500 g) seafood.

1/4 cup (2 fl oz/60 ml) olive oil

1/4 cup (2 fl oz/60 ml) lemon juice

2 bay leaves, crushed

2 cloves garlic, chopped

1 tablespoon chopped fresh rosemary

1/4 teaspoon cracked pepper

Combine oil, juice, bay leaves, garlic, rosemary, and pepper in food processor or blender and process until well mixed. Pour over fish and allow to marinate 30 minutes, or longer if time allows.

Drain, reserving marinade. Either barbecue, broil, grill, or panfry fish (see Introduction), basting well with marinade during cooking.

PEPPERED WINE MARINADE

MAKES ABOUT 1 1/2 CUPS (12 FL OZ/375 ML)

Very good with white-fleshed or oily fish fillets and steaks (cutlets), shrimp (prawns), cuttlefish, or squid (calamari). This recipe makes enough for 1 1/2 lb (750 g) seafood.

1 cup (8 fl oz/250 ml) dry white wine

1/2 cup (4 fl oz/125 ml) olive oil

2 teaspoons crushed pepper

grated rind of 1 lemon

2 tablespoons chopped fresh parsley

2 cloves garlic, chopped

Combine wine, oil, pepper, lemon, parsley, and garlic and mix well. Add seafood and allow to marinate 30 minutes, or longer if time allows.

Drain well, reserving marinade. Barbecue, broil, grill, or panfry (see Introduction), basting with marinade during cooking.

ALMOND AND BROWN RICE STUFFING

MAKES ENOUGH FOR 1 LARGE FISH

1 tablespoon butter

1 onion, chopped

1/3 cup (1 1/2 oz/45 g) flaked almonds

1 cup (6 oz/185 g) cooked brown rice

1 carrot, grated

2 tablespoons chopped fresh parsley

2 teaspoons chopped fresh oregano

grated rind of 1 lemon

1 egg, beaten

salt and freshly ground pepper

Melt butter in frying pan over medium heat. Add onion and cook until tender, about 4 minutes. Stir in almonds and cook until golden, about 2 minutes.

Transfer mixture to bowl and add rice, carrot, parsley, oregano, rind, egg, and salt and pepper to taste. Mix well. Fill cavity of whole fish and bake or barbecue (see Introduction).

RICE AND TABBOULEH STUFFING

MAKES ENOUGH FOR 1 LARGE FISH

1 1/2 cups (10 oz/300 g) cooked white rice

1/2 cup (3 oz/90 g) bulghur (cracked) wheat, soaked for 1 hour in cold water

1/2 cup (2/3 oz/20 g) chopped fresh parsley

1 tomato, chopped

1/3 cup (1/2 oz/15 g) chopped mint

2 scallions (spring onions/ shallots), chopped

2 tablespoons olive oil

2 tablespoons lemon juice

Combine rice, bulghur wheat, parsley, tomato, mint, scallions, oil and lemon juice and mix well. Fill cavity of whole fish and bake or barbecue (see Introduction).

Rice and Tabbouleh Stuffing

PINE NUT, RICOTTA, AND BASIL STUFFING

MAKES ENOUGH FOR 1 LARGE FISH

1 cup (2 oz/60 g) fresh breadcrumbs

3/4 cup (5 oz/150 g) ricotta cheese

1/4 cup (1 1/2 oz/45 g) pine nuts, chopped

1/4 cup (1 oz/30 g) grated parmesan cheese

3 tablespoons chopped fresh basil

salt and freshly ground pepper

Combine breadcrumbs, ricotta, pine nuts, parmesan, basil, and salt and pepper and mix well. Fill cavity of whole fish and bake or barbecue (see Introduction).

SPINACH AND PARMESAN STUFFING

MAKES ENOUGH FOR 1 MEDIUM FISH.

1 tablespoon butter

1 onion, chopped

1 clove garlic, chopped

2 cups (4 oz/125 g) chopped fresh spinach

1 cup (2 oz/60 g) fresh breadcrumbs

1/4 cup (1 oz/30 g) grated parmesan cheese

1/4 teaspoon nutmeg

Melt butter in frying pan over medium heat. Add onion and sauté until tender, about 5 minutes. Add garlic and spinach and sauté 2 minutes or until spinach is soft. Remove from heat. Add breadcrumbs, parmesan, and nutmeg, and mix well. Fill cavity of whole fish and bake or barbecue (see Introduction).

TOMATO, PECORINO, AND BASIL STUFFING

MAKES ENOUGH FOR 1 LARGE FISH

This mixture is ideal for stuffing whole fish, fish rolls, or squid (calamari).

1 cup (6 oz/185 g) cooked
long-grain rice
2 tomatoes, chopped
2 cloves garlic, chopped
3 tablespoons chopped
fresh basil
2 tablespoons chopped chives
¼ cup (1 oz/30 g) grated
pecorino cheese
1 egg, beaten
freshly ground pepper

Combine rice, tomatoes, garlic, basil, chives, pecorino, egg, and pepper in bowl and mix well. Fill cavity of fish and bake or barbecue (see Introduction).

Following page: Red Mullet, Olive Paste, and Onion Bruschetta (page 52)

INDEX

299

First published in the United States in 1995 by
Charles E. Tuttle Company, Inc.
of Rutland, Vermont, and Tokyo, Japan,
with editorial offices at 153 Milk Street, Boston, Massachusetts 02109.

Published in conjunction with Lansdowne Publishing Pty Ltd
Level 5, 70 George Street, Sydney Australia 2000

Managing Director: Jane Curry
Production Manager: Sally Stokes
Publishing Manager: Deborah Nixon
Project Co-ordinator: Kirsten Tilgals
Project Assistant: Amalia Matheson
Food Stylist's Assistant: Christine Sheppard

ISBN 0-8048-3071-1
Library of Congress Catalog Number 95-60447

Designer: Kathie Baxter Smith
Formatted in Stempel Schneidler on Quark Xpress
Produced in Singapore by Kyodo Printing Co (S'pore) Pte Ltd

Page 2: Seafood Plate with Green Mayonnaise, p.65

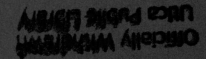